Trade Unions and the Management of Industrial Conflict

Rosemary Aris
Lecturer in Sociology
University of Warwick

First published in Great Britain 1998 by
MACMILLAN PRESS LTD
Houndmills, Basingstoke, Hampshire RG21 6XS and London
Companies and representatives throughout the world

A catalogue record for this book is available from the British Library.

ISBN 0–333–65798–5 hardcover
ISBN 0–333–65799–3 paperback

First published in the United States of America 1998 by
ST. MARTIN'S PRESS, INC.,
Scholarly and Reference Division,
175 Fifth Avenue, New York, N.Y. 10010

ISBN 0–312–17761–5

Library of Congress Cataloging-in-Publication Data
Aris, Rosemary.
Trade unions and the management of industrial conflict / Rosemary
Aris.
p.   cm.
Includes bibliographical references and index.
ISBN 0–312–17761–5 (cloth)
1. Industrial relations—Great Britain—History—20th century.
2. Strikes and lockouts—Great Britain—History—20th century.
3. Trade-unions—Great Britain—History—20th century.
4. Reconstruction (1914–1939)—Great Britain.   I. Title.
HD8390.A74 1997
331.88'0941'0904—dc21   97–26516
                                                                                        CIP

This book is printed on paper suitable for recycling and made from fully managed and
sustained forest sources.

10   9   8   7   6   5   4   3   2   1
07   06   05   04   03   02   01   00   99   98

Printed in Hong Kong

Contents

Acknowledgements

I would like to thank Tony Elger for his support and for his work on trade unionism which has been valuable in writing this book.

Abbreviations

ASE	Amalgamated Society of Engineers
ASLEF	Amalgamated Society of Locomotive Engineers and Firemen
BOT	Board of Trade
CGT	Confédération Générale du Travail
CWC	Clyde Workers' Committee
DORA	Defence of the Realm Act
GFTU	General Federation of Trade Unions
ILO	Independent Labour Organization
ILP	Independent Labour Party
IWA	International Workingmen's Association
IWF	International Workers' Federation
IWW	Industrial Workers of the World
L&SWR	London and South West Railways
MFGB	Miners' Federation of Great Britain
MNS	*Miners' Next Step*
MOL	Ministry of Labour
MOM	Ministry of Munitions
NDL	National Democratic League
NEC	National Executive Council
NIC	National Industrial Council
NSFU	National Sailors' and Firemens' Union
NUR	National Union of Railwaymen
SDF	Social Democratic Federation
SLP	Socialist Labour Party
SSM	Shop Stewards' Movement
STUC	Scottish Trades Union Congress
SWMF	South Wales Miners' Federation
TUC	Trades Union Congress
URC	Unofficial Reform Committee

Introduction

This book examines the role that trade unions and trade union leaders played in the British state's management of industrial conflict in the years 1910–21. This period is the focus for the study because, as Hinton has argued, 'the history of the British labour movement between 1910 and the early 1920s has a special claim to our attention. However it is measured – by the sheer growth of numbers in the unions; by the working days lost through strikes; by the upsurge of socialist organization, campaigning, ideas; by the intensity and range of debate over tactics and strategy of the struggle for socialism; even by the victory (albeit the hollow victory) of socialism within the Labour Party in 1918 – these years mark a climax of class-conscious self-activity among the workers which, in Britain, has not been surpassed'.[1]

This unprecedented outburst of industrial conflict was accompanied by an unprecedented increase in state intervention in industrial relations and it is generally agreed in the literature relating to this period that the First World War marked a turning point in the state's management of industrial relations. This combination of factors has made this period the subject of many studies in industrial relations, and there are many contradictory interpretations of the character of state intervention, the reasons for its growth and its impact, but this book builds on three influential approaches which offer varying accounts of labour unrest at this time. These accounts say something distinctive about the machinery of industrial relations which developed in this period, including the role of trade unions and collective bargaining systems. The rest of the introduction will outline these different interpretations and set out my alternative account, the specific contribution which this study makes and the set of questions which it addresses.

THE REVOLUTIONARY SCHOOL

The first of these interpretations belongs to what is commonly referred to as the 'revolutionary' school.[2] Representatives of the revolutionary school include Hinton, Price, Burgess, Holton and Hyman.[3] These authors develop a critique of orthodox interpretations of the evolutionary development of British industrial relations systems.[4] Whilst these analysts do not represent a coherent body, they all direct attention to the importance of informal workplace struggles and organization in the study of industrial relations in this period. This interpretation arose in response to the reappearance of unofficial organizations based on the workplace during the 1960s.[5]

In a broad-ranging reassessment of the changing structure of the working class and the implementation of collective bargaining, the revolutionary school produced what has come to be regarded as the dominant account of the role of trade unions in labour policy between 1910 and 1921.

For Hinton, state labour policy during this crisis was determined by the need 'to reinforce the disciplinary functions of the employer'[6], assisted by trade union officialdom, leaving the unofficial labour movement to 'resist the wartime offensive of the state and the employers against traditional working-class rights.'[7] Hinton argues that the outbreak of the war allowed the state to increase its powers of surveillance and coercion, and that by appearing to concede to the demands of organized labour it was able to co-opt trade union leaders into the 'Servile State'.[8] This increase in state compulsion, the acceleration of changes in working conditions and the 'betrayal' of skilled workers by their elected leaders led to the transmutation of forms of rank and file organization from a response to the problems of craft regulation into a radical challenge to the industrial and political status quo which was severely repressed by the state on the employers' behalf. The leaders of organized labour were, however, only recognized by the government so long as this recognition served the government's purposes. The trade unions had become 'a part of the social machinery of the State' but only in the most subordinate capacity, and without tenure . . . the primary result of this collaboration was not to extend working-class power into the state machine but to complete the process, already well advanced before the war, by which the leaders of the organized workers were divorced from their members.'[9]

Burgess argues that the increase in the numbers of trade unionists at the outbreak of war gave their organizations an official presence with government that had not existed before the war. This prompted government efforts to cultivate friendships with trade union leaders, to agree to separate negotiations with them and to 'manage' the implementation of government policy in a way that would win the unions' active co-operation. This incorporation of trade union leaders was an essential part of state manpower policy, designed to smooth the working of industrial relations during the emergency. It achieved the opposite effect by driving a wedge between the trade union leadership and the rank and file and weakening the control exercised by union leaders over it. This gave unrest an increasingly workplace-focused orientation, which became more menacing 'as the institutions of 'civil society' were steadily embraced beneath the umbrella of government tutelage. In consequence, the scope of social unrest became circumscribed to attacks on state power itself.'[10]

Price, Holton and Hyman focus attention on how the state's recognition of trade union leaders enabled employers to use these leaders to moderate the demands of their members and enforce unpopular settlements on the rank and file. Trade union leaders became part of the machinery designed to subordinate organized labour. For Price, the involvement of union bureaucracy in the collective bargaining process increased discontent and was the essential stimulus to labour unrest.[11] Union leaders exchanged traditional trade union practices for collective bargaining rights and this loss of power in the workplace intensified militancy amongst the rank and file.

Holton argues that in this period the state began to favour incorporation as a form of social control, in response to the extension of the labour movement's strength.[12] Moreover, the incorporation of union officials into state-sponsored conciliation schemes furthered the syndicalist cause, since union leaders distanced themselves from rank and file agitation and direct action seemed the only alternative. Sabel also argues that during World War I the subjugation of labour resulted from the manner in which union leaders collaborated with the state in administering the war economy.[13]

Hyman offers a more sophisticated analysis, arguing that instead of being characterized by a clearly defined bureaucracy separate from a coherent and self-conscious rank-and-file membership, intra-union relations were highly complex, with shifting interest groups and bureaucratic tendencies at many levels. He nevertheless reinforces Trotsky's view that class collaboration has been a long-term feature of trade unionism in Britain: 'it was not a case of workers' control over capital but of the subserviency of the labour bureaucracy to capital'.[14]

In summary, this approach argues, firstly, that state policy sought to incorporate the trade unions; secondly, that trade union bureaucracy defused the radical aspirations of the rank and file, imposing unpopular settlements upon them; and thirdly, that participation in national collective bargaining machinery by trade union leaders was a major cause of industrial unrest.

CORPORATISM

The second influential interpretation of this period is the corporatist view implicit in the work of Marwick[15] and explicit in Middlemas.[16] Middlemas takes a view of industrial events virtually identical to that of the revolutionary school but portrays the state in more neutral colours. Middlemas's central point is that in the period 1916–21 'a new form of harmony in the political system was established which changed the governance of the country quantitatively as well as qualitatively'[17]. Middlemas's idea of 'corporate bias' states that a triangular pattern of co-operation was established between government, labour and capital which led to the elevation of trade unions and employers' associations to a new kind of status: from being interest groups, they became governing institutions. The trade unions' new role was premised on their acceptance of the need to manage discontent and abandon the ideology of class conflict. By 1921, therefore, trade unions had crossed a threshold which had never existed before the war and behaved thereafter as estates of the realm.[18]

Middlemas argues firstly that trade unions were not incorporated in a collaborationist sense but came to share some of the political power and attributes of the state itself. Secondly, he argues that the Great War was a watershed in British politics – there were no significant continuities in the state's management of industrial unrest before and after the war.

REVISIONIST INTERPRETATIONS

The third major approach, purporting to offer a thoroughgoing revision of these conventional views, is represented by the work of Reid, Zeitlin, Wrigley Adams.[19] The revisionists argue against the revolutionary school's incorporation thesis. Reid, for instance, takes the view that the importance of independent shop floor organization has been exaggerated. Only a very small minority of unionists accepted the radical critique of officialdom and during the war the representatives of workers' grievances still came from official trade unionism.[20] There was, he argues, 'no serious revolutionary crisis,' no significant 'revolutionary impulse towards independent rank and file organization,' and 'no sustained government strategy to contain it.'[21] Zeitlin notes that in industries where labour was weak, conciliation machinery brought tangible gains for the unions which would not have been conceded had individual employers been given a free hand.[22] Revisionists thus suggest that incorporation was not a main cause of industrial unrest between 1914 and 1921. Adams argues that the importance of conciliation machinery as a cause of unrest has been greatly overstated. He substitutes the view of the revolutionary school with the notion that where workers rebelled against conciliation they desired its reform or extension into new areas rather than its destruction. The revisionists also pour scorn on the idea that trade union bureaucracy defused the radical aspirations of the rank and file. Reid and Zeitlin deny that the interests of the rank and file and the trade union leadership were necessarily divergent. Zeitlin questions the juxtapostion of a theoretically militant membership and a theoretically conservative leadership emphasizing the passivity and conservatism of the rank and file.[23]

These views about the relationship between trade union officials and their members represent a critique of an influential body of literature which is central to this study, known as 'rank and filism'.[24]

RANK AND FILISM

Building on the ideas of Michels[25] and the Webbs,[26] rank-and-filist literature emphasizes the fundamental division between the interests of the official trade union leadership and those of the membership. In this view the process of collective bargaining and the contradictory role of trade unions in capitalism are seen as the sources of the division. Broadly it is argued that, since the trade unions' long-term survival depends on bargaining with employers over the wages and conditions of their members, they must to some extent make themselves acceptable to employers. This acceptance is premised on their prior agreement on market criteria for wage settlements and managerial authority in the workplace. These compromises inevitably involve the unions in moderating the demands of their members, discouraging struggles for control at work and restricting demands to wage issues which are acceptable to employers. The need to uphold collective agreements, particularly where they are the result of formal procedures such as conciliation and arbitration, 'ultimately leads them to adopt an active role in sustaining managerial discipline in the factory.'[27]

Adherents of the rank-and-file interpretation, however, take the analysis further by arguing that workers, unlike trade union leaders, have no vested interest in the capitalist order and their exploitation in the workplace periodically leads them to struggle against managerial authority and the trade union structures and collective bargaining procedures which stifle autonomous action. For Zeitlin, the logical conclusion of this argument is that 'under propitious circumstances, as during and immediately after the First World War, such insurgent movements can come to challenge not only the structure of factory authority, but also the stability of the state itself.'[28] While acknowledging differences of interpretation among the 'rank and filists' as to the relationship between workplace militancy and politics, Zeitlin finds that they broadly subscribe to two underlying but highly problematic assumptions: firstly, that trade unions as organizations have an inherent interest in accommodation with capitalism 'and their members do not', and secondly that workers have a vast reservoir of latent power which is contained by trade unions. Although few rank-and-filists explicitly endorse this second assumption, Zeitlin notes that without it there would be no reason why the supposed caution of trade union leaders should become a point of criticism or why autonomous regulation and informality should always be considered as rational and natural.

For Zeitlin there are empirical as well as conceptual difficulties which present major problems for the rank-and-filists. Firstly there is the difficulty of separating the 'bureaucracy' and the 'rank and file' when there is no clear line of demarcation between them. Price, in particular, understates the heterogeneity of trade union leaders and grossly exaggerates the homogeneity of 'ordinary workers' and the 'rank and file'. Industries like building and engineering were deeply riven with sectional divisions, whether based on occupation, skill, locality, ethnicity or gender. Secondly, he argues, even if we could differentiate clearly, can we confidently identify trade union officialdom with moderation and the rank and file with militancy, when there is much evidence that leaders were often more militant than their members? Thirdly, he points to recent historical research which has shown the importance of central co-ordination in sustaining job controls and the responsiveness of even the most authoritarian unions to pressure from below. Fourthly, conciliation and arbitration procedures have been taken by rank-and-filist historians (Burgess and Price) to represent the nadir of union accommodation to the rules of the capitalist game, pegging wages to market criteria and subjecting workers to unchallenged managerial authority in the workplace. Several recent studies of the practical operation of these procedures are cited by Zeitlin as evidence that they were opposed by employers and, once they were in place, operated to safeguard workers' control over production.

Zeitlin notes that the various authors who adopt this approach are aware of these difficulties and have consequently hedged their positions with significant qualifications – but, he argues, in so doing they have not accounted for these difficulties within the framework of rank and filism, only expanded the paradigm's empirical reference at the expense of its explanatory power.[29]

This debate looms large in studies of industrial conflict before, during and immediately after World War I which was marked by widespread unofficial strike activity led by the shop stewards' movement. It is therefore central to this study, which takes up some of these issues by focusing on the role of trade unions and their leaders in the state's management of industrial conflict in this period. The study examines the role of trade unions in industrial relations policy through an analysis of the sources from which it derived at this time. This is necessary because recent extensive discussions have lacked detailed empirical work based on these sources for the whole of the period, and because analysis of the role of trade unions from the perspective of the state can contribute to the rank-and-filist debate by revealing and testing the adequacy of assumptions about the relationship between trade union leaders, trade union members and ordinary workers which underpinned state labour policy.

AN ALTERNATIVE VIEW

It could be argued that Keith Middlemas's 'Politics in Industrial Society' has already met these requirements.[30] This could be claimed, firstly, because this popular and influential account of the development of state intervention in industrial relations in this crucial period draws on primary archive sources for the whole of the period,[31] and secondly because it is 'formidably well researched' and 'took the state as its explicit object of study, not only repudiating the quaint swingometer episteme of mainstream political studies (and thus converging with the proliferation of Marxist theories of the state which appeared at this moment) but also bringing to this analysis a welcome commitment to historical and concrete explanation', thus 'diverging from the unmediated abstraction which characterized the greater proportion of this oeuvre.'[32]

Contrary to Middlemas's 'watershed' thesis, however, my research reveals significant continuities in the state's response to unrest before, during and after World War I. These continuities in state labour policy become apparent when the origins and development of the state's policy of conciliation and the theory of trade unionism which underpins it are analysed. This policy originated well before the period under study and continued to expand throughout it, making it more accurate to view the early 1890s as a more significant watershed in state industrial relations policy than World War I. My argument has important implications that prompt a reassessment of the nature of the political consensus which Middlemas argues existed until the 1960s.

Moreover, a focus on the state's policy of conciliation reveals a major defect of Middlemas's analysis at the methodological level. His account rests largely on a mixture of Cabinet papers, the private papers of prominent figures of the time and secondary sources. However, while I agree that Cabinet papers are a formidable authority, in that they consist of documents which are 'not written with a view to informing historians or sociologists, they are in fact secreted for the purpose of action. They are in a sense facts in themselves not merely the representation of facts,'[33] I would argue that this focus leads Middlemas to confuse political talk with administrative action and that a clearer understanding of the state's response to industrial conflict in these years must include an analysis of the papers of the Board of Trade.

In this respect the study takes seriously Davidson's[34] observation that although many social, economic and labour historians have concentrated on analysing the development of state policy towards labour unrest in the period 1880–1914, they have neglected the role of the Board of Trade. Davidson regards this as a serious omission, for several reasons: firstly, because the ability of the Labour Department of the Board of Trade (established 1893) to supply the relevant data and expertise made it 'the recognized information bureau on all that pertained to industrial conflicts, possessing systematic data on strikes and lockouts, trade combinations, employment and wage rates, easy access to more general economic data and an establishment which included several experienced negotiators.'[35] Secondly, government measures relating to industrial relations were largely determined by departmental ministers in conjunction with their permanent officials. There is no evidence to suggest that labour unrest was ever discussed in any systematic fashion by the Cabinet before 1911; after 1911, it was frequently debated in Cabinet but the lack of consensus among Cabinet members as to the correct strategy to adopt in the face of widespread industrial conflict meant that the initiative in formulating labour policy remained with the Board of Trade (BOT). Lastly, the social and economic objectives of the Board were seen by both employers and labour leaders as the prime determinant of state industrial relations policy.[36]

While Davidson's analysis provides valuable insights, however, his emphasis, like that of Middlemas, is largely on the personalities who populated the pre-war BOT. In this study I extend the analysis up to 1921 to include those institutions (the Ministry of Munitions and the Ministry of Labour) which inherited the task of formulating and implementing industrial relations policy from the BOT. From this it becomes clear that regardless of the changing incumbents and seemingly new departures in industrial relations policy, the latter remained remarkably consistent. This was because what was possible in industrial relations was circumscribed to a significant extent by the degree and character of worker organization and the state's ability to influence it without appearing to do so. It was this realization which first engendered the state's attempt to permanently manage industrial conflict through conciliation in 1896, when the Labour Department of the Board of Trade was designated the agency for the implementation of this policy.

In analysing the role of trade unions in industrial relations policy in this period from the perspective of the policy-making agencies themselves, I assess the limits of this policy in practice and address the points raised by critics of the rank-and-filist perspective.

Throughout the book the term 'state' will be used in preference to 'the government', since the former draws attention not only to the Cabinet but also to the institutions of the permanent Civil Service. It is not my intention to engage in abstract debate about the character of 'the state'.[37] However, as Miliband notes, a 'theory of the state' underpins all political analysis.[38] Later in this introduction I emphasize that the fundamental relationship in capitalism is that between labour and capital and the state is taken to be that set of institutions which politically regulates the terms of that relationship. Underpinning this approach is the view that the labour-capital relation is not just economic but also legal and political. Although it seems that exploitation in capitalism takes place purely through the buying and selling of labour power, this economic relation is underpinned by property relations. Property relations are legal relations and the law is backed up by political power or force supplied by the state. This should not be taken to imply that the state is a unified actor. On the contrary, as this study shows, the state is a set of hierarchical institutions with overlapping powers and contradictory objectives.[39]

Industrial conflict is taken to be expressed through strike activity, collective bargaining and arbitration. Analyses of information gathered by state agencies about these were the starting point for the formulation and implementation of labour policy. The state combined this information with the views about the attitudes and mood of workers expressed by those directly concerned with industrial conflict.

The concept of the 'working class' has been a major preoccupation and a source of controversy among sociologists for more than a hundred years, and there is an extensive sociological literature on the subject.[40] It is important to be aware, however, that for the state in the period under study the term had a precise meaning. A good illustration of this precision is to be found in the report by the Labour Department of the Board of Trade to the Royal Commission on Labour in 1894. In this report the term 'working class' refers to 'the industrial class . . . especially that portion of the five and a half million males (in England and Wales) who are adult workmen (over ten years of age) and engaged in productive as contrasted with distributive enterprise. The class engaged in transport adds an appreciable but very vague and fluctuating contingent and the industrial population of Scotland and Ireland has to be taken into account.'[41] No modern-day sociologist would sanction such a narrow definition of class, not least because of its blindness to gender and ethnicity. Nevertheless, this is what is meant in discussions of the working class in state papers at this time, even during the First World War when women formed an appreciable proportion of the 'industrial class'.

PLAN OF THE BOOK

The book is organized in the following way. Chapter 1 analyses those theories of trade unionism which influenced the study and provides the theoretical context for the empirical examination of trade unions and their role in industrial relations policy between 1910 and 1921. It could be argued that industrial relations covers more than just trade unionism, and, of course, it does; but the core of industrial relations is trade unionism. As Allen has emphasized, industrial relations arise out of the prime economic relationship in society, which is the buying and selling of labour power, and there is perpetual interaction between the buyers and sellers, for three reasons.[42] Firstly, there is an enormous imbalance of economic power between the two classes – there are many sellers and relatively few buyers, and the latter are dominant over the former in every sphere of activity through their ownership of the means of production. Secondly, this imbalance is accentuated because members of the labour market possess varying degrees of freedom to exploit this power position for their own advantages; and lastly, there are unremitting pressures on buyers and sellers to use this freedom. The sellers or workers depend on the price of labour power for their own subsistence and are therefore forced to maximize it while the buyers or capitalists treat that price as a cost and so constantly try to minimize it. The result is a dynamic conflict situation: class struggle. Trade unionism is the manifestation of this conflict – it constitutes an attempt by otherwise relatively powerless individuals to redress the power imbalance.[43]

Chapter 2 analyses the reasons why the state came to tolerate trade unions and to promote and participate in conciliation – a method of dispute resolution in which the participation of trade unions was central. It examines the roles which the Labour Department of the Board of Trade and trade unions were to play in this policy and the obstacles encountered in its implementation. My aim is to uncover the understandings of industrial conflict, of trade unionism and of trade union officials on which state industrial relations policy rested in the period 1910–21.

Chapter 3 explores the development of revolutionary politics in trade unions, especially the 'new unions', with particular emphasis on the emergence of syndicalism and industrial unionism between 1890 and 1910. The aim is to provide a background for understanding the tactics and strategies adopted by workers, their leaders and the state, which are analysed in the later empirical chapters.

Chapter 4 is taken up with the 'Great Unrest' of 1910–12. The extent to which this large-scale industrial conflict was influenced by the movements previously discussed is explored from the perspective of the BOT. The chapter charts the effects of this conflict on workers, trade unions, trade union leaders and on state industrial relations policy.

Chapter 5 focuses on the Munitions of War Act. Here the emphasis is on the extent to which worker resistance contributed to this legislation, modified its impact, strengthened worker organization and led to state initiatives, notably the creation of the Ministry of Labour and the implementation of the Whitley Scheme, which were designed to restore the authority of trade union leaders over their members.

Chapter 6 looks at industrial conflict in the years 1916–18 from the perspective of the Ministry of Labour. The Ministry of Labour inherited a crisis in the management of industrial conflict along with the mantle of state conciliator. The Ministry paid particular attention to the ways in which the implementation of the Munitions of War Act by the Ministry of Munitions hampered the management of industrial conflict. This analysis of the major industrial conflicts in the period 1916–18 provides important insights into the relationship between different departments of state.

Chapter 7 focuses on the resurgence of large-scale industrial conflict and the threat of a general strike in the immediate post-war period. This chapter centres on the Ministry of Labour's detailed analysis of the prospects for a general strike, which reveals the limits and possibilities of both state and trade union action.

The concluding chapter draws together the major themes of the book. An appendix provides a discussion of the status of the most heavily used and cited government records in studies of this period, which suggests that these should be looked at more critically.

NOTES

1. Hinton, 1973, p. 13.
2. Reid, 1985, p. 46.
3. Hinton, 1973; Price, 1980; Burgess, 1980; Holton, 1976; Hyman, 1979.
4. Dunlop, 1958; Flanders, 1968; Poole, 1981.
5. Batstone, Boraston & Frenkel, 1977; Hyman, 1979; Nichols & Beynon, 1977.
6. Hinton, 1973, p. 35.
7. Ibid., p. 41.
8. For a discussion of this concept, see Belloc, 1913, pp. 175–176, and Hinton, 1973, p. 44.
9. Ibid., p. 54.
10. Burgess, 1980, p. 166.
11. Price, 1980.
12. Holton, 1976, p. 33.
13. Sabel, 1981.
14. Hyman, 1979, pp. 54–67.
15. Marwick, 1967.
16. Middlemas, 1979.
17. Ibid., p. 19.
18. Ibid., pp. 20–21.
19. Reid, 1985; Zeitlin, 1985; Wrigley, 1987; Adams, 1989.
20. Reid, in Tolliday & Zeitlin, 1985, p. 67.
21. Ibid., p. 68.
22. Zeitlin in Mommsen, 1985, p. 332.
23. Ibid.
24. Zeitlin, 1989.
25. Michels, 1911.
26. Webb, 1911.
27. Zeitlin, 1989, p. 46.

28. Ibid.
29. Ibid.
30. Middlemas, 1979.
31. Adams used local trade union sources and focused on local disputes. Hinton focused on local shop stewards' movements and Reid focused on the British shipbuilding industry. The analyses of Burgess and Hyman rest on secondary sources. Price focuses on the building industry. McLean (1983) concentrates on a particular geographical area at a particular time.
32. Schwartz, 1987, p. 111.
33. Webb, 1932, p. 100.
34. Davidson, 1978, pp. 571–591.
35. Davidson, 1982.
36. Ibid.
37. For an extensive discussion of the character of the state, see Carnoy, 1984; Holloway and Picciotto (eds), 1978; Jessop, 1990 and Clarke (ed.) 1991.
38. Miliband, 1969, pp. 3–4.
39. See especially Chapters 5 and 6 of this study.
40. For an indication of the size of the literature, see Crompton, 1993.
41. Fifth and Final Report of the Royal Commission on Labour, 1894, C7421, p. 27.
42. Allen, 1971, p. 9.
43. Dobb, 1959, p. 160.

The Role of Trade Unions

Trade unions can be defined as representative organizations of workers which are based upon but transcend the collectivism of particular workplaces and localities.[1] Their essential function is to overcome the individual worker's weakness by substituting a collective bargain for separate individual bargaining.[2] This wider formal organization transforms the possibilities of shop floor representation and action by mobilizing support, providing organizational resources and framing united policies – a feature which has been appreciated by state agencies as well as social commentators. As Hyman[3] emphasizes, united collective organization *for* workers also implies 'power over' workers, to coordinate activity and ensure unity. Hyman accepts that collective organization allows workers to create social power much greater than their power as individuals, but points out that the organization of conflict also makes conflict manageable by employers and by governments. It does this by ensuring that 'grievances are brought into the open, channelled to the appropriate authorities, expressed in a form which makes compromise possible and articulated by a bargaining partner with whom an agreement can be reached which employees will feel some commitment to observe. Thus an inescapable function of trade union action is, in Mills's terms, "the management of discontent".'[4]

It is equally important to note that although workers organized in trade unions have objective common interests,[5] the most fundamental of which is their common relationship of opposition and antagonism to capital and the owners of capital, consciousness of this class identity is obscured in reality by the immense variety of work contexts and work relations which characterize capitalism.[6] The latter may foster an inward-looking unity among workers such that they see themselves primarily as boilermakers, shop assistants, employees of a particular firm or workers in a particular industry rather than in class terms.[7] They may be more conscious of those interests which divide them from other workers than of those which unite them. When workers organize in trade unions these divisions are naturally expressed in the organizational boundaries which shape the lines of demarcation within and between trade unions.

Other major sources of division which have negative effects on worker organization are those of gender and ethnicity.[8] Historically, trade unions have made use of two main strategies: firstly, they have excluded women and ethnic minorities from paid employment, and secondly, they have confined women and ethnic minorities to jobs which are graded lower than those of white men in order to raise the price of their members' labour power.[9]

The historical development of trade unionism in Britain is also a limiting factor. The aims of early trade unions or craft societies were sociability and the provision of friendly benefits. Their role in industrial relations was secondary and they developed an industrial relations role primarily as defenders of traditional working rules and practices against either employers or other groups of workers. It was rare for them to initiate action to change working conditions. Effective craft unionism was based on the principle of unilateral control, whereby the union reserved the right to determine the rules of the trade and the rates of pay and to enforce these through its own members, who would boycott or leave employers that did not respect union conditions. Unions could do this because they had a monopoly of labour supply – they controlled entry to trades through apprenticeship and the enforced demarcation of their own area of work, and benefit funds allowed them to support workers who could not find work on union conditions.[10]

The barriers erected by craft unionism were only decisively breached when shifts in the labour process in the 1890s facilitated the discovery of bargaining leverage by key groups of unskilled workers and encouraged a reorientation of some craft unions towards a wider membership in the context of de-skilling. Although this was a form of unity, it tended to consolidate sectionalism by embracing a diverse membership with varied interests. In the following decades, mass offensive unionism, influenced by syndicalist ideas and with considerable instability of membership, demonstrated that mass organization and centralized administration did not automatically denote conservatism. However, while these general unions acted as mobilizing organizations responsive to rank-and-file pressure during their initial phases of formation, recruitment and mobilization (and often during periods of prosperity when the confidence of unskilled workers was boosted) they developed rapidly into oligarchic 'bossdoms' under the impact of employers' associations, war administration and later the depression.[11]

There were also limits to the 'general' character of the unskilled organizations: they did not encroach on the craft societies' territory or on that of the industrial-type unions – coal, cotton and the railways. They confined themselves to filling the gaps left by the earlier structure of trade unionism. Their open character tended to decline once they had established effective organization; they tended to become conscious of having sectional interests and to operate by excluding other sections of workers. Furthermore, large-scale organization created a structure of organizers with distinctive experiences and priorities which posed issues of accountability and control.[12]

As Elger notes, these issues have usually been addressed in terms of arguments about the oligarchic and democratic features and tendencies of trade unionism although they are also intimately connected with competing notions of the whole rationale of unionism and differing strategies of organization and recruitment.[13] Several classic positions on these issues were developed by analysts of the labour movement who were also participants in the early period of mass working-class unionism and political organization during the last decades of the nineteenth century.[14]

The Webbs offered a relatively 'optimistic' account of the institutional resolution of a conflict between democracy and 'efficiency' in the development of British trade unionism. They emphasized that as unions became involved in extended and centralized collective bargaining, they confronted the limitations of the traditional pattern of 'primitive democracy' characteristic of the early craft societies (identified with mass meetings, referenda on policy issues, annual elections and rotating headquarters). With this development, they argued, unions faced the dilemma of dictatorship by experts or parochialism and inefficiency. However, this dilemma could be circumvented through a formal apparatus of representative democracy. Elected representative assemblies could be substituted for 'primitive democracy' as controllers of union executives, allowing unions to advance as efficient democracies.[15]

Michels built on the Webbs to provide the classic 'pessimistic' account of the domination of ostensibly democratic trade unions and labour parties by an oligarchy of union and party leaders. In his view, oligarchy and conservative union policies were the outcome of professionalisation and bureaucracy. For Michels, trade unions must organize on a mass scale and become sophisticated in negotiations to be effective. The resulting complex of bureaucratic tasks requires specialist officials. Union moderation then becomes the norm, since the need for tangible results through trade-offs prompts officials to adopt a conciliatory bargaining stance. This moderation is reinforced by their concern with their new-found status and by concern to recruit less committed workers into unions to maintain and increase membership. Organizational survival becomes central. 'Uncontrolled dominance', he argued, was therefore inevitable and trade union leaders' power allowed them to impose their conservative policies, even where these were 'disapproved of by the majority of workers they are supposed to represent.' This abuse of power – oligarchic control – provoked little resistance because, in the absence of adequate information or experience, members accepted that their leaders possessed a 'customary right' to their positions and were willing to allow them to speak for them.[16]

Historical and contemporary analyses of British unions have qualified and contextualized the Michelsian diagnosis of oligarchy.[17] They have shown that the relation between leadership and rank and file is more complex than he implies. Hyman has pointed out, firstly, that if members are assumed to be subject to the informed official leadership, this implies that workers' orientation to trade unionism is instrumental and hangs on the latter's ability to deliver a satisfactory level of benefits. The frustration of these expectations may lead to a rank-and-file revolt. This is an important constraint on leadership autonomy. Secondly, the generally accepted view that unions ought to act democratically and ensure the support of their members restricts the scope of leaders' activity. Thirdly, the fact that union leaders were often lay activists before they became officials ensures that the extremes of cynical manipulation are usually avoided. Fourthly, although Michels is right to emphasize the difficulty of direct membership control at national levels of decision making in unions, this does not exclude membership participation and control at other levels. For Hyman, other weaknesses of Michels's argument include his neglect of the constant interaction between unions and the oligarchic organizations of capital which put pressure on them to become similarly oligarchic. Employers and the state are often irritated by union leaders who want to consult their members before making decisions. There is also the external influence of capitalist organizations on workers which socialize them into anti-democratic values. This is reinforced by workers' direct experience of the uniformly oligarchic organizations and institutions of capitalist society and compounded by the mass media which projects anti-democratic ideas on specific issues.[18] Lastly, unions vary considerably in the extent to which they are subject to the pressures that Michels emphasizes. Nevertheless, critics of Michels have recognized that the growth and scale of trade union organization means that unions certainly confront tensions between such priorities as survival, mobilization, representation, participation, accommodation and discipline, and that 'the only way to successfully defeat the oligarchic tendencies of trade unionism is to overthrow capitalism itself.'[19]

Given the divisions within trade unions and the conflicting priorities with which trade unions are faced, a fundamental question arises for these writers: what part, if any, can trade unions play in the struggle for the revolutionary transformation of society? There are contrasting views linked to different analyses of the practical objectives of unions and the interests of trade unionists. Pluralist analyses, from the Webbs onwards, focus on the role of trade unions as key participants in the process of collective bargaining, not as agencies of social transformation. Unions are seen as agencies of mobilization, representation and discipline through which workers gain a significant though subordinate role in the joint regulation of employment conditions and substantive improvements in wages and working conditions within the established framework of (capitalist) employment relations. Such pluralist diagnoses go beyond the perspectives of 'business unionism' by emphasizing that the first of these objectives represents a form of 'industrial citizenship', but they also define the relationship between unions and politics as strongly circumscribed by the priorities of collective bargaining.

Flanders's analysis remains indicative of some central assumptions of industrial relations pluralism. He argues that the centrality of joint job regulation underwrites a clear division of labour between trade unionism and labourist politics. Since trade unions are primarily bargaining institutions, they should not prioritize politics above effective bargaining, either by attempting to substitute for the specific political role of the Labour Party or by subordinating themselves to the claimed requirements of 'national efficiency'. Within this framework, however, Flanders recognizes that unions must retain some sense of being a social movement and not merely an institutional structure if they are to effectively mobilize active support. This may mean championing the cause of the unorganized or advocacy of an egalitarian incomes policy. Pluralism takes an optimistic view of industrial relations, assuming first, a roughly equal balance of power between employers and workers organized in trade unions; second, that workers have a responsibility to observe agreements, and, third, that any outstanding differences between them are resolved by the procedures of collective bargaining.[20]

As Fox points out, however, collective bargaining does not restore the balance of power between employers and workers, because it is concerned with restricted issues and not the fundamental disparity of power between the propertied and the propertyless. Trade unions aim at marginal improvements for their members and defend them against arbitrary management action. They do not attack management on the basic principles of the social and industrial framework such as private property, the extreme division of labour and the massive inequalities of financial reward, status, control and autonomy in work or try to secure a foothold in the majority of decisions on management objectives, markets, capital investment and rate of expansion. They rarely seriously challenge the treatment of labour as a commodity to be hired or discarded at management's convenience. The reasons why the trade unions do not challenge the status quo are to be found in their understanding of the magnitude of employers' power supported by government and the relative passivity of the rank and file.[21]

In contrast to pluralist analysis stands the 'optimistic' Marxist tradition, which emphasizes the potential for radicalization and a class-based oppositional or revolutionary politics which may arise out of union activity and experience. This view focuses on the instabilities and contradictions built into processes of collective bargaining and the manner in which substantive gains are circumscribed by the power of private capital and the state. It is argued that the very process of struggle, involving solidarity among workers and confrontations with employers and the state, may produce 'explosions of class consciousness'.[22] Other writers have questioned the view that trade union activity can escalate almost automatically into a radical social movement characterized by mass mobilization and a highly politicized class-consciousness. Hyman notes the long-standing tension between the 'pessimistic' and 'optimistic' Marxian analyses of the unsettled relationship between trade unions, social mobilization and politics.[23]

This tension stems from the ambiguous legacy left by Marx and Engels in their treatment of trade unions. Engels saw trade unions as 'the military school of the working men in which they prepare themselves for the great struggle which cannot be avoided.' Marx later qualified this view, arguing that although unions 'work well as centres of resistance against the encroachments of capital' they should guard against restricting themselves to a 'guerrilla war against the effects of the existing system instead of simultaneously trying to change it.'[24] Later both Marx and Engels were scathing about the co-option of union leaders and the bourgeoisification of elite sections of the organized workers. In spite of their criticism, however, Hyman suggests that Marx and Engels were optimistic in regard to the emergence of a mass politics out of union struggles.

The 'pessimistic' view is apparently codified by Lenin in his famous contrast between trade union economism and revolutionary class consciousness. Lenin argued that trade unions were primarily concerned with economic and sectional interests and fostered only a 'trade union consciousness' subservient to bourgeois ideology which is older, more developed and has many more resources available for its diffusion than its socialist rivals. For Lenin, revolutionary class-consciousness could not develop spontaneously out of trade union economism and would have to be brought to the working class via the revolutionary party.[25]

It could be argued that classical Marxist theorists, in their concern to establish the need for a revolutionary party to organize and politically motivate the working class (in contrast to those 'economist' intellectuals who adhered to Marx's early work in believing that capitalism's contradictions alone would engender revolutionary change), tended to neglect the relationship of consciousness to workers' experience of exploitation and the fact that, as the power base of trade unionism is the working class and not capital, it can reflect but not impose workers' patterns of consciousness.

Attempts to explore how far revolutionary class-consciousness grew out of workers' experience of their exploitation gained momentum in Britain in the late 1960s, when Goldthorpe et al. found that workers' experience outside work determined their orientations to it and this engendered a fragmentary consciousness which displayed no notion of common interest as a working class.[26] Later research modified these conclusions and found little evidence of orientations of any sort as an organizing principle of workers' lives. Instead it was argued that workers had multi-stranded priorities but were primarily concerned with pay, job security and work content, and the relative importance of these varied with life-cycle factors and economic conditions. This focus produced a pattern of consciousness based on a rudimentary sense of class antagonism ('them and us') overlaid with fatalism, cynicism and acceptance – 'contradictory consciousness.'[27]

These arguments gave rise to Marxian analyses which capture important features of the patterns and mechanisms of consciousness and the potential for radicalization in workplace struggle. Beynon found that this contradictory consciousness was sometimes transcended and developed into a volatile 'factory consciousness' in the course of struggle, but it stopped short of revolutionary class-consciousness because of trade union intervention. 'In all of these struggles the role of trade unions has been to de-escalate rather than extend the struggle between capital and labour.'[28]

In another version of 'rank and filism' Mann points out that this union response is not a betrayal of the working class by its leaders.

Instead it is rooted in workers' experience of exploitation. Through unions workers bargain on a terrain defined by capital which is characterized by the ideological separation between economics and politics, production and consumption, although not without struggle. This struggle teaches them that economic demands sometimes get results but control issues do not, so workers take what they can get and dismiss what is denied them as unimportant – 'pragmatic accommodation'. Their experience gives them a sense of class identity and location but not a sense of the totality of class relations or of any alternative society which would be a prerequisite of revolutionary class-consciousness. Unions reflect this dual consciousness to the extent that they pursue economic and job control issues separately and the latter defensively – and as long as they do this, no matter how aggressively, they are a profoundly conservative force which works to weaken class-consciousness.[29] For Hyman, however, it is precisely unions' economic focus which produces situations of radical instability for capital, because it hangs on capital's ability to satisfy workers' demands. The level of demands which can be accommodated varies according to the economic context and stagnation means that improved wages cannot be financed out of economic growth.[30] Trade union activity also raises issues of power and control, or at least 'the demand not to be controlled disagreeably', which can form the basis for far more explicit 'political' demands and runs through all trade union activity.[31]

While the above contributions represent the major positions within the industrial relations debate on union and class activity, there have been some important challenges to certain of their assumptions from other analysts of class relations. In particular, De Ste Croix has argued that to restrict the notion of class struggle to occasions where an overt struggle on the political plane, involving class consciousness on both sides, can be shown to exist, is inadequate.

'The very common conception of class struggle which refuses to regard it as such unless it includes class-consciousness and active political conflict (as some Marxists do) is to water it down to the point where it virtually disappears in many situations. It is then possible to deny altogether the very existence of class struggle ... merely because in each case the exploited class concerned does not or did not have any 'class consciousness' or take any political action in common except on very rare occasions and to a very limited degree. But ... bring back exploitation as the hallmark of class, and at once class struggle is at the forefront, as it should be.'[32]

It then becomes clear that

> the essence of the relationship of classes in a class society founded
> on the existence of private property in the means of production, is
> the economic exploitation which is the very raison d'être of the whole
> class system . . . If the division into economic classes is in its very
> nature the expression of the way in which above all exploitation is
> effected . . . then there is to that extent an unceasing struggle be-
> tween exploited and exploiting classes.'[33]

For De Ste Croix, even if workers were precluded from playing any
sort of political role and had no chance of taking industrial action in
their own defence (which was not the case from the mid-nineteenth
century) the very existence of an exploited class has important consequences, not only in the economic sphere but also socially and politically. The very existence of classes involves tension and conflict between
the classes, and

> 'even if only the masters could carry it on effectively: they would
> always be united, and be prepared to act . . . the masters conduct a
> permanent struggle . . . in the very act of holding down their slaves . . .
> but in a sense even slaves who are kept in irons and driven with a
> whip can conduct some kind of passive resistance, if only by quiet
> sabotage and breaking a tool or two.'[34]

Given this, De Ste Croix argues, the only definition of class struggle that makes sense is one that starts from the fact of exploitation
and takes account of its nature and intensity. Class struggle is a permanent feature of human society above primitive levels. It does not
necessarily involve collective action by a class as such and it may or
may not include activity on a political plane, although such activity
becomes increasingly probable when the tension of class struggle becomes acute.[35]

As the next chapter will show, a similar understanding of class relations informed the state's management of industrial conflict in late
nineteenth century Britain. It led the state to favour conciliation rather
than confrontation and to build a framework of procedures for the
permanent management of industrial conflict, the cornerstone of which
was established trade unionism.

NOTES

1. Elger, 1989.
2. Dobb, 1959, p. 160.
3. Hyman, 1975, p. 195.
4. Mills, 1956.
5. These flow from lack of ownership or control over the means of production, being forced to sell their labour power in the labour market, being subordinated to a heirarchy of managerial control, insecure employment, lack of autonomy in work, poor pay and working conditions.
6. Hyman, 1975, p. 42.
7. Mann, 1973.
8. Kelly, 1988.
9. Walby, 1986, p. 244.
10. Turner, 1962, pp. 180–182. Lane, 1974. Hobsbawm, 1964.
11. Turner, 1962, pp. 201–232. Hyman, 1971.
12. Elger, 1989.
13. Ibid.
14. Ibid.
15. Webb, 1897.
16. Michels, 1968.
17. Crouch, 1982. Kelly, 1988.
18. Ibid.
19. Clarke, 1978, p. 18.
20. Flanders, 1968.
21. Fox, 1978, pp. 130–151.
22. Kelly, 1988, Chapter 5.
23. Hyman, 1971.
24. For an overview, see Lapides, 1987.
25. Lenin, 1902.
26. Goldthorpe et al., 1968.
27. Blackburn and Mann, 1979.
28. Beynon, 1973.
29. Mann, 1973.
30. Hyman, 1971.
31. Goodrich, 1975.
32. De Ste Croix, 1983, p. 57.
33. Ibid., p. 66.
34. Ibid.
35. Ibid., p. 44.

2 The State, Trade Unions and Industrial Conflict

In the first half of the nineteenth century, trade unions were illegal organizations, although they persisted, especially among craft workers, either secretly or with the tacit acquiescence of employers. The Combination Acts were repealed in 1824, allowing workers the right of free association and encouraging the spread of worker organization. Prosecutions of trade unionists continued, however, through the use of other laws, so that associations and strikes concerned with issues other than wages and hours remained criminal conspiracies at common law.

In the last half of the nineteenth century the British state sponsored a move away from confrontation towards conciliation in the management of industrial conflict and sought to involve the trade unions in this policy.

The shift in attitude towards trade unions began with the Royal Commission on Trade Unions set up in 1867 in response to the Sheffield outrages and the growth of the trade union movement, which had 'roused alarm among the governing classes.' The Commission's investigations were hampered by the fact that there was very little information available about the extent and nature of trade unionism and industrial conflict, and commissioners had to rely heavily on the testimony of trade union leaders and employers. Trade union leaders estimated that trade unionism embraced 'every branch of skilled labour and a very large proportion of the working men of the kingdom' observing that there had been a striking and steady increase in trade unionism over the previous twenty years and that this was not the spasmodic growth of a temporary movement but the progress of a stable institution.[1]

Witnesses also talked of the growing antagonism between employers and workers and increased organization on both sides manifest in ever more violent episodes of industrial conflict. Employers complained that trade unionism had fostered this spirit of antagonism. They had lost control over their employees. The Commission agreed that employers were no longer 'regarded by both law and usage as the governing class . . . [and that] . . . a substitute has now to be found for it.'[2] There was also the question of whether 'the State should not on common public grounds

24

require associations of this permanence and importance to be conducted under some guarantees . . . of publicity.'[3]

The terms of reference of the Commission were outlined as follows, 'seeing that the bulk of the artisan population consider it in their interest to form themselves into these associations, in what way can they be rendered most conducive to public policy?'[4]

Commissioners were told of the striking and steady increase of well-organized and powerful trade unionism among skilled workers but recognized that this had gone hand in hand with improvements in their general character, compared with earlier inquiries (1824, 1825, 1838) and that violent incidents were a rarity. This type of trade unionism was not the problem. In their view, violence was common among associations of workers which were badly organized and unrecognized and clung to the ways of the old secret trade unions. The latter did not provide benefits for their members and preserved the criminal features of the surreptitious unions under the old law.[5]

Evidence brought before the Commission showed that trade unionism and industrial conflict were not synonymous. Strike activity did not increase as the strength of a trade union increased. The reverse was true. Once trade unions established themselves, strikes decreased and instead of a bid to constantly increase wages, a regularity of wages and hours ensued. The strongest, richest and largest unions were in those trades which exhibited established wage rates and few disputes. For example, unions in the engineering trade had a large membership and a large reserve fund, but wages had remained static for twenty-five years except when varied by employers. The shipwrights' and printers' unions exhibited the same characteristics.

In addition, the evidence showed that trade unions were 'a benefit of immense public utility and must spare the community a heavy burden in the poor rates and infirmaries alone' since 'every fresh expansion of industry is accompanied by a vast train of destitution.' Unions offered sick benefits, accident benefits, funeral funds, superannuation and unemployment benefits. They kept a great body of workers out of pauperism by keeping records on the state of trade and by sending labour from places where work was scarce to where it was plentiful or assisting their emigration. Well-organized trade unions like these were 'plainly useful both to capitalists and to the community'[6].

It was noted that the best types of union owed their superior organization to men like the Secretary of the Amalgamated Society of Engineers, who 'must impress all who have the opportunity of knowing him as a man of ability and character.'[7] Of trade union officials generally, it was emphasized: 'we cannot suppose that the officials . . . look on the acts of illegality and violence with any less feeling of abhorrence than we do ourselves . . . employers know of no case of violence . . . which they could connect with the principal union officials.'[8]

Strikes were shown to be most frequent and disorderly in the absence of any established union. Examples were cited of strikes, lockouts, outrage and riots in the coal mining districts of South Wales and Derbyshire, where no regular union was in force: 'experience has shown how readily a body of men who are dissatisfied with their wages subscribe a small fund for the purpose of striking, and form a rude union which scarcely exists, or is intended to exist beyond the immediate occasion.'[9] It was concluded that strikes and violence 'are ordinary incidents of the association of working men in masses' to which trade unionism of the kind referred to above 'brings an increased sense of order, subordination and reflection.'[10]

The employers' claim that violence and industrial conflict was caused by workers' determination to remain outside unions was rejected. No workers had come forward to substantiate this claim, and

'this may be interpreted, either as implying that the labouring classes in general are not discontented with the restrictions that trades unions appear to impose on industry or as implying that the influence of those unions is so very extensive, their ramifications so minute, and the general dislike to oppose an established class feeling so strong, that the real sentiments of the workmen opposed to unions have been, to a great extent, withheld from us.'[11]

The Commissioners concluded that this was a small element in industrial unrest, that only a very small minority of workers wanted to remain outside trade unions and that this was probably due to the influence of outside agencies such as the Free Labour Registration Society (a body organized by employers for the express purpose of counteracting trade unions). Many strikers were wage labourers struggling for subsistence who saw unionism as a way forward. The biggest obstacles to this and a major cause of unrest were, in the Commissioners' view, the oppressive practices of employers and the legal containment of trade unions.

Overall it was believed that all the disadvantages of trade unionism, as far as employers and the community were concerned, disappeared when they reached a high degree of organization and 'a well-recognized code of general rules exists, with a competent authority to maintain and explain them. The element of due notice before a change on either side alone effects the greatest results in removing sources of dispute. The difference between one state of things and the other appears to us to be that between a morbid and a healthy state of industrial relations . . . when the great advantages of the system of a code of rules and prices is further supported by a board of arbitration, it appears to us the nearest solution of the labour and employment question which has yet shown itself.'[12]

The Commissioners concluded that conciliation and arbitration boards offered 'a remedy [for industrial conflict] at once speedy, safe and simple'[13] and that the success of this remedy depended on the promotion of 'responsible' trade unionism. Responsible trade unionism was a discipline on the natural tendencies of workers to organization, strikes and violence and a substitute for employers' loss of direct control over them.

So, instead of the repression of trade unions as many employers expected, the members of the Commission discussed the merits of conciliation and arbitration and their Report recommended giving unions legal recognition on the grounds that repressive legislation 'belongs in spirit to ages when the State was morbidly jealous of anything which could threaten its authority . . . [it is] . . . a relic of feudalism and contrary to the spirit of modern legislation.'[14]

The Trade Union Act was passed in 1871. A trade union could not now be considered unlawful because its objects were in restraint of trade. This legislation established trade unions on firm social and legal foundations but 'the foundations . . . were still extremely narrow, and equally narrow was the prevailing conception of their tasks.'[15] The Trade Union Act aimed at creating an environment which favoured the expansion of 'responsible' trade unions led by officials with authority over their members who would negotiate with employers and contain industrial conflict. This legislation entitled a recognized union to bargain collectively with the employer concerned. On the other hand, it denied the right to bargain collectively to unions which were not recognized by employers. It thereby imposed legal restraints on rank-and-file activity. Also, as Hyman emphasizes, it allowed employers to determine the scope of collective bargaining. An employer would naturally favour a union which had no inclination to challenge seriously the right of management to control production. Even without such selectivity, the terms on which an employer recognized a union could include restrictions on its right to pursue certain issues in negotiation. And even where no explicit restrictions existed, union representatives would not normally present demands which jeopardized the bargaining relationship.[16]

Conciliation and arbitration as ways of resolving disputes between employers and workers were pioneered in the hosiery industry in the 1860s.[17] The increase in popularity of conciliation and arbitration between employers and workers was interpreted at the time as a sea-change in industrial relations such that 'confidence and good will have replaced suspicion and open hostility.'[18] Later it was characterized as 'an evolutionary triumph of liberal principles and civilized restraints, with workers coming gradually to "learn" what was required of them in this best of all liberal worlds. Organized labour, after a turbulent and irrational period, grasped the wisdom of rational peaceful negotiation and fashioned systems which took their place in the emerging panoply of civilized institutions, with alternative strategies deservedly sinking down into the dustbin of history as pathetic and doomed digressions.'[19] While noting that the use of conciliation and arbitration marked an important development in industrial relations, contemporary writers have been less effusive or unanimous in their assessments of them.

Workers achieved some concessions and worker organization was strengthened by the existence of joint procedures for settling disputes (acceptance of joint boards was a condition for survival of trade unionism)[20] but it is clear that in terms of wages employers had most to gain from them.[21] Phelps Brown argues that two factors explain employers' participation in conciliation and arbitration at this time: the growing strength of worker organization and employers' interest in standardizing wages, as this removed one element in competition. Phelps Brown clarifies the issue thus:

'the unionists were at least strong enough to bring a number of mills out together, and would go back only when a common settlement had been made for them all. If the employers had begun by feeling that the wider the combination was, the greater the threat to them, they soon found it was really the other way round: except where they were pinned down by foreign competition, they might have little to fear from a wage settlement if only it was enforced on all of them alike, and a strong union was their guarantee that it would be. Not a few reached the conclusion that it was a positive advantage to them to have a floor put under price competition in this way. Those who had little love for the union were still willing to meet it to negotiate a rate, because of all union activities this interfered with them least. They would resent hotly any encroachment on their prerogatives as managers of their own businesses, but collective bargaining only meant that they were paying the same price as their competitors for one factor of production, just as they did when they bought a raw material in the same market.'[22]

ARBITRATION

Arbitration was used more than conciliation in the 1870s because it circumvented the issue of recognition and placed the onus of deciding claims on arbitrators. The majority of arbitrators were lawyers, politicians and employers who shared the conventional view of political economy. This, combined with union leaders' willingness to negotiate, 'placed a definite restriction on the possibility of any considerable change in the workers' position.'[23]

The criteria most often used by arbitrators for determining awards favoured employers and included the general state of trade, the competitive needs of a district and changes in the selling price of the product. The first of these offers no precise criterion – 'what the trade is and what it can bear are relative matters, to be determined only after taking into account a large number of factors . . . A great deal depends on obtaining figures from employers on which to base a judgment. As a general rule, employers have been extremely reluctant to supply this evidence, and when it has been furnished it has been too fragmentary to be of much use.'[24] The second standard could mean that no district ever got a wage advance.[25] It was nevertheless often used by arbitrators. The most popular criterion was changes in the selling price of the product. An influential arbitrator, Rupert Kettle, asserted in 1869 that 'price forms the only legitimate fund out of which wages can be paid, and the enquiry should be strictly confined to this.'[26] Few arbitrators considered profits as a standard for wage awards, sharing the employers' view that profits were no concern of the workers. Few recognized the question of a subsistence level, and where arbitrators did recognize this standard 'it was usually sacrificed to their need to make an award reflecting the change in the state of trade.'[27]

In the period 1873–1896 few arbitration awards gave wage increases – most were either reductions or rejections of claims for increases. In the industries analysed by Porter in this period – the hosiery and lace trades, boot and shoe, cotton spinning, iron and coal mining – arbitration awards showed a correspondence to the trend of average industrial prices and to short-run changes in the level of economic activity. Porter finds only two instances of wage increases and twenty-eight reductions. Product prices were the main information provided by employers. Arbitrators were forced to accept these and, since the main feature of the Great Depression was the fall in prices, award wage reductions. In addition, where other criteria were used, such as changes in output, these were based on a comparison of the present level of activity with that of a previous year, and since the majority of awards in the Great Depression took place against a background of temporarily declining economic activity, the pressure to reduce wages was reinforced.[28]

Arbitration as a method of settling wage disputes was at its height in the 1870s during the Great Depression. After 1879 the number of wage disputes taken to arbitration began to decline sharply owing to 'considerable difficulties'.[29] Since it seemed invariably to correspond with wage reductions, trade union members became disillusioned with arbitration and resort to arbitration became much less frequent, except in poorly organized trades where workers depended on some form of state arbitration or a state tribunal of some kind.[30] In strongly organized trades, like coal, iron, cotton, hosiery and lace, there was a shift away from arbitration towards conciliation.

Trade union leaders became enthusiastic supporters of conciliation boards and pointed to the gains made through them, not least the reduction of strikes.[31] However, there were also important disadvantages for workers in conciliation.

CONCILIATION

A major restriction characteristic of agreements reached through joint conciliation procedures was the length of agreements negotiated by union leaders, which prevented workers from taking advantage of prosperous trade to press for wage increases. By negotiating long-term agreements as trade was increasing, employers could keep wages down as profits were rising and production was less likely to be disrupted by disputes. Long agreements also prevented local union branches from making wage claims, so that for militant local unionists union discipline was as important as employer opposition.

In addition, conciliation machinery required a period of notice after the expiry of agreements before a claim could be made. The Nottingham

Hosiery Board required one month's notice, while most sliding scale agreements provided for two or three months' notice. This prevented employers from being caught in the middle of an order. There were also restrictions on the size of wage rate fluctuations at any one time or within a certain time – typically, five per cent at any one time or within five years.

In some industries employers placed restrictions on what could be discussed on conciliation boards. For example, the terms which followed the Boot and Shoe lockout in 1895 (negotiated with the assistance of the BOT) restricted the work of the boards to the interpretation of existing agreements to prevent the discussion of 'abstract principles of socialism.' The employers' chairman described the terms as 'a charter of rights for the manufacturers, under which three fourths of the disputes which affected the industry would be rendered impossible.'[32]

Procedural delays involved in making a claim through conciliation machinery also constituted a barrier to effective action. For workers, who were obliged not to strike while their claims were being processed, this could mean a wait of months or even years as in the case of the 'abnormal places' dispute in South Wales.[33]

The restrictive effects of conciliation agreements on workers' wages in a boom were not matched by equivalent restrictions on employers when their relative power was greatest in a depression – for instance, in the coal mining districts of the Federated Area and South Wales, where a conciliation agreement (which was virtually a sliding scale with a maximum and minimum rate) operated after 1894 and 1903 respectively. The divergence between the level of wage rates when these rates reached the maximum permitted by the agreement was greater than the divergence between the level of prices and wage rates in a depression when the minimum rate was in operation.[34]

In practice, then, both arbitration and conciliation tended to improve the position of employers and trade union leaders rather than the workers' position in industrial bargaining. It was this effect of conciliation and arbitration, together with its beneficial effect on strike activity, which recommended them to the state. Members of the Royal Commission on Trade Unions applauded responsible trade unionism when it was shown that it could peacefully ensure that 'wages could remain static for twenty-five years except when varied by employers'.[35] The establishment of numerous boards of conciliation and arbitration in the 1870s was welcomed by the BOT, because they produced 'the relative moderation in the demand of the workmen for a share in the profits of the extraordinary trade expansion then in progress.'[36]

Although a range of legislation was passed to encourage the spread of conciliation and arbitration, the Commission's hopes for the generalization of this method of dispute resolution were not realized. The Councils of Conciliation Act was passed in 1867 to promote the setting-up of councils of conciliation where employers and workers' representatives could meet to thrash out voluntary agreements, which would then be legally enforceable. In 1872 A.J. Mundella (hosiery manufacturer, MP and later President of the BOT) succeeded in passing the Arbitration (Masters and Workmen) Act to try and encourage the trend towards arbitration. This Act provided for agreements drawn up between employers and workers as a result of conciliation or arbitration to be made binding on both. It facilitated compulsory arbitration, but was weaker than previous legislation in that it was necessary for both parties to agree. A decision could not be imposed on either party. This legislation and previous legislation (such as the Arbitration Act 1824) had been 'complete failures' because 'employers and employed have preferred to settle disputes in their own way without calling in extraneous authority.'[37] There was also a growing belief among union members that their leaders had become too willing to compromise their interests to preserve conciliation machinery, and this discontent began to be expressed in unofficial action, resulting in several conciliation boards being broken during and after the Great Depression of the 1870s.[38]

By the late 1880s the reluctance of many employers to recognize trade unions, the failure of attempts to reduce strike action with conciliation and arbitration procedures, the expansion of worker organization and escalating industrial conflict led to a systematic re-examination of industrial conflict and of the relationship between trade unions and industrial conflict, and subsequently to another Royal Commission.[39]

THE LABOUR CORRESPONDENT OF THE BOARD OF TRADE

In 1886 the Board of Trade was empowered by Parliament to collect and publish statistics in relation to labour. Later, in 1888, the Board of Trade was officially charged with producing annual reports to the government on strikes and lockouts in Britain. In these reports various officials of the Board of Trade, under the heading of 'Labour Correspondent' mapped out the terrain of British industrial relations for the government as well as producing statistics on industrial conflict.

In the first report on strikes and lockouts, the Labour Correspondent set out the obstacles in the way of improved industrial relations. He noted that there had been many failed attempts 'to prevent altogether or settle as speedily as possible, the quarrels which arise between capital and labour.' These failures were serious because

'the regularity and continuity of labour represent largely the wealth and life of the nation and all violent or unnecessary stoppages affect like a disease the whole organism of trade.' Part of the problem was that not enough was known about industrial conflict and 'very little has been done to collect information as to these disputes, which is a pity, for we might now have had available a vast mass of statistics on the subject in the highest degree useful, full of interest, of warning and of teaching to all.'

It was not enough, however, to send questionnaires to employers and trade unions as the BOT routinely did. In addition, and to avoid 'a tendency which threatens to wreck the whole system of social statistics', namely the knowledge of the use to which the results of the investigation would be put, the Board of Trade was careful to seek its data 'in absolute records compiled for other purposes.' It was emphasized that statistics on wages were best obtained from employers. This was not just because only employers kept wage statistics from year to year but also because 'they are less likely to be influenced by personal feeling or class prejudice to make false or misleading statements.' Workers, on the other hand, 'might be influenced by common class feeling to make their wages as low as possible in order to make a showing on their side of the social question'.[40]

It was also necessary to combat the 'astonishing' lack of interest displayed in strikes by the general community where 'even the largest labour fights are little more then a nine days' wonder.'[41] The main stumbling block, however, was 'the present industrial system' where 'it was the object of the contending parties on the one hand, to buy as much for as little as possible and on the other to sell as little as may be for the highest attainable price.' This meant that conflict was inevitable.[42]

Not only was conflict inevitable, but labour quarrels in Britain were more frequent, larger in scale and more pertinaciously fought out than in other countries.

There were two reasons for this. Firstly, the fighting organizations of employers and workers were more highly developed in Britain than elsewhere. Secondly, the right of workers to dispose of their own labour was established, and whatever 'the wisdom or justification of strikes and lockouts from the moral and economical point of view, there is now no legal hindrance to their operation.'[43]

In the first report on trade unions in 1887, the Labour Correspondent of the BOT (John Burnett) set out to correct some widespread misunderstandings about them. He emphasized that the gradual self-organization of labour had been one of the most striking facts in the industrial history of the nation in the previous sixty years. The trade union movement was 'expressly and specially the creation of labour itself and for its own purposes' and had now become so much a part of the social life of the nation and so much a fundamental principle of social and political liberty that it was difficult to realize that the right of combination in Britain was so recently granted.[44]

Burnett went on to point out that, contrary to popular belief, trade unions were a feature of the rise of capitalism and bore only a superficial resemblance to the guilds of the Middle Ages. The feudal guilds were unions of all the men in a trade, masters and workers alike, and the object of the combination was to look after the interests of all. The growing diversity of interests between employer and worker due to the development of industry led to the destruction of the guilds over time and the formation of opposing trade unions, whose object was to look after the interests of the section of workers they represented without any special regard for others. The rise of trade unions and the decline of the guilds was a manifestation of the fact that a mutuality of interests no longer existed between employer and employed. For the Labour Correspondent, this situation was to be regretted. Nevertheless, it was an improvement on 'the state of social anarchy' which had prevailed in Britain after the breakup of the guilds and which reached its climax in the late eighteenth and early nineteenth centuries. This was 'an age of petty legislative restrictions and regulations. Acts of Parliament attempted to regulate nearly all the relations of capital and labour.'[45] The hours of labour were fixed by law and wages were assessed 'in the same spirit of paternal government.' Employers flouted the law in practice and prompted workers to combine to enforce the law, whereupon employers 'strove to enforce the laws which made combination illegal.' The resulting conflicts between capital and labour were frequent, fierce and vindictive. This, combined with the rapid development of industry, rendered the condition of large masses of the people 'miserable in the extreme.'[46] The trade unions were a welcome corrective to this: 'there is now nothing in their modes of working which will not bear the fullest light of day' and 'the more there becomes known about them, the more useful they are likely to become'.[47] From the standpoint of the BOT, there was 'little doubt their members are the flower of their respective trades' and that their leaders 'are cautious and moderate in the extreme . . . these men do not act the part of social disturbers or industrial incendiaries inflaming the passions of their constituents . . . they confine themselves to remarks which are distinguished by reason and moderation.'[48] A main concern was that, contrary to the findings of the Royal Commission in 1867, trade unions 'cannot by any means be said to include within their ranks anything like the great body of workmen of the kingdom.'[49]

The Labour Correspondent then turned his attention to strikes. Strikes were a common feature of industrial life in Britain; they were characterized by the British worker's love of representative forms of government, and

'as a rule they are conducted upon very businesslike principles and their management is often marked by executive ability of a very high order, especially among the trades which have permanent officials who are thoroughly conversant with all the technicalities of their trade and who are able to speak and write with clearness and force.'[50]

The causes of strikes were more complicated, and though many seemed to revolve around what constituted 'a fair day's work and a fair day's pay', closer investigation revealed that the true causes of strikes were not always apparent.[51] Also, it was commonly believed that strikes were started by the central executives of trade unions and not by workers themselves – that workers were forced to strike by their trade unions and left work 'unwillingly and in opposition to their own wishes and inclinations.'[52] Research revealed, however, that in nine out of ten cases strikes were first suggested by the men themselves in their separate shops and localities and information only afterwards found its way to the authorities of the trade societies. Far from being in favour of strike action, the executive committees of all the chief unions were to a very large extent hostile to strikes and exercized a restraining influence. Moreover, 'to such an extent is this power of repression occasionally exerted that the members of trade unions are often found to declare that their executive bodies are too slow in taking action in cases of dispute.'[53]

Trade unions were regulated by elected committees at both local and central levels, and

'a general knowledge of these principles of trade union government and a long observation of the methods of procedure adopted in trade movements are sufficient to show that agitation first commences with the actual workers, next it extends, if it be not an entirely sudden and impulsive outbreak, to the lodges, committees and executives of the union before it assumes definite shape.'

It was emphasized that in recent years the control of central executives over strike movements had gradually become stronger and unofficial strikes were less likely to be recognized or supported by the union. In all the large unions, especially those with national coverage, 'safeguards of this kind must be devised to restrain rash and hasty action on the part of any locality.'

Their funds must be safeguarded. The good of the whole union must be placed before the wishes of any section or district. This was the executive's responsibility, and so the leaders, although they shared their members' concerns, were bound by 'a heavy sense of responsibility in all they do and theirs is a much more sobering and restraining influence on their constituents than is generally supposed.'[54]

In spite of their beneficial influence and their role in the prevention of strikes, however, union leaders received little credit for their role from the general public and often small thanks from the rank and file of trade unions. The Labour Correspondent emphasized that he did not want to give the impression that trade union leaders were infallible. Both leaders and their members were apt 'to make mistakes and to miscalculate the strength of the forces in front of them and behind them.' He only wished to clarify the dynamics of trade unions and strike action, to show that 'the old ideas of secret tribunals and despotic delegates ordering men to work or not to work at their good pleasure are things of the past and in nearly every case it is right to assume that when a body of men come out on strike they do so of their own free will.'[55]

The investigations of the BOT showed that it was now widely realized that legislation against strikes and combinations had been ineffective: over the previous twenty years there had been a considerable move towards preventing and settling industrial disputes by arbitration and conciliation. It was made clear that

'these methods of arranging difficulties have only been made possible by organizing forces on both sides and have, as it were, been gradually evolved from the general progress of the combination movement.'[56]

The beneficial effects of these peaceful methods were most evident in the coal industry and in certain branches of the iron trade, but tentative experiments had begun in other industries. The lead had been taken by the miners of Northumberland and Durham and the ironworkers of the north of England: 'Before these trades were highly organized, strikes were frequent, prolonged and bitter. Now they meet their employers and talk over questions affecting their labour "upon something like equal terms" and conciliation and arbitration characterize the relationship between them rather than strike action.'[57] Neither conciliation nor arbitration was the perfect solution to strikes and lockouts. These could not be entirely prevented. In certain cases agreements were not unanimously accepted and were themselves the cause of disputes – but these were mostly local and limited. With these qualifications, however, conciliation and arbitration procedures had been 'an important factor' in managing industrial conflict: 'they minimize the number of disputes, moderate their acerbity and shorten their duration.'[58]

Figures were provided in support of these claims. There had been 509 strikes in 1888. Although difficulties had been encountered from employers and trade unions in gaining information about them, the information which was available showed that the majority of strikes (57.3 per cent) were in the cotton trade and in the mines. The reason given for striking in the majority of cases (62.25 per cent) was the need for increased wages. Enquiry forms sent out by the BOT also asked employers and unions for suggestions for the prevention and settlement of disputes. Of the 100 employers who completed these, one third advocated arbitration; one sixth were in favour of sliding scales; four called for the abolition of trade unions; two sarcastically recommended 'giving to labour all that it may demand until, as one suggests, capital is exhausted'; two called for the removal and punishment of paid agitators with hard labour; 'common sense' was recommended by some, and only one employer recommended co-operation.[59]

The responses of trade unions and employers to BOT enquiries 'were much more in harmony than might have been expected.' Of the 72 trade unions which replied, one third were in favour of arbitration; nearly one third were in favour of conciliation; two were in favour of sliding scales; two advocated government interference; six thought more and better worker organization was the solution; one was for profit sharing; one advocated a union of employers; eight thought there should be a list of prices faithfully adhered to and several advocated workers' control of the means of production.[60]

Against this background, the BOT advised that the most constructive option for the government was 'to become familiar with the organization and take a lead in those movements likely to conduct us to a state of things in which it shall become more and more difficult to resort to the strike and lockout as the only arbiters in the struggles of employer and employed.'[61] Subsequent years, however, saw an explosion of industrial conflict which made this analysis seem unduly optimistic.

THE 'NEW UNIONS'

In 1889 there were 1,145 strikes. This wave of industrial conflict was markedly different from previous years. It was notable for the revolt of the unskilled labourer. It marked the consolidation of unskilled worker organization such that 'it is now common to speak and write about the "old" and the "new" trade unionism as distinct and separate from one another and to see the "new" trade unionism as 'a labour movement almost without parallel in English history.'[62] For Burnett and the BOT, however, this movement differed 'in no matter of principle ... from many that have gone before it'.[63] It was not something entirely different in essence from other trade unions which preceded it. It was 'stronger, more concentrated and possibly embraces a much wider area and a larger number of people' – but the most significant characteristic of the movement was the effective use of the sympathetic strike, which 'has never been so strongly in evidence before'.[64] This tactic was not new, but it was a form of strike more common in the USA than in Britain and 'it is certain that those who struck on sympathetic grounds did not return to work without receiving substantial concessions for themselves.'[65]

Six branches of industry furnished 60 per cent of the strikes, although most trades were subject to disputes. The most troublesome sectors were textiles, mining, shipbuilding, engineering, docks, seafaring and firefighting. Of the total number of strikes, 41.6 per cent were successful, 32.1 per cent were partially successful, 18.1 per cent were unsuccessful and no results were available for the remainder.[66] Workers in well-organized trades had been very successful in enforcing their demands. A minority of trades passed peacefully through this upheaval and significantly these were trades in which boards of conciliation, arbitration or sliding scales existed.[67]

An important factor underpinning the conflict of 1889 was the fact that depression had given way to a prosperous state of trade at the end of 1888, accompanied by a significant increase in demand for labour of all kinds. A striking example of the upturn was shipbuilding and boilermaking, where unemployment fell from just over 26 per cent in 1885 to just over two per cent in 1889.

Another significant development in 1889 was the drive towards building links between labour movements internationally. At the London International Congress 'a strong socialistic element had made its appearance and several notable London Socialists were appointed by trade unions or sections of trade unions as delegates to the Paris Congress to be held the following year.' It was concluded that although 'the bulk of English trade unionists can't be said to have taken much interest' in these developments, it was significant that the socialists went to Paris 'as a party, acting together and with definite aims for the first time, to use the labour organizations for the purposes of their own movement.'[68]

The Labour Correspondent was relieved to report that although strikes of unskilled labour continued in 1890 and were 'often obstinate and prolonged, they were devoid of the novelty, excitement and dramatic incidents of the great strike of dockers in the previous year'. Nevertheless ten per cent of the strikes in 1890 were of dock, wharf and riverside labour and 'this is a very large proportion' for a newly organized association.[69] There were 1028 strikes in total, a large number of which were general strikes. Of the total, 37.1 per cent were successful (41.6 per cent had been successful in 1889); 22 per cent were partially successful (32.1 per cent in 1889); 31 per cent were unsuccessful (18.1 per cent in 1889); for 9.7 per cent results were unknown (8.2 per cent in 1889). Sympathetic strikes were less numerous and less successful than in 1889 – 63.1 per cent of these were defeated. The BOT concluded that overall the statistics showed less favourable results from strike action for workers in 1890 than in 1889. It was suggested that this may have been due in part to the increase in strikes caused by refusal of trade union recognition or by refusal of trade unionists to work with non-unionists. There were 59 strikes under this head in 1890, mainly involving unskilled unions, and only 23 per cent were successful.

Apart from the waning success of the unskilled workers' organizations, there was another encouraging factor in the conflict of 1890. This was the significant increase in the popularity of conciliation as a way of resolving disputes and 'strange to say, this prevails most strongly amongst the new organizations of unskilled labour, which are otherwise generally most extreme in their modes of action.'[70] The BOT had again canvassed the opinions of trade unions and employers as to the best means of avoiding or settling disputes. The replies showed a marked change in outlook from the previous year. The majority of those who replied were in favour of conciliation boards. Some employers were in favour of state boards of conciliation and arbitration. One trade union 'even goes so far as to ask for a government board of conciliation.' The Labour Correspondent concluded that

'in the vast majority of cases the suggestions put forward are made with good faith and seriousness which proves how fully the gravity of the situation is realized and there is manifest a full recognition of the fact that a better state of affairs is only to be brought about by conciliatory means.'[71]

One of the less encouraging features of the general labour movement in the year 1890, however, was the prominence of the campaign for the eight-hour day, which 'has been steadily pressed to the front as the most urgent problem of labour politics.' The 'one special feature of this movement' for the BOT was its international character and 'the workers of all the most important nations are endeavouring with more or less energy and enthusiasm, to press this industrial problem upon the attention of their respective governments.'[72]

The unprecedented increase in trade union activity and industrial conflict in 1889 and 1890, together with the intelligence provided by the Labour Correspondent of the BOT, led to the Royal Commission on Labour in 1891.

THE ROYAL COMMISSION ON LABOUR 1891–94

In its report in 1894 the Commission noted that the initiatives taken by the Royal Commission of 1867–69 had been based on the idea that well-organized and responsible trade unions and employers' organizations were the key to improved industrial relations. The latter had worsened significantly in the intervening period after a promising start and the Commission concluded that this deterioration was the outcome of various factors.

Firstly, the expansion of responsible trade union organization, as proposed by the Royal Commission on Trade Unions, had been much smaller than envisaged. This owed much to the fact that many employers still endeavoured to employ workers who were not organized.

Secondly, a main aim of the Trade Union Act 1871 was to challenge the traditional structure of authority relations in trade unions – to reverse the flow of union authority from below so that disputes could be subject to executive control. This was central to the effective operation of conciliation and arbitration. For the most part, however, power was still with the rank and file in trade unions and not with the executives. It was emphasized that in some cases, such as that of the Durham coal miners, so many references had to be made in the case of general questions to the local lodges or branches, to be decided by ballot, that the central body were little more than delegates acting under immediate instructions and had to refer points to their constituents, even in the midst of negotiations with employers.

In other cases, especially where a trade was scattered in various branches all over the country and through districts differing widely in local circumstances from each other, much power and discretion was frequently left with the district or executive committees or local branches. The only power the central executive of most unions of this kind seemed to have was the power of withholding funds if strike action was taken by a local branch or district, and this power was seldom exercised.[73]

The ideal trade union from the Commission's point of view was characterized by

'such a proportion of men in a trade as will give it controlling power in the trade and enable it to treat with employers as representative of the whole and to make agreements and decisions binding on the whole trade. It will have a strong executive council, thoroughly representative of the members and implicitly trusted by them. This machinery will enable the society to negotiate with employers with the least possible friction, either from time to time or by way of a permanent joint board, for the purpose of settling hour and wage rate questions and other points of dispute and to give undertakings and enter into agreements on which employers can rely.'[74]

Some trade unions came near to this ideal, but these were mostly in skilled trades which were more adapted to organization (it was easier to convert the natural craft already in existence into a formal and permanent trade union) or in other less skilled trades where the monopoly possessed by an industry and its consequent facilities for organization were more developed owing to extraneous causes (e.g. legislation). Coal mining was cited as a good example of this. The natural monopoly which, in some trades, was due to workers' special skill had been obtained by coal miners not only because the industry was concentrated in certain districts and they had practical possession of the villages adjacent to which they worked, but through the provisions of the Coal Mines Regulation Act 1887, which rendered it impossible for employers to bring in new men, in case of a strike, to take the place of the strikers.

Thirdly, there were serious deficiencies in organization among employers. Employers' organizations tended to be formed in response to the growing strength of workers' organizations. They were forced to combine to resist them. There were some longstanding employers' associations, originally formed to watch legislation affecting trade or for tempering competition by agreement among themselves, which had become instruments of mutual protection against worker organization. Generally, however, employers combined unwillingly and competition between them usually ensured that their combinations were short-lived. Many employers did not join employers' associations.

Fourthly and most importantly, there was the substantial rise in the numerical representation and importance of organization among unskilled labour since the reports of the Royal Commission on Trade Unions.[75] This was the organization of the previously powerless, who saw in trade unionism and conciliation and arbitration the way to address their powerlessness. It had caused new difficulties. Unskilled organizations were usually weak. They rapidly arose, enrolled many members and rapidly declined. Their members had no natural monopoly over their work as in the skilled trades and employers could easily replace them. They relied solely on strike action to achieve their aims. The unskilled unions' prosperity and numerical strength depended on success in conflicts. When strike action was unsuccessful they lost many members, because they could not offer the benefits which provided solidity and permanence to the established trade unions. Their low-paid members could afford only small subscriptions.

In spite of these weaknesses, however, the unskilled unions had become a source of concern for several reasons. Unskilled union members tended to use violence to prevent non-union labour taking the place of locked-out unionists. They sought the support of unskilled labour in other trades, other trade unions and the state in industrial conflicts. Large schemes of amalgamation and federation had appeared with the intention of achieving sympathy strikes. This had extended the range and damage caused by industrial conflict. Finally, the growth of organizations with membership extending beyond a single establishment across an entire industry had loosened the control of employers over their workforce in individual firms. It was noted that attempts had been made to counteract this by profit-sharing schemes, mutual benefit and accident funds to 'reproduce the old-fashioned sentiment of unity only on a basis of more equal relations suited to the altered spirit of the time' and to make firms 'independent industrial polities constituted on the footing of partnership' but the notion of co-operative industrial partnership had failed. Established trade unions had seen these initiatives as an attack on them and resisted them.[76] It was emphasized that many recent conflicts in the ranks of unskilled labour had been aimed at compelling employers to recognize their organizations. Employers, however, saw no need to recognize them and totally resisted their attempts – they were easily replaced by non-union labour and labour imported from country districts. This was causing great bitterness and violence.

It was concluded that the solution to the problem lay in setting up a body to impose a regulatory framework on industrial relations. That body already existed within the Board of Trade. The Conciliation Act, passed in 1896, empowered the Labour Department of the Board of Trade to devise, maintain and explain a code of general rules for the regulation of industrial relations. Before 1896 intervention in trade disputes was not formally included in the BOT's functions, although it intervened and undertook conciliation procedures informally with a view to the settlement of strikes or lockouts which were either imminent or in progress – they were a method of settling disputes, not of preventing them.[77] The BOT's main role had been to provide the state with 'copious particulars as to the numbers, funds, expenditure and objects of trade unions.'[78]

After the Conciliation Act, conciliation came to mean much more than a practice involving the services of a neutral third party in a dispute to help the parties reach an amicable settlement. The aim of conciliation came to include intervention by the BOT to actively foster trade union recognition and collective bargaining – to intervene permanently to prevent disputes from developing into strike action. The Labour Department began to set up a dialogue with existing conciliation boards, to co-operate with them and to promote the setting-up of new boards. Where the BOT was called upon to assist in the settlement of disputes, it embodied the settlement in the form of a collective agreement together with procedural arrangements for future agreements and a clause providing for the appointment of a state conciliator should the parties fail to reach a settlement by negotiation.[79]

The state now actively sponsored the recognition of trade unionism through the imposition on employers of a duty to bargain with trade unions recognized as 'representative.' Contemporary writers differ on the significance of the state's intervention at this point. Middlemas sees the pre-war Labour Department of the BOT as an 'enlightened bureaucracy, sympathetic to the interests of labour, which took up the cause of trade unionism 'to ameliorate some of the disadvantages suffered by trade unions in industrial bargaining.'[80] However, the evidence confirms Davidson's view that official decisions were constrained by a broader imperative. It suggests that the extent to which the state sought to redress the balance in favour of organized labour through conciliation was very limited and circumscribed by the need to safeguard the competitiveness of British industry which, it was thought, would be jeopardized if the state sought to moderate the role of market forces in the determination of wages. This is manifest in the fact that in the overwhelming majority of disputes handled by the BOT in the period 1896–1914 labour failed to achieve its objectives. It was more successful in those disputes in which the BOT was not involved. In addition, the majority of disputes handled by the BOT in this period stemmed from trade union demands for wage increases and better working conditions at a time of declining real wages, such that the high percentage of compromise settlements under the Conciliation Act represented a serious failure on the part of labour to realize its aims.[81] There was an 'underlying identity between the bureaucratic objectives of the Board and the self-interest of employers: a concern for the preservation of the free market, for the security of capital and for the continuity and cost-competitiveness of industrial production.'[82] The main difference between officials of the BOT and employers was over the means by which these objectives might be achieved. Many employers favoured repressive measures involving penal or military sanctions, while the BOT saw intervention in wage determination together with welfare legislation as 'the most effective antidote to socialism and the preservative of industrial capitalism'.[83]

CONCLUSION

The picture of trade unions and their leaders drawn above by the BOT paints them as 'plainly useful to capitalists and the community.'[84] Trade union leaders provided a remedy for industrial conflict superior to legislation and the use of force. The strong influence of craft unionism and the limited impact of socialism on worker organization in this period are underlined. Trade union leaders were 'managers of discontent'.[85]

The investigations of the BOT confirm an important distinction between trade movements and trade unions made in Price's analysis of nineteenth-century worker organization.[86] Trade movements were separate and distinct from any union organization. They emanated from organizational efforts in a few shops which brimmed over to a district or town and the sources of authority flowed upwards from the mass to the leadership. Price shows that employers' complaints about the restrictions which unions imposed on their activities (e.g. control over labour supply, rules restricting output, rules against overtime, opposition to machinery, enforcement of standard rates and the regulation of apprenticeship) have been misunderstood. These restrictions were commonly associated with trade union organization. There was, however, a disjuncture between the number of trade unionists and their supposed power and influence. The restrictions employers encountered were typically those of the workgroup and bore little relationship to union existence and function.[87] Price emphasizes that 'union' was likely to have meant any attempt by workers to act in union.[88]

This distinction was recognized by officials of the BOT and it was precisely the readiness of workers to organize and act independently and sporadically in 'the absence of consistent or informed commitment to any one set of beliefs' which defined these combinations and was most threatening.[89] These characteristics of independent worker organization restricted employers and explained why trade union organization was not extensive, and why trade union leaders in many cases exerted limited power over their members. They made conciliation a less effective strategy for managing industrial conflict. They made state intervention more likely and at the same time restricted the shape it could take.[90]

This situation was aggravated by the rise of unskilled workers' organizations and the wave of industrial conflict which accompanied it was seen mainly as a response to unskilled workers' exclusion from collective bargaining by established trade unions and by employers. The unskilled workers adopted tactics inimical to 'responsible' unionism which bore many of the hallmarks of earlier worker organization. They were often violent but essentially weak and transient. However, some of the 'new unions' had developed new tactics in their struggle which relied on numerical strength and on amalgamation and federation for the purpose of sympathy strikes. They recruited members across the boundaries of individual firms. This struggle had also acquired an international dimension and was being exploited by socialists to further their own cause. This was a novel combination of factors which had extended the range and damage, both actual and potential, of industrial action. There had been important developments in both the structure and tactics of working-class organization, but they were driven by unskilled workers' desire to be included in collective bargaining to improve their wages, not to transcend capitalism itself.[91]

The solution was state intervention to spread 'responsible' trade unionism and collective bargaining, and this was systematically and successfully promoted by the Labour Department of the BOT over the whole period 1896 to 1913. By 1910 the BOT could report to Parliament that 'the method of collective bargaining may be said to prevail throughout the whole of our manufacturing industries and to a very considerable extent in regard to the employment of dock and riverside labour and of labour employed in transportation and sea fishing'.[92] In 1896 105 conciliation boards were known to be in existence; by 1913 there were 325.[93]

The remainder of this study charts the efficacy of this solution to industrial conflict, and especially the adequacy of the view of trade unions and trade union leaders which underpins it, throughout a period of unprecedented industrial conflict. The next chapter begins this exploration by looking at key influences on the development of trade union organization, in particular syndicalism and industrial unionism, from the late nineteenth century in Britain. The aim is to provide a background for understanding the tactics and strategies adopted by workers, their leaders and the state, which are analysed in the later empirical chapters.

NOTES

1. Flanders, 1968, p. 14.
2. Ibid., p. 18.
3. Eleventh and Final Report of the Royal Commission on Trade Unions 1869, p. 33.
4. Ibid., p. 12.
5. Combination Acts 1799, 1800.
6. Report of the Royal Commission on Trade Unions, 1869.
7. Ibid., p. 35.
8. Ibid., p. 36.

9. Ibid.
10. Ibid.
11. Ibid.
12. Ibid.
13. Ibid., p. 235.
14. Report of the Royal Commission on Trade Unions 1894.
15. Ibid.
16. Hyman, 1975, p. 111.
17. Conciliation is a practice which involves the services of a neutral third party in a dispute as a means of helping disputing parties reach a settlement. The responsibility for settling disputes rests with the parties themselves. Arbitration is a procedure whereby a third party, not acting as a court of law, is empowered to take a decision which disposes of the dispute. (International Labour Organization 1980)
18. Crompton, 1876, quoted in Allen, 1971.
19. Fox, 1985, p. 167.
20. Tarling & Wilkinson, 1975, p. 9.
21. Allen, 1971, pp. 72–73.
22. Quoted in Hyman, 1975, p. 111.
23. Porter, 1970, p. 462.
24. Burns, 1926, pp. 385–387.
25. Porter, 1970, p. 464.
26. Ibid.
27. Ibid., p. 465.
28. Ibid.
29. Report of the Royal Commission on Trade Unions 1894, p. 51.
30. Ibid., p. 51.
31. Porter, 1970, p. 470.
32. National Union of Boot and Shoe Operatives Monthly Report Nov–Dec. 1900 quoted in Porter, 1970, p. 473.
33. Evans, 1911.
34. Porter, 1970, p. 473.
35. Ibid.
36. Ibid.
37. Report of the Royal Commission on Trade Unions 1894, p. 56.
38. Ibid.
39. Kay, 1979, p. 114.
40. Memorandum explaining the Progress of Arrangements for Collecting and Publishing Statistics Relating to Labour, 20th December 1888, p. 132.
41. Report on Strikes and Lockouts in 1888 by the Labour Correspondent of the Board of Trade, 1889, LX 703, p. 705.
42. Ibid., p. 706.
43. Ibid.
44. Report by the Labour Correspondent of the Board of Trade on Trade Unions, 1887 (1st Report) LXXX1X (C5104) 13th June 1887, p. 719.
45. Ibid.
46. Ibid., p. 720.
47. Ibid.

48. Report on Trade Unions by the Labour Correspondent of the Board of Trade (2nd Report), LXXX1V (C5808), 24th July 1888.
49. Ibid., p. 729.
50. Ibid., p. 710.
51. Ibid., p. 708.
52. Ibid., p. 709.
53. Ibid.
54. Ibid.
55. Ibid.
56. Ibid., p. 719.
57. Ibid., p. 721.
58. Ibid., p. 722.
59. Ibid., p. 737.
60. Ibid., p. 744.
61. Report of Strikes and Lockouts of 1888 by the Labour Correspondent of the Board of Trade (1889), LXX703, p. 705.
62. Report on Strikes and Lockouts (1890), p. 452.
63. Ibid., p. 454.
64. Ibid., pp. 454–455.
65. Report of Strikes and Lockouts in 1889 by the Labour Correspondent of the Board of Trade (1890), LXV111, pp. 449–478.
66. Report on the Strikes and Lockouts in 1889, p. 478.
67. Sharp, 1950, p. 290.
68. Report on Strikes and Lockouts in 1889, p. 467. There were twenty-one English delegates – those singled out for special attention were Wm Morris, H. Hyndman, Cunninghame Graham, Dr and Mrs Aveling, T. Burt MP and C. Fenwick MP.
69. Report on Strikes and Lockouts in 1890 by the Labour Correspondent of the Board of Trade (1890–1891), LXXV111, pp. 673–677.
70. Ibid., p. 714.
71. Ibid.
72. Ibid., p. 715.
73. Price, 1980.
74. Royal Commission on Labour, 1894: Fifth and Final Report, p. 29.
75. Ibid.
76. Ibid., p. 38.
77. Memorandum on The Progress of the Labour Department of the Board of Trade, April 1893.
78. Royal Commission on Labour, 1894, p. 27.
79. Askwith, 1920. Sharp, 1950, p. 297.
80. Middlemas, 1979, p. 59.
81. Davidson, 1978, p. 590.
82. Ibid., p. 590.
83. Ibid., p. 591.
84. Chapt. 1, p. 73.
85. Mills ?
86. Price, 1980.
87. Price, 1980, p. 62.
88. Ibid., p. 67.

89. Ibid., p. 706.
90. Ibid., p. 36.
91. Ibid., p. 38.
92. Sturmthal, 1972, p. 56.
93. Report on the Strikes and Lockouts of 1896, Cmd 8643, 1897. Report on the Strikes and Lockouts in 1913, Cmd 7658, 1914–16.

3 Trade Unions and Revolutionary Politics

For much of the nineteenth-century, trade union organization in Britain was dominated by craft workers in exclusive craft associations. Unions in the craft industries were built on apprenticeship and on customs which had persisted from before the Industrial Revolution.[1] Craft societies built on custom to delimit a preserve of craftsmen's work, defined sometimes by the material, sometimes by the tools and machinery and sometimes by the product. This preserve was defended against the unqualified, against changes in the organization of production or techniques and against encroachment by other crafts.[2] Craft rules occasionally led to conflict but widespread conflict and bargaining with employers were untypical of craft unionism. It was craft unions' contention that craftsmen should regulate 'what we alone have a right to regulate, the value of our labour.'[3]

Every craft union provided friendly benefits. Firstly, there were advantages in disguising a trade society as a friendly society when the latter was accepted by employers and protected by the law. Secondly, they were a vital element in craftworkers' control of working conditions. Benefits made union members a cohesive force and 'any member who had been paying in for some years was likely to feel he had an investment not likely to be sacrificed.'[4]

The strike was used to prevent infringements of the rules in particular shops and to extend a society's control of shops not previously organized. The technique of withdrawing small groups of men or individuals known as the 'strike in detail' was used to enforce craft rules without large-scale conflict with employers. Strikers were supported by unemployment benefit, not strike pay.[5]

Throughout the nineteenth century, however, craft unions were increasingly threatened by technical change and the social conflict which this engendered. In industries created by the industrial revolution, such as the railways, there were no hallowed customs and no traditional basis for apprenticeship. Other industries, particularly coal, iron and cotton, were so profoundly altered that protective customs, where they existed, were swept away. New skills were acquired by experience and by promotion from less skilled to more skilled without formal apprenticeship.[6]

Workers in these industries earned more than labourers but these industries were subject to trade fluctuations. Craft unions' resistance to the assault on their exclusiveness and workers' relative weakness in these industries gave rise to the formation of separate and comparatively open trade unions (industrial-type unions) which were more dependent on the strike and collective bargaining.[7] They were vertically open in that they organized workers with varying degrees of skill, but horizontally closed in that they did not attempt to organize outside the boundaries of their own industries and they excluded labourers.

Early organizations of labourers tended to be transient, both because of their insecure position in the labour market and because of craft opposition.[8] As the previous chapter has shown, the year 1889 marked an enormous burst of trade union growth and industrial conflict, especially in industries and occupations which had previously been poorly organized or unorganized. These were the 'new unions', commonly understood as socialist-led unions of unskilled labourers who revolted against the exclusive and selfish trade unionism of the crafts.[9]

However, not all of the new unions were composed of the unskilled and low-paid, or were against friendly benefits and had low subscriptions. New unionism was not based on a single principle of organization but aimed at filling in the gaps left by existing forms of trade unionism by organizing unions for the general run of workers in one or more industries. This was not a new departure and had been pioneered long before by the weavers, the boot and shoe operatives, the railway servants and to some extent, the miners.

The new unions, however, recruited on a wider scale among seamen, dockers, gasworkers, chemical workers and transport workers. They recruited less skilled workers in industries where only the skilled were organized. The new unions adopted this general form unintentionally. As they set out to organize particular groups of workers, they found other workers keen to join and their industrial coverage expanded. These unions therefore became general, not as a result of any coherent policy or tactics but because union officials welcomed the subscriptions of those 'clamouring to join.'[10] There is much evidence of ruthless behaviour by union bureaucrats to maximize membership numbers. Dockers' and seamen's unions set about crushing and eliminating rival unions and poaching their members.[11]

Not all new unions were socialist and/or militant. Nevertheless, most analysts, including Clegg, Fox and Thompson, believe that most of the new unions used militant and coercive tactics[12] and the new unions have been typically viewed as being committed to a 'fighting policy based upon class solidarity and directed by implication at any rate against capitalism itself.'[13]

The source of this fighting policy has been traced by influential commentators to new union leaders such as Tom Mann, Will Thorne and Ben Tillett who introduced 'a socialism far removed from the jolly fellowship of Robert Blatchford, the hygienic bureaucracy of the Fabians or the idylls of Keir Hardie.'[14]

The new unions' reputation for socialist-inspired militancy has been undermined by recent research which suggests that this is due partly to a reliance on florid reporting (prevalent in the middle-class press at the time) rather than to the actions of the leaders and partly to a failure to distinguish between the new unions as institutions and the high number of strikes in the 1889–90 period, which were undertaken by workers who may or may not have been members of a union.[15]

The revolutionary aims of the better-known workers' leaders tended to be confined to the level of rhetoric. Will Thorne, general secretary of the gas workers' union, despite his Marxist credentials and systematic provocation by employers, consistently advised caution, was against strike action and was surprisingly supportive of the employers' need to discipline his own union members.[16]

Crowley shows that 'advocacy of arbitration was to become rather more a characteristic of the 'new' unions than the old.'[17] The gasworkers' first rulebook in 1889 emphasized that it was 'the duty of this society to endeavour to form boards of conciliation and arbitration for the settlement of labour disputes' and employers were to be approached for concessions by means of 'respectfully worded requests.'[18]

The leaders of the dockers' union seemed just as keen for their members to prioritize the needs of employers and in June 1990 the dockers were attempting to form an arbitration committee with employers. At their first annual conference, Tom Mann argued for conciliation and arbitration.[19] For Ben Tillett, a board of conciliation was

'the only means to bridge the gulf between capital and labour . . . [and assist] the strengthening of the bonds of good feeling and robustness, which must inevitably tend to the moral, social and industrial advancement of the individual and the nation alike.'[20]

The evidence suggests that the London dock strike was the spontaneous action of the dockers themselves; they struck before most of them had joined a union and Tillett was surprised to find them clamouring for action. Further, during the strike the leaders urged caution, actively searched for opportunities to reach a settlement and, once the strike was over, worked to prevent any further conflict. Subsequent disputes were entered into by the dockers against the union's wishes.[21]

The seamen's union was also moderate: in July 1889, its leaders emphasized that they had no intention of permitting another strike 'if it can possibly be staved off by arbitration or otherwise.'[22]

Recent studies of new unionism, then, support the rank-and-filist view. They find a clear distinction between the moderate union leadership and the frequently militant workers who could also be violent because of the need to stop blacklegging. They conclude that the new unions, their rules and their officers were on the side of moderation from their inception. It was the rank and file which forced strikes on a usually reluctant leadership. As Matthews has emphasized, 'Thorne and Tillett might take the lead in a strike and talk aggressively, but this only served to obscure the origins of the militancy.' More often than not union officials were looking for ways to call off strikes to preserve funds and safeguard their own livelihoods and 'the leadership had plenty of past evidence that if the union collapsed they could easily end up back in the retorthouses or at the dock gates.'[23] In this context 'the union is the brake on the wheel which prevents too great precipitation and liability to consequent failure.'[24]

This work is a useful corrective to dominant accounts of the dynamics of industrial conflict in the late 1880s in Britain. But it must be remembered firstly (as Matthews points out) that there were many hard-working and reliable union officials and activists among the leadership of the new unions and that the struggle was foisted on a leadership which was internally divided. Leaders were engaged in a struggle of their own. There was division, confusion and competition among prominent figures in the struggle for leadership of this expanded worker organization and intense sectarian rivalry over the strategies and tactics of the conflict itself. This fragmentation most clearly emerges in the struggle between the advocates of syndicalism and industrial unionism around the turn of the century in Britain, which is traced below.

SYNDICALISM

The word 'syndicalism' has traditionally provoked strong sentiments among labour movement watchers – but at the movement's height in the decade before World War I, it engendered widespread fear and criticism across continents and was seen as a 'new red spectre' with a menacing and subversive programme:

'rarely has a movement aroused such universal agitation, awakened such worldwide discussions and called forth such expressions of alarm as this one, that seemed suddenly to spring from the depths of the underworld fully armed and ready to do battle.'[25]

In France before 1895, syndicalism meant trade unionism and the French 'syndicats' (or unions) were merely associations of skilled workers who combined in pursuit of higher wages and shorter working hours. Revolutionary syndicalism – the movement which is widely seen as the engine of unrest throughout parts of Europe before World War I – (and which I will refer to throughout the study as 'syndicalism') emerged in France in the 1880s with the passing of the Waldeck-Rousseau law in 1884 which granted legal freedom to the formation of unions. This law was part of a government policy aimed at encouraging moderate trade unions and industrial conciliation and discouraging militant action.

The body of ideas known as revolutionary syndicalism was set out at the Amiens Congress of the Confédération Générale du Travail (CGT) in 1906 in the famous Charter of Amiens. The Charter explained that the CGT brought together, independent of all political schools of thought, 'all workers who are conscious of the need to struggle for the abolition of the wage system.' This declaration involved 'a recognition of the class struggle which, on an economic foundation, puts the workers in revolt against every form of exploitation and oppression, material and moral, that is operated by the capitalist class against the working class'.[26]

The Charter recognized that the class struggle had both a reformist and a revolutionary character, so that

'in its day-to-day demands, syndicalism seeks the co-ordination of workers' efforts, the enhancement of workers' well-being through the achievement of such immediate reforms as the shortening of hours and the raising of wages. This effort, however is only one aspect of the work of syndicalism. It prepares for complete emancipation, which can only be achieved by expropriating the capitalist class. It advocates the general strike as the means of action to that end and holds that the union which is today the instrument of resistance, will in future be the unit of production and distribution, the basis of social reorganization.'[27]

The struggle between the two classes was understood as a creative force which would ultimately emancipate the workers because class struggle itself promoted workers' awareness of themselves as an exploited class. Syndicalists aimed at assisting this process by organizing workers into trade unions. Trade union organization was seen as the most fundamental and permanent of all human groupings, because it was based on the satisfaction of economic needs. Since all workers had this interest in common and it transcended all other interests, organization on this basis must promote solidarity and encourage class-consciousness.

For leading French syndicalists, the union was also the instrument of direct struggle with employers. It enabled workers to mount 'direct action' against employers. Direct action was action taken by workers without external intervention – 'the manifestation of the consciousness and of the will of the working men themselves.'[28] Various activities constituted direct action in syndicalist terms. Syndicalist leaders saw every act, every union campaign to achieve any economic gain as a successful battle in the class war – sabotage, strikes, boycotts; agitation for the regulation of apprentices, support for minimum wages, shorter hours, the enforcement of health and safety legislation, equal pay, suppression of piecework or work in convents, prisons and military garrisons, and propaganda. These were activities, the syndicalists believed, which weakened capitalism, benefited workers materially and psychologically and produced solidarity. But the ultimate form of direct action – the raison d'être of syndicalism – was the general strike, through which the new society would be achieved. Syndicalists believed that labour alone was absolutely necessary to production, so that when the workers decided to withdraw their labour all of society, including employers and the state, would be forced to capitulate. There was, however, no clear idea of the form the general strike might take; some saw a general strike as short, decisive and probably violent, others saw it as a peaceful 'strike of folded arms',[29] and yet others understood it as a general strike in a single trade or industry or a local general strike of all trades.[30]

French syndicalists did not aim at refashioning the state and rejected political action. The state was the tool used by capitalists to exploit workers and had to be destroyed. Struggle on a political level was useless, since all political parties were a fraud and 'Parliament was a sink of jobbery, corruption and compromise. The Socialists were no better than the rest, perhaps worse. Claiming to represent labour, they diverted workers from the real issues and dropped their cause after they had arrived through their votes . . . only the workers' own action could emancipate them.'[31] In any case, as there was to be no state in the new society, there was no need to try to control it in the present one; the point was to undermine it.

Criticism of the syndicalist aim – the autonomous ownership and control by trade unions of the production carried on in their trades – predates the formation of the CGT. In 1894, writing on Robert Owen's *New View of Society*, the Webbs pointed out that even if Owen's idea of combining all workmen in a trade as commercial producers was possible, it would only redistribute the capital of the country without altering or superseding the capitalist system.[32]

Criticism of syndicalist methods focused firstly on the assumption that nothing could be done through the state. Syndicalists saw the capitalist as the enemy against whom a war of attrition must be fought through strikes and sabotage. It was pointed out that the capitalist is the effect and not the cause of capitalist property, so that 'the day after the strike the wage earners remain wage earners and capitalist exploitation continues.'[33] Capitalist property is a social institution which cannot be transformed except by political action.[34] Even if

'the proletarians take possession of the mine and the factory, it will be a perfectly fictitious ownership. They will be embracing a corpse, for the mines and factories will be no better than dead bodies while economic circulation is suspended and production is stopped. So long as a class does not own and govern the whole social machine, it can seize a few factories and yards if it wants to, but it really possesses nothing. To hold in one's hand a few pebbles of a deserted road is not to be master of transportation.'[35]

The general strike was criticized as just another name for insurrection. Workers, it was pointed out, could not seize the means of production and institute a new social system without being confronted by the use of force by the state. It was emphasized that a general strike would not be a battle on the industrial front between workers and employers but a battle between the armed forces of the state and the workers. Even if the workers were an organized and conscious unit with the resources to withstand a prolonged and total strike, the state would not necessarily be forced to capitulate. The aid of the middle class, the police, farmers and the armed services would be enlisted in production. Furthermore, of all classes the workers themselves were most vulnerable to a general strike. Wages were the only thing between them and starvation.[36]

As to sabotage, it 'places the . . . struggle once more in the hands of individuals, not of the mass – it divides the working class.'[37] Employers dealt with sabotage through *agents provocateurs* and spies, often featuring the *lumpenproletariat* or slum proletariat described by Marx as that layer of society whose conditions of life especially fit it 'for the part of a bribed tool of reactionary intrigue.'[38] They infiltrated the unions to urge more violence and/or enable employers to construct blacklists; it became impossible for workers to trust one another. Sabotage provided scope for employers to corrupt the workers of rival employers to gain competitive advantage. In short, 'resort to the individual act is given a new sanction at the expense of collective action.'[39]

THE DISSEMINATION OF SYNDICALISM IN BRITAIN

Syndicalism appeared in Britain in 1910 under the sponsorship of Tom Mann. Mann had spent the previous eight years in Australia and New Zealand, where he was active in the labour movement. Mann's involvement in industrial conflict in Australia led him to conclude 'that the present system of sectional trades unionism is incapable of effectively combating the capitalist system under which the civilized world is now suffering, and such modifications and alterations should be made in the existing unions as will admit of a genuine federation of all organizations with power to act unitedly for industrial purposes.'[40]

On his return to Britain in May 1910, Mann declared his intention to advocate 'Industrial Unionism' owing to the weakness and sectional character of the existing trade union movement and stressed the importance of industrial organization over political action. However, he emphasized that he did not aim to destroy or disrupt the trade union movement but to improve it. Soon after, Mann and Guy Bowman (journalist, translator and leading light of the Social Democratic Federation) left for Paris to investigate the workings of the CGT. Mann was so impressed with the 'French Policy' that on his return to England he produced the first issue of the *Industrial Syndicalist* (in partnership with Bowman) in which he compared the aims and methods of the American Industrial Workers of the World and the French Confédération Générale du Travail and found the former wanting.[41]

The terrain of revolutionary politics in Britain had changed while Mann was away and in some quarters he was seen to be re-establishing his career as a labour leader by cynically exploiting the work of more committed candidates for the organization of the working class and the representation of its interests.

For the Socialist Labour Party in Britain, Mann's influence was pernicious. Prior to his departure for Australia Mann had spent some years in the Social Democratic Federation learning his socialism from such teachers as William Morris, Hyndman and others. He left and became a paid officer of the Independent Labour Party – 'that milk-and-water, wishy-washy sidetracking organization. Let us be quite clear. After he got to know what socialism really meant, he accepted paid offices to divide the movement!'[42] Mann's secretaryship of the ILP terminated after the leading members of the ILP (mainly women) rejected his views on marriage.[43] He then associated himself with the National Democratic League, 'a Radical freak show, promoted by the late W.M. Thompson, the then editor of *Reynolds News*. The NDL was an attempt to dodge the working class away from the Socialist Movement and hitch them on to the discredited rump of the Liberal Party!'[44]

The SLP 'allowed the beanfeasting and speechmaking with which his [Mann's] return to London was celebrated to pass unnoticed, although the spectacle of this champion of industrial unionism hobnobbing with the bitterest opponents of industrial unionism might well have justified an exposure of his duplicity and insincerity.' This course was adopted because 'we wished to see what line he would take; whether he would recognize the work that had been done for industrial unionism in this country and ally himself with its pioneers, or whether he would "jump the claim". He has "jumped the claim".'[45]

The explanation for Mann's behaviour was clear to the SLP:

'in Australia the term *Industrial Unionism* was good enough for Tom Mann; in South Africa the same term served his purpose. In this country, however, industrial unionism had been so bitterly opposed, and industrial unionists so vehemently attacked, that it required greater courage than Tom Mann possesses to fight under that name. So after a trip to Paris our worthy industrialist found that the word "syndicalism" was synonymous with the word "unionism" and inscribing 'industrial syndicalism' on his banner, he has valiantly gone forth to battle safe from the attacks of those for whom industrial unionism is anathema . . . whatever Tom Mann may do is done primarily in the interest of Tom Mann and only incidentally in the interests of the working class.'[46]

The SLP described Tom Mann as now engaged on 'a raging tearing propaganda of Industrial "Syndicalism". Taking Marx's name on his lips, he calls upon the workers to unite, and, says he, 'we will lead them a devil of a dance, though who "they" are is not clearly indicated' (it was suspected that 'they' might be the workers in view of the contents of Mann's pamphlets and the *Industrial Syndicalist*). In this literature Mann railed against the evils of sectional unionism but had no remedy to offer except 'improvements' in the existing trade unions. Mann maintained that industrial syndicalism could wipe out poverty under capitalism, that it could obtain wages for the unskilled equal to those of the skilled 'as fair play demands' and that it could solve the unemployment problem by compelling the reduction of hours so that the unemployed would be absorbed.

The SLP concluded that the

mass of contradictions and absurdities which is being foisted off on the workers as industrial unionism' must astonish many of Mann's contemporaries who are expected to teach that unemployment (that indispensable condition of capitalist production) can be abolished by reducing the hours of labour and that the raising of the wages of the unskilled depends on its abolition. The suggestion that "fair play" has anything to do with determining wages is almost too absurd to merit criticism. Tom Mann must be aware that no greater economic fallacy exists but persists in propagating this nonsense in a series of pamphlets, the opening number of which states that what is called for is that the working class movement should aim at the abolition of the wages system.[47]

Analysis of Mann's writings and speeches reveals that the difference between syndicalism and industrial unionism was not always very clear to Mann himself (it is doubtful whether more than a handful of British socialists knew much about French syndicalism)[48] and confirms that he used the terms interchangeably to describe a position which was neither industrial unionist nor syndicalist, but quite compatible with a more efficient reformism.[49] His position had not substantially changed over the previous twenty years. It had its roots in the strike wave of 1888–92 in Britain, when organized labour had begun to shift away from localism towards industry-wide organization in response to the concentration of capitalist power. As White records, Mann did not support or encourage militancy and industrial conflict in the new unions. He felt that stable and permanent trade unionism was more important for the rank and file. His was the outlook of the skilled craftsman and labour aristocrat. He wanted to eliminate the 'riff raff' and raise the standards of those who remained. He admonished workers, saying

'it is no use gushing over the out o' works. We want men who grasp the problem, who see that if we are to raise the status of our members we must keep them with sufficient wages to provide food and keep up their physical strength. The other men at the dock gates must clear off. With us there is no room for them; no doubt there are other social movements to provide for them, but our movement is to eliminate them.'[50]

Mann even set up a temperance society for union members. The strike wave was a major formative event in Mann's life; it catapulted him straight to the top of the British labour movement and crystallized his ideas.[51] The apparent anomalies after 1910 are a consequence of his promoting himself and his ideas in the guise of revolutionary syndicalism under the influence of Guy Bowman. It was Bowman and not Mann who was the 'most prominent British Syndicalist.'[52]

Mann was a rhetorical target. The vitriolic attack on him by leading members of the Socialist Labour Party was driven by the belief that he was the embodiment of all the obstacles to an authentic socialist movement in Britain past and present. They believed that socialism had been practically non-existent in Britain before the SLP was founded. The reasons for this and for the difficulties encountered in the SLP campaign to educate, agitate and organize British workers could be summed up in their phrase 'Tom Mannism'.

For the SLP, there were three main obstacles to the realization of socialism in Britain. The first was the form of British trade unionism (craft unionism): 'we condemn trade unionism, not for the mistakes that it makes. . . . but for the mistake that it is.'[53] This form of organization was entirely unfit to achieve or help the revolutionary process. The fundamental errors of trade unionism were acceptance of the wages system and organization in autonomous craft sections. It did not recognize the interests of workers as a class. Only a small section of workers were organized in trade unions. It was the greatest obstacle to the organization not only of unskilled workers but the large and growing body of semi-skilled workers. Even within the ranks of the workers in individual crafts, the trade union was an obstacle to organization because of the high subscriptions and apprenticeship conditions which it imposed on its members. Finally, the British trade union 'in some cases specifically, in all cases in practice, "socialist" resolutions notwithstanding, disclaims any intention to overthrow capitalism. It recognizes "the just rights of the employer" to exploit labour and seeks merely to secure for its members as favourable terms of exploitation as possible'.[54]

The second obstacle was the workers' leaders, in particular trade union officials. Most middle-class intellectuals were in the labour movement because it offered them the chance to 'shine' and 'gather coppers'.[55] This was to be expected. Trade union officials were another matter. They were often corrupt, often treacherous and in general dominated by capitalist thought, serving capitalist rather than working-class interests. Their belief in the permanence of capitalist economic and political conditions made them naturally anxious to secure as good a position for themselves as possible in capitalist society. The multiplication of trade union sections and therefore of trade union officials induced a competition among them as to which of them could best serve the interests of the discerning and place-granting capitalist class and outdistance his rivals in the race for capitalist favour. Their bourgeois pretensions and reactionary activities were the authentic outcome of trade union philosophy and organization.[56] Their adherence to middle-class values of thrift, temperance, self-help and respectability meant that 'the tablets of the British working man's mind are scribbled all over with the craziest pot-hooks put there by generations of freaks – it will take giants' hands to wipe these off.'[57]

Moreover, by 1910 there was a realization that the new unions had become 'popular bossdoms'.[58] They were dominated by a hierarchy of full-time professional officials who nominated their own successors and who often assumed a dictatorial position in relation to their members, whose interest and participation in union affairs could be minimal.

The third obstacle was syndicalism. It was important for the SLP to distinguish industrial unionism from syndicalism. Syndicalism was the 'newest anarchism'[59] and anarchism was a theory of society that 'finds vastly more affinity with the capitalist class than it does with the socialist.'[60] The anarchists and the ruling class shared a common conception of the role of the proletariat in politics and this was 'as food for cannon.'[61]

The struggle between anarchism and socialism had given birth to the SLP. It caused a split in the International Workers' Federation: by 1871 the IWA became largely polarized into two opposing camps, the anarchists and the socialists. At the congress of the IWA at The Hague in 1872, the seat of the General Council of the IWA was moved from London to New York to protect it from the anarchists led by Bakunin.[62] The IWA was dissolved at the Congress of Philadelphia in 1876 and reconstituted as the Socialist Labour Party by the largely German immigrant members of the defunct International. This was the first Socialist party to be established in America and until 1890, when Daniel DeLeon, a convert to Marxism, joined the SLP, it had remained a negligible force in the American labour movement.

The Socialist Labour Party emerged in Britain in 1903 after George Yates, a member of the Scottish SDF, became disillusioned with the increasing reformism of the Second International and the SDF and set out to build a new party composed of like-minded people and to publish *The Socialist*, expressing their opposition to the SDF. The British SLP faithfully reflected Daniel DeLeon's beliefs; some members corresponded with DeLeon and the SLP distributed his writings in Scotland.[63]

The SLP maintained that DeLeon's industrial unionism was the path for true socialists to follow. The aim of the movement was to organize a class union not a trade union, not a loose affiliation of class unions but one union under one constitution composed of industrial departments to include the many and closely related grades of labour. This would unite the entire working class organized by industry and would not be 'merely for those for whom there are jobs ... and ... those who can pay dues.'[64] The object of this industrial organization was to enable the working class as a class to take control of and hold as their own collective property, all the means of production and to constitute the organization of the 'Socialist Republic' of which the central directing authority was to be a Parliament of Industry composed of the representatives of various departments of production elected from below.[65]

Struggle within existing trade unions was pointless because they were 'the limbs of capitalism' controlled by the 'labour lieutenants of capital' and 'a belated reproduction of the old guild system' which 'deserves no quarter at the socialist's hands.'[66]

The industrial union had no more power to increase real wages than the craft union. The main weapon of the industrial union, as of the craft union, was the strike – but the strike had no revolutionary potential because

'the workingman who goes out on strike does first of all leave in the hands of the capitalist the plant of production. By that mere fact he admits that the employer is the rightful owner, at least as much is implied. The revolutionary act of the working class will not be a strike.'[67]

Political organization was imperative to facilitate the work of the industrial organization, because the present function of the state was to defend the interests of the ruling class and the workers could only disarm the capitalist class by taking the state out of its grasp.[68] Once the means of production were communally owned, the state would re-assume its beneficient functions of aiding and assisting in production. A state or central directing authority was necessary because 'the nature of the machinery of production, the subdivision of labour which aids co-operation and which co-operation fosters, and which is necessary to the plentifulness of production that civilization requires, compel a harmonious working together of all departments of labour and thence compel the establishment of a central directing authority.'[69]

Workers' desire for reform was understandable, but 'steps in the right direction' – so-called 'immediate demands' – were precarious. The notion that the capitalist class would allow itself to be 'pared off to death' was a fatal illusion because 'the tiger of capitalism will protect its superfluities with the same ferocity that it will protect its very existence. Nothing is gained on the road of palliatives, all may be lost.'[70]

DeLeon waged war against syndicalism (as embraced by the Chicago Industrial Workers of the World) saying he had no sympathy with 'men who talk dynamite, bombs, blood and thunder.' He decried the syndicalist leadership of the IWW for its 'glorification of individual theft as expropriation by instalments' and for equating individual crimes with 'legitimate measures of mass warfare.'[71] Bill Haywood (President of the IWW) was comparable to Bakunin, who was 'unresponsive to the sharp distinction between individual and collective, private and public, single and mass action.' This was anarchism.[72]

ANARCHISM AND SYNDICALISM

Writers such as Hunter[73] and Levine,[74] have emphasized the extent to which revolutionary syndicalism was indebted to the anarchist philosophy in general and to Bakunin in particular. Michael Bakunin was involved in the 1848 revolution and was jailed by Prussia, Austria and Russia for inciting revolution and unrest. A key element of Bakunin's philosophy, later summed up by Paul Brousse in the phrase '*Propaganda of the Deed*', was that the propaganda of words and theories spread by socialist books and newspapers had little effect on workers. It was necessary 'to destroy something – a person, a cause, a condition that hinders the emancipation of the people . . . [this] is a powerful means of awakening the popular conscience . . . it makes more propaganda in a few days than a thousand pamphlets. The government rages pitilessly but by this it only causes further deeds to be committed . . . [it] drives the insurgents to heroism. One deed brings forth another, opponents join the mutiny, the government splits into factions, harshness intensifies the conflict, concessions come too late, the revolution breaks out.'[75]

By the 1860s Bakunin had gathered a substantial following and in 1868 he set up an organization to rival the International Workingmen's Association called the International Alliance of Social Democracy. Bakunin formed this organization in a bid to supplant the IWA. He failed and joined the IWA with his supporters to promote 'anarchism as the end and terrorism as the means' to worker emancipation, in opposition to Marx.[76] This organization declared itself in support of the political, economic and social equality of the classes (which were to continue to exist). It aimed at achieving this by the destruction of government and the abolition of the right of inheritance. In Bakunin's view, church and state had spawned such a strong web of ideas and mechanisms for their own support that they had achieved an all-enveloping tyranny of mind and body which made a free society impossible until these 'monstrous oppressions' were destroyed.

Bakunin saw Marx as the author of a new and even more monstrous tyranny – state socialism – in which the state was to become the sole owner, capitalist, banker, moneylender, director of all work and distributor of its products. For Bakunin this made Marx the enemy of the entire human race, because 'the state will always be an institution of domination and exploitation . . . a permanent source of slavery and misery . . . The workers have only three escape routes from their misery – the church, the rum shop or revolution.'[77]

In 1871 Bakunin formulated the methods through which the workers would achieve the destruction of the state and freedom – firstly, through the organization and federation of strike funds to enable workers to organize and maintain strikes. He saw the strike as the beginning of the social war of the proletariat against the bourgeoisie. Strikes would engender solidarity and consciousness of common interests and new principles which are 'destructive of religion, of juridical right and of the state, of authority, divine as well as human.'[78] All forms of political action were rejected and it was proposed that producers' groups should assume control of all industrial production on behalf of the community. There was to be no centralized organization and groups were to retain total freedom to do whatever they liked.

There are important differences between anarchism and syndicalism, but they have much in common. As Hunter[79] points out, anarchism is a doctrine of individualism; syndicalism is a doctrine of working-class action, anarchism is a remnant of eighteenth-century philosophy, while syndicalism is a product of an immature factory system. But beyond this we are left with the words of Yvetot:

'I am reproached with confusing syndicalism and anarchism. It is not my fault if anarchism and syndicalism have the same ends in view. The former pursues the integral emancipation of the individual, the latter the integral emancipation of the working man. I find the whole of syndicalism in anarchism. When we leave the theories of syndicalism to study its methods, we find them identical with those of the anarchists.'[80]

For the SLP the struggle between the syndicalists and the industrial unionists in Britain was the same struggle over aims and methods as that between the anarchists and the socialists in Europe and America. Syndicalists rejected democracy, rejected political action, advocated self-destructive methods and so 'the syndicalist becomes the logical descendant of the anarchist and must mislead and ultimately abandon the working class'.[81] This was the root of the SLP's concern to correct the confusions instigated by Mann and labour leaders generally and propagated by the capitalist press.

CONCLUSION

By 1910 neither the SLP nor Tom Mann had made as much impression on workers in England as they would have liked. The mass of organized workers seemed slow to perceive and act in their own interests, as outlined relentlessly in the speeches and writings of members of the SLP and Tom Mann. The protagonists concluded that this was due not to flaws in their own analyses of workers' role in capitalism but to the absence of class-consciousness among organized workers. For Mann, workers had somehow not evolved sufficiently.

Mann located himself in the tradition of Owen, whose project had failed eighty years previously because 'the workers were not equal to resorting to such highly trained methods; and they have had to spend twice forty years in the wilderness because they were neither mentally nor physically qualified to enter the promised land'.[82] In the same way that he saw the workers as the fatal flaw in Owen's scheme, the obstacle in the way of Mann's aim of worker emancipation was not the state or employers but workers themselves. It was the 'remarkable gullibility', sectionalism and ignorance displayed by organized workers which led to their being taken in by the establishment.'[83] It was 'the trade unionists themselves . . . [with] their minds so fully occupied with the idea that Parliament is the all-important institution.'[84] As to trade union leaders, they had no idea that there was such a thing as class struggle and they 'are fearful lest identification with the workers' real movement should debar them from sharing the contents of the Egyptian fleshpots.'[85] Mann argued on the one hand that the existing trade union movement could be reformed but concluded at the same time that it was 'solely because of the inability of the workers to agree upon a common plan of action' that capitalism prospered, so that 'if only the workers would agree and act then they would become all-powerful . . . there will be no power on earth to stop us so long as we do not fall foul of economic principles.'[86] The solution was the education of workers and Mann and Bowman set up the Industrial Syndicalist Education League 'to propagate the principles of syndicalism throughout the British Isles with a view to merging all existing unions into one compact organization for each industry, including all labourers of every industry in the same organization as the skilled workers.'[87]

The SLP rejected the notion of the working class as a 'dumb driven herd', but at the same time workers were seen as biddable and credulous. They were easy prey for leaders such as Tom Mann because capitalist 'cultural domination' had created a slavish psychology within the British working class.[88] Following DeLeon,[89] the SLP believed that the latent class-consciousness and creativity of the working class had been suffocated by intellectuals and by the leaders of 'pure and simple trade unions.'[90] Without their ministrations, capitalism itself would make a class-conscious socialist working class through its contradictory tendencies.[91] This was why the SLP devoted much of its effort to attacking other socialist groups and exposing their deficiencies to the workers.

The analysis of trade unions and their leaders provided by the SLP bears a striking resemblance to that presented by the BOT in the previous chapter. Trade unions in Britain were entirely unfit to achieve or help the revolutionary process. Trade union leaders were the 'labour lieutenants of capitalism'. Both accounts agree on the strong influence

of craft unionism and the limited impact of socialism on worker organization in this period. They see trade unions and trade union leaders
as an antidote to revolution. The SLP account, however, highlights the
divergence and tensions among leaders and would-be leaders of worker
organizations and the extent to which trade unions fragmented organization and stifled class-consciousness. Although this enabled theorists
of the SLP (and others using this approach) to win propaganda battles
by exposing the 'deficiencies' of other contenders for power, it is an
unsatisfactory explanation as to why the mass of organized workers
seemed unwilling or unable to understand and act in their own interests
as defined by the SLP. It overestimates the extent and influence of
trade unionism in this period and underestimates the revolutionary potential of the working class.

For officials of the BOT it was not so much class-consciousness
as its opposite which was the problem. It was precisely the readiness of workers to organize and act independently and sporadically
in 'the absence of consistent or informed commitment to any one set
of beliefs' which defined these combinations and was most threatening. This was 'dry material' which could be set ablaze 'by a chance
spark.'[92]

Goldthorpe has described these characteristics of worker organization as amounting to a 'potential for action of a more concerted kind,
both industrial and political, the ultimate threat of which is to create a
major degree of economic dislocation and civil disturbance.' The realization of this potential requires and reflects certain conditions, namely
the readiness of a working class to 'hold up the country to ransom',
the relative weakness of its moral and social integration into the existing order and reserves of grassroots solidarity on which concerted organizational strategies can draw.[93]

The dry material was set ablaze in 1910 when all of Goldthorpe's
conditions for the realization of the disruptive potential of the British
working class appeared to be present. Many see syndicalism as the
chance spark which fuelled the massive strikes in the years from 1910
to 1914 and brought the country to the point of revolution, which was
only 'forestalled by some bullets at Sarajevo.'[94] This view suggests a
major miscalculation of the limits and possibilities of trade unionism
in Britain on the part of the BOT and the SLP and implies a restruc-
turing of their respective policies. Others, however, have seen syndicalism in this period as 'a slogan of the struggle and not a programme
for social transformation'[95] and as 'a mirage of historians treading the
infertile deserts of labour history in search of a *révolution manquée*'.[96]

With these interpretations in mind, the next chapter will focus on the 'Great Unrest' which provided the first real test of the view that trade unions were the key to the management of industrial conflict.

NOTES

1. Turner, 1962.
2. Phelps-Brown, 1960.
3. London Union of Compositors quoted in Clegg, 1964, p. 5.
4. Phelps Brown, 1960, p. 7.
5. Ibid., p. 9.
6. Phelps-Brown, 1960, pp. 15–16; Clegg, 1964, p. 15.
7. Phelps-Brown, 1960, pp. 120–122.
8. Elger, 1989.
9. Clegg, 1964.
10. Ibid., p. 92.
11. Matthews, 1991, p. 27.
12. Clegg, 1964, p. 91.
13. Cole, 1948, p. 103. See also Hobsbawm, 1964.
14. Phelps-Brown, 1960, p. 320; Clegg, 1964.
15. Matthews, 1991, p. 28.
16. Ibid., p. 29.
17. Crowley, 1952, cited in Matthews, 1991.
18. Matthews, 1991, p. 29.
19. Clegg, Fox and Thompson, 1985, p. 93; Schneer, 1982, p. 52.
20. Dockers' Record, September 1890, quoted in Matthews, 1991.
21. Stedman Jones, 1976, p. 347; Pelling, 1971, p. 98; Schneer, 1982, p. 40; Matthews, 1991, p. 30.
22. Taplin, 1974, p. 82.
23. Ibid., p. 32.
24. George Howell, quoted in Matthews, 1991, p. 31.
25. Hunter, 1969.
26. Cole, 1954, p. 337.
27. Lorwin, 1954, p. 27.
28. Levine, 1912.
29. Ibid.
30. Mitchell, 1987.
31. Ibid., pp. 30–31.
32. Webbs, pp. 147–148.
33. Hunter, 1913, p. 268.
34. Ibid., p. 275.
35. Jaurès, 1913, pp. 124–125.
36. Ibid.
37. Spargo, 1913, p. 173

38. Ibid.
39. Ibid., p. 173.
40. Brown, 1974.
41. *The Industrial Syndicalist*, Vol. 1, No. 1, July 1910.
42. *The Socialist*, March 1911.
43. Tsuzuki, 1991, pp. 101–108.
44. Ibid.
45. Ibid.
46. Ibid.
47. Ibid.
48. Cole, 1971, pp. 266–267.
49. Holton, 1976, p. 29.
50. Speech by Mann at Toynbee Hall, quoted in White, 1991, p. 40.
51. White, 1991, p. 35.
52. Pribicevic, 1959, p. 20.
53. **Craft Unionism or Industrial Unionism: Which?** Socialist Labour Press, Edinburgh. ND
54. **The Socialist Labour Party: Its Aims and Methods.** Socialist Labour Press, Edinburgh, 1908.
55. King & Blatchford, 1897.
56. **Craft Unionism or Industrial Unionism: Which?** Socialist Labour Press, Edinburgh. ND
57. DeLeon, 1929, p. 133.
58. Turner, 1962, pp. 290–1. *Clarion*, 28th April 1911. The notion of popular bossdom (though not the phrase) was first used by Daniel DeLeon.
59. Hunter, 1913, Chapter 10.
60. See Conlin, 1969, for a discussion of the IWW's reputation for violence and sabotage.
61. DeLeon, 1901.
62. Braunthal, 1966.
63. Challinor, 1977, p. 10.
64. Ibid., p. 19.
65. *The Socialist*, October 1910.
66. DeLeon, 1904.
67. Seretan, 1979, p. 183. Seretan highlights many analysts' failure to distinguish DeLeon's doctrine from the generic term 'industrial unionism' – this has been a source of confusion about the movement.
68. DeLeon, 1896, p. 6.
69. Ibid., p. 7.
70. DeLeon, **Two Pages from Roman History**, ND, p. 40.
71. DeLeon, 1929, pp. 96–97.
72. Conlin, 1969.
73. Hunter, 1914.
74. Levine, 1912.
75. Quoted in Hunter, 1914, p. 52.
76. Ibid., p. 154.
77. Bakunin, quoted in Hunter, 1914, pp. 181–182.
78. Hunter, 1914, p. 185.
79. Ibid., p. 245

80. Ibid., p. 247.
81. Ibid., p. 271.
82. The Industrial Syndicalist, No. 1, July 1910, pp. 3–4.
83. Ibid.
84. Ibid.
85. Ibid.
86. Ibid.
87. Mann, quoted in White, 1991, p. 148.
88. Young, pp. 341–343.
89. DeLeon, 1909.
90. DeLeon, 1905.
91. DeLeon, 1891.
92. PRO CAB 37/107/70, 25th July 1911.
93. Goldthorpe, 1978, p. 208.
94. Halevy, 1952; Dangerfield, 1936.
95. Hobsbawm, 1984, p. 277.
96. Phillips, 1971.

4 The 'Great Unrest'

The first main phase of the 'Great Unrest' began with the rapid escalation of discontent in the South Wales coalfields. In this area wages were fixed not by individual or collective bargaining but by the price of coal. From 1907 declining wages, worsening conditions and increasing difficulties in mining coal due to difficult geological conditions made the issue of 'abnormal places' a continuing focus of discontent for Welsh miners. Miners who worked difficult coalfaces found that price lists which were negotiated for normal conditions failed to give them a living wage, and yet in 1908 a legal decision ruled that employers need not pay special rates to men working in abnormal places. Discontent also simmered around the issue of 'small coal'. Miners were paid for the production of 'clean large coal' only, although they inevitably produced a quantity of small coal – sometimes a very large quantity. Miners were not paid for the production of small coal which coal ownwers nevertheless sold in the same way as they sold the large coal. In 1908 the Coal Mines Regulation Act introduced an eight-hour day for miners. This effectively meant a cut in wages, because the reduction of hours further reduced miners' ability, especially for men working in abnormal places, to secure a living wage. They could not work longer hours to make up the shortfall. Employers responded to the decline in productivity by exploiting loopholes in the legislation, by operating multiple shifts and attacking established work practices and customs.[1]

The leaders of the South Wales Miners' Federation were wedded to conciliation and the sliding scale system of fixing wages. In April 1910 they signed a five-year agreement with the coal owners which did not confront the abnormal places issue or payment for small coal and sanctioned far-reaching changes in working arrangements demanded by the coal owners.[2]

On 1st September 1910 the Cambrian Combine closed the Ely pit, part of the Naval Collieries, after the failure of the South Wales Conciliation Board to settle on a price for the working of a seam which was subject to difficult geological conditions. By 19th September all of the pits of the Cambrian Combine were on strike in sympathy and in defiance of a decision taken by the South Wales Miners' Federation that work should be resumed pending a ballot of the whole coalfield.

The strike continued to spread until 10,000 men were out on strike. By November 1910 the Rhondda and Aberdare valleys and the Tonypandy area were the scene of bitter conflict. Confrontation and sabotage were widespread. Various tactics were used by the miners to end the dispute, including mass picketing, attacking collieries which were still operating, mine managers' homes and 'blacklegs' brought in to keep the collieries working. Employers resisted with the help of local and imported police and later troops. Violent battles developed, notably at Tonypandy, where strikers responded to police tactics by looting shops. There were many casualties.[3]

Throughout this dispute another conflict raged internally between the Cambrian Combine Committee and the SWMF executive council, between the young socialists of the Rhondda and adjacent valleys and the older leaders steeped in Liberal traditions. The old leadership was typified by William Abraham (known as Mabon). Abraham was a Liberal MP, a devout Christian and preacher who expounded from the pulpit on 'the identity of interests between capital and labour'.[4] This established style of leadership had been increasingly threatened by militant and active miners. What Mabon called conciliation was now called 'class collaboration' by the newer leaders such as Noah Ablett and Noah Rees, who were members of the Plebs League established in Ruskin College to extend Marxist education.[5] Established leaders now found themselves in a position where they were no longer able to lead, but they were sufficiently established to prevent leadership falling into the hands of others. They looked to the Board of Trade for help but 'that department of government trod these paths very gingerly, so long as the coal owners were loath to brook 'interference' by the Board of Trade'.[6]

The Labour Department of the Board of Trade did intervene and attempted to mediate between the coal owners and miners, but was unable to break the deadlock. The strike continued, with the SWMF being financially supported by the Miners' Federation of Great Britain. The MFGB attempted to reach a settlement through a meeting with the coal owners in which it was agreed that the employers' terms should be given a year's trial. This was unanimously rejected by the SWMF, whereupon the MFGB withdrew its support on 31st August 1911 and the miners returned to work on the terms offered by the employers in the previous October.

Meanwhile, on 14th June 1911 the National Sailors' and Firemen's Union had declared a general strike at Southampton in support of demands for a conciliation board, a minimum rate of wages, reduced

working hours and various changes in working conditions. The shipowners brought in blackleg labour and by the 20th of June the strike
had spread to Goole and Hull, where the dock labourers struck in support of the seamen and put forward claims of their own. The strike
spread to Manchester and Liverpool, where the Seamen's Union stopped
the White Star Line's 'Olympic' on her maiden voyage in order to
force the Shipping Federation to recognize the union for collective
bargaining purposes and thereby negotiate improvements in pay and
conditions. The strike came to include dockers and workers in factories and processing plants who initially struck in sympathy but later
framed demands of their own. The circumstances of the strike suggested the presence of syndicalism to many commentators on the transport
strikes of 1911 and the prior Cambrian Combine strike. The Board of
Trade investigator J.F. Moylan discerned the influence of syndicalism,
promoted by a small group of hitherto unknown young syndicalists,
which threatened the position of established union leaders.[7]

The transport strike was characterized by hostility towards mediation attempts by union leaders and the Board of Trade and widespread
violence, including assaults on blacklegs, attacks on the offices of shipowners and a Labour Exchange operated by the Shipping Federation.
George Askwith of the Board of Trade reported that 'the union leaders
have little control and are now frightened'.[8] About 400 extra police
were drafted in from other areas but on 1st July workers rejected a
further settlement and the meeting broke into a riot. A further 500
police were sent to the area to maintain control.

On 18th July shipowners in Cardiff attempted to use Chinese labour
to unload the S.S. 'Annan' and police were unable to control the subsequent riot in which the quayside was set alight. Extra police were
imported and the next day Cardiff was virtually in the grip of a general
strike when workers in many trades came out in sympathy with the
waterfront workers. The Chief Constable expressed the view that this
sympathetic strike owed much to the 'considerable influence . . . exercised by bodies of men and women going from place to place with a
view to inducing those inclined to remain at work to join their ranks'.[9]

By mid-July negotiations were in progress to end the strike, but
before these had been completed more conflict broke out in early August
in London. Waterfront union leaders had accepted the terms of the
Devonport Agreement, which gave substantial increases to most groups
of waterfront workers, but this agreement was rejected by the dockers
(who wanted more) and this led to unofficial strike action throughout
the London dock system. Official union calls for a return to work went

unheeded. The BOT intervened as the strike paralysed the docks and food supplies dwindled. Agreements were reached by the end of August which gave wage rises to workers not covered by the Devonport agreement and concessions were made on the issue of the employment of casual labour under pressure from the BOT. Before the month was out, however, conflict surfaced amongst railway workers in Liverpool in response to the pressure of falling real wages and hostility towards the Conciliation Boards set up in 1907.

Unofficial strike action taken by Merseyside railwaymen centred initially on goods services, where many workers were employed in railway depots on the docks and had close contact with waterfront workers. By mid-August 15,000 railwaymen were out on strike. They were quickly followed by coal porters, lightermen and carters, until a total of about 80,000 workers were on strike. Port employers responded with a general lockout and the strike committee declared a general strike.[10]

This was the biggest rail strike in history. There was mass picketing and violence. There were attacks on blackleg labour and on goods in transit and fires were started in dockyard areas. The Liverpool City authorities formed a committee of public safety and called in large numbers of police and troops, until by the middle of August there were 3,000 troops, several hundred imported police and two gunboats moored on the Mersey with their guns trained on the city. At the same time the War Office dispatched troops to many industrial areas, both with and without the request of the civil authorities, and the Home Secretary (Winston Churchill) announced that Britain was under the control of the military authorities.[11]

The strike came to a head in the third week in August, when a peaceful mass demonstration of 80,000 workers (including women and children) sponsored by the National Transport Workers' Federation was broken up with a 'merciless use of violence that horrified those who saw it'. Troops with fixed bayonets and loaded rifles fired on the crowds; one man was killed and many others wounded.[12] Agreements were reached in the wake of this conflict after mediation by the BOT and a general return to work began. The settlement provided for the setting-up of a Royal Commission to look into the Conciliation scheme of 1907 and all strikers were to be reinstated without penalties.

On 18th October the Commission produced its Report which was rejected by the unions, who called for a meeting with the railway companies to discuss it; they refused. The unions prepared to ballot their members on whether to renew the strike. In the House of Commons the Labour Party condemned the railway companies' intransigence and put forward an amended resolution calling for a meeting to discuss 'the best means of giving effect to the Report.'[13] The vote was carried and the railway companies agreed to attend a meeting under state auspices. A settlement was reached on the basis of a modified Report and the strike threat was lifted.

The new improved Conciliation Scheme of 1911, however, still refused trade union recognition. It only instituted a system of Boards peopled by worker representatives who had to petition management. Nevertheless, railway companies were forced to negotiate indirectly with the unions, because workers could choose their representatives from any source and in practice these tended to be trade union officials.

ANALYSIS OF THE INDUSTRIAL CONFLICT

Amid calls for the government to take more stringent action to stem the tide of industrial conflict, the BOT was asked to submit a report on the situation to the Cabinet in July 1911. The report was to provide a basis for the reconsideration of existing state policy towards industrial conflict. The BOT presented a comparative and historical study of industrial conflict in Britain in order to identify any new factors which could account for the severity of the outbreak.

The report began by summarizing the key features of the conflict. The largest and most virulent strikes which marked the outburst involved 'the three classes of labour in which the community as such is most deeply entrusted'. The labour unrest was mainly the consequence of the fact that between 1900 and 1910 wages were static but prices rose considerably. Workers' leaders, employers and the government were unprepared for the ferocity of the explosion of industrial conflict at this time.[14]

Moreover, the industrial unrest displayed certain characteristics which, according to the BOT, distinguished it from earlier periods of industrial conflict. The attention of the Cabinet was drawn to the speed and success of the strike movements and the readiness with which the better organized trades, like the miners and railwaymen, gave support to each other and the transport workers. The report cited the seamen's strike as an example. This strike was called on 16th June 1911 and had been threatened for some time, but it was not generally expected to be serious. The Shipping Federation was aware that if a strike did break out it would present problems because of the shortage of seamen, but no-one foresaw the extent of the support the strike attracted from transport workers or the cohesiveness of the different groups of workers involved. The Seamen's Union was a weak institution and the Transport Workers' Federation embryonic – and yet this strike achieved far-reaching concessions and engendered such a belief in collective action among the workers that they felt they had the power to stop the trade of any port. This victory owed much to the fact that shipowners were reluctant to leave ships idle while trade was good – but the shipowners could not be held responsible for the spontaneous character and improved organization which forced them to concede the seamen's demands. Similarly, although the increase in the cost of living (but not in wages) could explain disturbances in the labour world generally, it could not explain the changed character, organization and improved success rate of industrial action. For the report's authors the explanation had to be sought in wider industrial and political developments over the previous thirty years.

Throughout this period there had been an increase in casual employment, combined with an increased risk of unemployment. In the conditions of modern competitive industry employers tended to see the labour force as something to be switched off and on like electric current, as required, and failed to see that any decrease in the certainty and continuity of employment causes unrest.

The workers of 1910 were better educated, propaganda had a bigger impact and workers were more concerned with social questions than hitherto. Books such as *Merrie England*, written by Blatchford, had sold by the million and had a profound effect. The cheap press and advances in communication had made workers more homogeneous, more aware of their common interests and more inclined to act collectively – aware that there was strength and safety in numbers. It was recognized that older unionists' complaints about the younger union men being 'rotten with socialism', undisciplined and spoiling for a fight were not unfounded – but it was concluded that most of the workers concerned 'do not realize what a fight to the finish means' and they had only a superficial understanding of socialism.[15]

That workers had developed new methods but not new aims in their struggle was not comforting for the BOT. These new methods had been assisted by the growth of specialization in industry, which had increased interdependence among the various branches such that 'the dockers can stop the whole trade of a port and a few hundred collierymen can threaten to stop all the coal mines in Scotland.'[16]

Further, the bias towards collective action was reinforced by 'a change in middle and upper class attitudes, among whom Victorian theories

as to capital and labour have become obsolete.' There was now a disposition to try to see things from the worker's point of view and 'to
wonder, not why he is discontented, but that he has been patient for
so long'.[17]

Finally, and most importantly for the BOT, there had been a marked
decline in the influence of the established trade union leaders who
were central to the successful management of industrial conflict. In
the joint opinion of Askwith and Mitchell of the Board of Trade, 'a
new force has arisen in trade unionism and on every hand there is
evidence to show that the power of the old leaders has been superseded.' This new force had been very influential among workers. This
was illustrated by the fact that there were practically no successors to
the moderating influences exerted by trade union leaders such as Burt,
Fenwick, Knight, Burnett, Bowerman, Bell, Maudsley, Mabon and
Chandler. When any of the more moderate union leaders retired they
were replaced by very different types of men and the moderates still
in office had practically no influence. This change was obvious in the
Northumberland miners' decision to abolish the three-shift system 'in
defiance of an agreement only just reached, the triumph of the rank
and file of the boilermakers over their executive, the recent printers'
dispute, the complete annihilation of the policy pursued by Mr Bell in
connection with the railways, the ascendancy of Mr Crinion as the
dominating influence in Lancashire, the capture of the South Wales
Miners' Federation by the Tonypandy men and the almost complete
obliteration of Mr Chandler as a force in trade unionism. The new
force was "industrial unionism", having Tom Mann as its most active
advocate, the central practical idea of which is the sympathetic strike'.[18]

Industrial unionism had been gathering momentum since the Belfast
strike of 1907. At that time Askwith and Mitchell feared that the tactics pursued by the strike leaders would be adopted by other leaders in
future disputes and they predicted then that grave consequences would
ensue 'should there be any widespread acceptance of the sympathetic
strike policy'.[19] After the Dublin strikes of 1908, however, the Irish
transport workers' leaders were discredited. The repudiation of the Irish
leaders by English trade unions and the opposition to sympathetic strikes
by older and trusted union leaders led Askwith and Mitchell to conclude that 'this always more or less popular idea of the sympathetic
strike' would again be sidetracked'.[20] Recent developments had shown
this to be wishful thinking. The sympathetic strike was now widely
advocated by English workers, who pressed their leaders to adopt this
tactic. Mitchell believed that the success of the movement for better

conditions among transport workers was attributed by the men to those who struck in sympathy and that the old leaders' opposition to the sympathetic strike was due to their desire to conserve their union funds to fight their own battles. This conservative policy was thought to be rapidly weakening and there was a strong feeling amongst trade unionists that trade union policy generally would become more aggressive and united – which meant the more extensive adoption of the 'general strike' policy. Signs of this were discerned in the miners' constant demand that the MFGB should put its twentieth rule into operation. This rule stated that 'whenever any county, federation or other district is attacked on the wage question, all members connected with the Society shall tender a notice to terminate their contracts if approved of by a conference called to consider the advisability of such joint action being taken.'[21]

Mitchell also pointed to the significant development amongst transport workers whereby all sections (seamen, dockers, carters, labourers) were united in one organization – the Transport Workers' Federation – which gave its leaders (J.H. Wilson, Tom Mann and Ben Tillett) enormous power. All indicators showed the probability of railwaymen joining these new forces, as during the Hull and Manchester disputes. Mitchell believed that workers were increasingly attracted to the new policy and would seek its more extensive application. In the hands of the leaders named, he argued, 'who are supported almost without exception by the younger local leaders who have largely displaced the older and more moderate men, anything might happen in the near future, indeed possible consequences of a very grave nature have been put forward – for instance, a refusal to handle goods by railwaymen is only a step removed from refusal to handle special trains (troop trains)'.[22]

By 1911 the overall conclusion of Askwith and Mitchell was clear. The most threatening aspect of the industrial conflict was the coherence and scale of worker organization, and while

'it may be said that difficulties such as are being experienced are cyclical and pass away after a period of unrest, there is a fundamental difference between past periods of unrest and the present one which renders this view complacent. The earlier movements were spasmodic and had little national cohesion. The present one is essentially national and frankly aims at complete stoppage with all the advantages of organized bodies in their separate trades acting together. During the last thirty years the regiments have been formed and disciplined and are now, practically for the first time, acting together as an army. Thirty years ago the "general strike" was a very shadowy proposal. Now it is a definite objective deliberately advocated by the same men who have achieved at least some success in the present struggle. We are in fact thirty years older and labour men, like others, learn from experience . . . these being our general views of the situation we are driven to the conclusion that some effort should be made to maintain control. Successful as the Board of Trade may have been in finding a solution of difficulties which appeared insurmountable, it must be remembered that these difficulties are becoming daily greater and one failure may mean the letting loose of forces which would irreparably damage our trade and commerce.'[23]

MAINTAINING CONTROL

On 9th August 1911 the President of the BOT, Sydney Buxton, endorsed this appraisal of the situation and put forward the BOT's recommendations for maintaining control.[24] Buxton noted that the unrest and its consequences had directed public attention to the question of the improvement of the official machinery for preventing or shortening industrial warfare and suggested that the public would welcome and support any well-considered measure for dealing more effectively with the question, especially if it could be utilized to anticipate and thus to prevent disputes from culminating in a strike or lockout.

Buxton acknowledged that industrial disputes were now national and not merely the concern of the parties directly involved, and that the question was not whether the state should interfere in trade disputes but what form this interference should take. The President was dismissive of the many crude suggestions which had been offered as solutions to the industrial conflict and of the unrealistic expectations of the existing machinery set up to deal with the problem. He called for the greatest circumspection in taking any steps to address the problem, since 'a step taken in the wrong direction might do great damage and undo much of the patient work which has been gradually accomplished in recent years by administrative action on the part of the Board of Trade.'[25]

Having established the ground rules, Buxton considered the plans put forward by the influential cotton employer Sir Charles Macara for an Industrial Council to encourage the co-operation of unions and employers at national level to improve industrial relations. Macara's plan for an Industrial Council was not new. There had been successive attempts to form similar structures, all of which had been thwarted, usually by employers.[26]

Buxton's interpretation of Macara's plan suggested that it too was destined for rejection. He noted that it involved the transfer of the BOT's jurisdiction over labour disputes to an independent court under an 'Industrial Judge' which would mean the repeal of the Conciliation Act to divest the BOT of its duty and the 'transfer of these powers to an independent and therefore an irresponsible Tribunal'.[27] This would have little chance of being accepted by Parliament, in Buxton's view. Even if it was accepted, he went on, there would still be the difficulty that the new Tribunal, in order to safeguard its independence, would have to be permanent in constitution and withdrawn from the control of Parliament, like the Courts of Law. He felt that the parties concerned would not agree to such a proposal. In addition, it was probable that in the case of a permanent body such as this, its method of handling a particular dispute or its refusal to intervene, or the nature of its decision would in some cases give cause for dissatisfaction to one or both sides. It would not be safeguarded, as it currently was, by the anonymity of the Board of Trade, the periodical changes of Ministers or the power which a great administrative department could exercise of shifting about or supplementing the officers in charge of particular branches of work. The industrial court could find itself out of favour for any of these reasons and it would simply cease to be invoked, with the result that recourse to the mediation of the BOT would begin again (as before the Conciliation Act) and there would be two rival official agencies – which would be highly inadvisable.

Macara proposed either that disputes could be subject to compulsory conciliation or arbitration before a stoppage of work took place or that the official machinery available for conciliation, enquiry and (in suitable cases) decision could be improved. Only the latter was feasible for Buxton, since 'it is quite certain that neither public opinion nor the opinion of employers nor of workmen would assent to the compulsory enforcement of an arbitration award.'[28] He emphasized that the British tradition had 'favoured elasticity of machinery proceeding by way of conciliation, enquiry and agreement with no reference to arbitration except by consent and with arbitration awards (so-called) resting solely on moral sanctions.'[29]

Buxton was adamant that there should be no change in the management of industrial conflict. The BOT must continue to promote amicable settlements between parties to disputes. This would overcome the suspicion of single arbitrators while avoiding the dangers of setting up a court consisting permanently of the same people. But most importantly, the strengths of the existing system lay in the fact that the BOT was flexible and unhampered by formal rules and able to respond in any particular case with solutions which seemed most appropriate. There was no court consisting of named individuals who might become the focus of discontent at an unpopular decision.

Seemingly in the face of Buxton's protests, an initial round of talks between government, employers and workers' representatives took place on 15th August 1911 and the Industrial Council was established on 10th October 1911. The employers' representatives included Charles Macara himself and many of the moderate trade union leaders mentioned in the earlier reports by the BOT as being no longer representative of workers involved in the current unrest.

Charles argues that this plan was taken seriously because of the personal standing of Macara and the pressing need for the government to be seen to be doing something to address unprecedented industrial conflict, but mainly because the time was right for an industrial council. Charles cites published work by Askwith (arbitrator for the Labour Department of the BOT and Chief Industrial Commissioner of the Industrial Council) in support of his view that the industrial council's moment had arrived – a moment in which 'solid common sense, the real desire to work in general harmony governed the basic relations between employers and employed.'[30]

The internal deliberations of the BOT provide a different perspective on the formation of the Industrial Council. The proposal was adopted in spite of its limitations because it gave Buxton an opportunity to address a key obstacle faced by the BOT in the management of industrial conflict.[31] This was the belief that the BOT was subject to political influences favouring one or other parties to a controversy. This belief had reduced the effectiveness of the BOT in dealing with trade unions and employers.[32] In Buxton's view the setting-up of the Council provided a pretext for the reorganization of the BOT, which would allow the political disadvantage to be eliminated without changing the existing system.

Under the auspices of the Industrial Council the Board's responsibility for action was delegated to an officer, called the Chief Industrial Commissioner. It was explained that this officer held a position in relation to the BOT analogous to that of the Comptroller-General of Patents. The Patent Office, it was made clear, was administratively a branch of the BOT, but the Comptroller was a judicial person who was solely responsible for certain classes of acts and decisions and was not under the direction of the President of the BOT. An Industrial Office was constituted on similar lines, presided over by the Commissioner, with a suitable staff and an advisory council all appointed by the BOT, so that it would be unnecessary to refer to the BOT with regard to action to be taken in any particular dispute.

In addition to the powers conferred upon the Chief Commissioner as chairman of the commissioners, his role was to carry out on behalf of the BOT the duties conferred upon the Board under the Conciliation Act and any other work now carried out by the Labour Department of the BOT so far as conciliation in labour disputes was concerned. It was emphasized that the avowed object of the Government in appointing Industrial Commissioners with an impartial Chairman would be 'to avoid the appearance of undue Governmental interference with the problems which the trades of the country should specially interest themselves in settling.'[33]

The President of the BOT emphasized that this or any other plan must not be put before the employers and workers who were to meet the Prime Minister, since it might be fatal to success if it appeared that the BOT had already worked out a plan before the conference. It was most important not to give this impression 'but rather to elicit the suggestions of the various representatives than to present them with a scheme as from the Board of Trade.'[34]

What was to be made clear to them, at the right time, was that the government, in taking this course, did not desire to hinder any voluntary methods or agreements then in force or likely to be adopted for the prevention of stoppage of work or the settlement of disputes. On the contrary, it was to be emphasized that the government aimed at providing an opportunity in every trade of referring such difficulties as might arise to investigation, conciliation or arbitration more extensively than had previously been the case. The object and effect of the new departure was to decrease the current great waste of national resources by industrial war. Further, it was to be emphasized that this organization would provide machinery which might facilitate the adoption of legislation along the lines of the Canadian model, if thought advisable.

The Council was chaired by George Askwith, now knighted and given the title of Comptroller-General of the Labour Department of the BOT and Chief Industrial Commissioner. Buxton, in his speech to the first meeting of the Council on 26th October 1911, told the trade union leaders that they had been chosen 'because you were known by the positions you held, to be representative men.'[35] He stressed that the 'last thing' he desired was 'to lay before you a cut and dried scheme.'[36] Meanwhile, industrial unrest was closely monitored at the request of the Prime Minister (Asquith) and two further reports were submitted to the Cabinet by the President of the BOT and the Chief Industrial Commissioner in 1912.[37] These reports assessed the impact of the great strikes on the workers themselves, on the trade unions, on the country and on the state's management of industrial conflict.

It was noted, firstly, that the railwaymen's strike of the previous August had been a failure from the workers' point of view and they were very disappointed. These workers

> struck in order to obtain 'recognition' which would at once lead to a large increase in wages. They did not obtain recognition in the sense in which they interpreted it, namely direct negotiations as in other trades between the company and the officers of the trade union. They did not obtain any advance in wages in any grade from the strike itself though, after the strike was over, and no doubt partly in consequence of the strike, the companies produced a considerable amount of conscience money for the lower grades.[38]

However,

> the railwaymen live in hopes that by means of the newly constituted conciliation boards, which meet in May, further considerable concessions will be obtained. Unfortunately their demands are being put very high and are almost bound to lead to disappointment. The leaders at least propose to continue to act under the constitution which came into being under the Royal Commission but the leaders are not strong men and their influence is by no means supreme.[39]

Meanwhile it was noted that the coal strike had in some ways eased the position. On the one hand the generous consideration shown on the whole by the railway companies to the men during the unemployment caused by the [coal] strike tended to materially improve the relations between the men and the managers. On the other hand, the funds of the Amalgamated Society [of Railway Servants] were depleted to the extent of some £100,000 by the coal strike and to this extent the union had been crippled as a fighting force.

With regard to the miners, it was thought to be too early to estimate the effect of the strike on their future action. It was noted that 'the men are sulky, suspicious and disappointed' because 'the promises freely made by their extreme leaders of a week or two's holiday and the early concession of their full demands by the owners, under pressure from the community, have not been fulfilled.' Fortunately 'neither the community nor the government had been terrorized or brought to their knees but quite the contrary'. However, the moderate leaders had allowed themselves to be overawed by the extremists. The Executive and the Conference [MFGB] had continually shrunk from taking responsibility or failed to give a lead. The result was that among the trade union leadership 'both forwards and moderates have come out of the conflict discredited and have greatly diminished influence.' The Federation itself had been shaken to its foundations; it was thought possible that it would not survive the shock and that a process of local disintegration might now set in. Further, it was noted

'the miners have now experienced, very much against their will in the case of a large minority and against the anticipations of all, the discomforts and sufferings of a strike and their funds are for the most part exhausted. It is at least doubtful therefore whether, whatever may be the decisions of the Joint District [conciliation] Boards or of the chairmen (and in some cases at least they are bound to be disappointing), the Federation, the leaders or the miners will be in a position, or care to put up another at the present.'[40]

The transport workers were a very different matter for the President of the Labour Department. The success of the seamen in the previous summer

'in a strike which precluded anticipation by the Shipping Federation, was astonishingly rapid and thorough. The dockers and others followed suit and also obtained large concessions. The result was a very great increase in the membership and in the funds of the respective transport trade unions, great elation on the part of the men and a confident belief in their power of forcing a successful strike, either for themselves or for others in co-operation with them. I do not myself believe that syndicalism as such has acquired any hold in the country, though the South Wales miners' strike caused alarm and the recent prosecutions have given it an unlooked-for advertisement.'[41]

What was more worrying for the President was the 'sympathetic strike idea' which 'has made great strides and the more extreme of the transport workers (both leaders and men) are under the impression that they could, by a sympathetic strike of all the import transport workers including the railwaymen, 'hold up' the country and enact practically any terms they chose.' However, the relative failure of the railway strike and the failure of the miners to exact their terms had shown that

'the country is not so easily held up as was supposed. The object lesson of the miners' strike, that the brunt of the suffering of a general strike falls on the working classes themselves has probably somewhat cooled their ardour. Further, the more moderate leaders at all events are anxious not to endanger what they gained last year by a precipitate and unsuccessful fight.' Finally the Transport Workers Association 'is a very heterogenous body and its organization is not yet a year old'.[42]

Although these factors indicated that industrial conflict would probably not escalate, 'there is at least a possibility that the seamen might come out as a protest against the prosecution of Tom Mann, at one time a prominent member of the union.'[43]

Tom Mann had been arrested in March 1912 in connection with the 'Don't Shoot' exhortation to the army in *The Syndicalist* of January 1912. Mann did not write or publish this article; it had been written by Fred Bower, a syndicalist stonemason and had already been published in the *Irish Worker* in July 1911 without raising any controversy.[44] The government was reluctant to arrest Mann, but in the words of Herbert Samuel (a minister in the Liberal government), it seemed that Mann invited arrest since his 'language was as seditious as the speaker could well make it and he would probably welcome a prosecution for seditious language.'[45]

The BOT feared Mann's arrest would restore his standing with workers and revive the flagging conflict as Mann intended,

'though such action would greatly embarrass other unions, as the strike would be political and not industrial, it would undoubtedly just now receive great sympathy and possibly receive sympathetic backing from other unions on the ground that it was a protest against "free speech" and against "strike breaking".'[46]

In general, it was concluded that there were certain disquieting features of the situation which found their clearest expression in the transport workers' organization and had profound implications for the management of industrial conflict generally.

Firstly, any strike which before would have been purely local in character or confined to a trade, 'may now easily develop into a strike on a large scale'.

Secondly, a strike affecting the utility services 'will not only be sympathetic but will, in all probability, be begun without notice and in total disregard of any agreement, legal or otherwise.'

Thirdly, a change for the worse had come over the trade union movement in respect of the attitude of the men towards their leaders and towards agreements:

> 'a change of attitude not confined to the less skilled and more 'rabble' trade unions. The leaders no longer possess the confidence and are not allowed the executive authority that used to be reposed in them. A recommendation by the leaders used, for the most part, to be loyally adopted and carried out . . . [but] . . . the leaders have lost influence and consequently self confidence and naturally are unwilling to take the same responsibility as they would gladly have taken and did take under former conditions.'

As to the newer leaders, they 'have little respect for agreements and their own signatures. All this makes collective bargaining far less certain, effective and peacemaking.'[47]

Fourthly, 'the Labour Party has almost completely collapsed as an effective influence in labour disputes'. They were not consulted and were not involved in the current disputes. They tried 'to act as a go-between for the men and the government but they had very little actual influence over the action of the men or on the result. During the miners' strike the miners' representatives professed to belong to the Labour Party in the House but the Labour Party exercised no influence over them at all. The miners used them as a "cat's paw."' This was 'a distinct loss to industrial peace', since the influence of the Labour Party 'if it still existed, would be moderate and constitutional on leadership and action . . . they may be forced to seek to regain their influence by taking up a more aggressive attitude on labour questions.'[48]

THE MINERS' NEXT STEP: 1912

Much of the above prognosis was informed by the publication early in 1912 of '*The Miners' Next Step*' (MNS) by members of the Unofficial Reform Committee (URC) of the SWMF who, in the wake of the

Cambrian Combine defeat, aimed at transforming the union and bringing about radical changes in the coalfield. This pamphlet was the outcome of an attempt by members of the URC to resolve the problems of trade union organization later outlined by Michels.[49] Both Michels and the authors of the MNS were influenced by the work of Daniel DeLeon. DeLeon supplied many of the examples used by Michels and the Plebs League took its name from DeLeon's pamphlet, *'Two Pages From Roman History'*.[50]

Key problems addressed by the writers of the MNS included the tendency for trade unions to develop into oligarchies, the development of leaders' distinctive interests because of their position within an organization and the *embourgeoisement* of working-class leaders. They believed that, despite good intentions, the power wielded by leaders inevitably corrupted them. They became dishonest in some instances but, more importantly, they exchanged the goals and ideals of the rank and file for prestige and position.[51] Oligarchy was an irresistible tendency because 'in order to be effective the leader must keep the men in order or he forfeits the respect of the employers and 'the public' and thus becomes ineffective as a leader.'[52]

Contrary to DeLeon's conviction (echoed by Michels) that nothing could be done to reform existing trade unions, the authors of the MNS sought the solution in organizational change. Following DeLeon, they proposed the formation of one industrial organization to fight, gain control of and ultimately administer the whole of the mining and related industries of Britain. They aimed at the elimination of employers and control and administration of the industry by workers, and they believed that this could only be achieved gradually and in one way – through the organization of all industries to that end. Nationalization would not achieve this and shareholders would still own and rule the coalfields. Nationalization 'simply makes a National Trust, with all the force of the government behind it . . . to see that the industry is run in such a way as to pay the interest on the bonds with which the coal owners are paid out and to extract as much profit as possible in order to relieve the taxation of other landlords and capitalists.'[53] At this point the authors parted company with industrial unionism and advocated, as the first step towards their goal, the welding together of all of the existing semi-autonomous organizations which made up the SWMF into one organization with one central executive. This, it was argued, would overcome sectionalism and facilitate the rapid and simultaneous stoppage of the mining industry. In line with syndicalist thought, there was to be a new constitution and political programme for the SWMF whereby decision-making power was to reside in the rank and file. The local union lodges were to have 'effective control of affairs'. They were to be 'self-reliant units with every stimulus to work out their own local solution in their own way.'[54] The conciliation policy of the SWMF was rejected, not just because of its inability to improve wages but because of the position in which it placed the union leadership. Conciliation Boards and wages agreements 'only lead us into a morass.' What was necessary was 'a continual agitation in favour of increasing the minimum wage and shortening the hours of work until we have extracted the whole of employers' profits.'[55]

The authors of the MNS devoted little space in their manifesto to the power of the state or the role of political parties. Gilbert (1992) has highlighted the tension between the two models of democracy proposed in the MNS. He explains these omissions and inconsistencies in terms of the practicalities of organizing the workers of South Wales. The Cambrian Combine dispute demonstrated the weaknesses of sectional struggle. The MNS called for the centralization of fighting power so that the full strength of the organization would in future be mobilized and no section would have to fight alone.[56] However, the South Wales miners were particularly attached to the notion of district autonomy. This was the result of a number of factors, not least the social geography of South Wales. This was an area of small-scale communities based on interpersonal contacts and local institutions. The union lodge was a central institution in these communities. It was 'an exceptional trade union' which concerned itself with much more than industrial matters and exerted an overriding influence over daily life in South Wales.[57] So, through the democratization of decision making and the centralization of fighting power, the authors of the MNS hoped to reorganize workers embedded in these local communities and to reconcile their distinct 'immediate interests' with their interests as members of a wider working class. However, the bid for effective centralization of fighting power was 'to be shipwrecked on the rock-like sense of district autonomy to which the South Wales miners were particularly attached'[58] and in the wake of the publication of the MNS Labour MPs, miners' MPs (Mabon, Brace, Richards and Williams) and socialists (including Keir Hardie and Snowden) 'fervently voiced their opposition to syndicalism: and syndicalism in that year . . . was equated with *The Miners' Next Step.*'[59]

THE MINERS' STRIKE, 1912

In September 1911 the Miners' Federation of Great Britain demanded a national minimum wage from the coal owners represented by the Mining Association. The latter agreed only that local negotiations might take place. The miners accepted this but threatened national strike action if a settlement was not reached in all areas. Negotiations in Scotland, South Wales, Northumberland and Durham ended in stalemate, whereupon the Miners' Federation took a strike ballot which resulted in overwhelming support for a national strike. This strike took place on 1st March 1912, involved one million workers and was the largest Britain had yet seen.

The BOT intervened and proposals were drawn up for the settlement of the dispute, endorsing the miners' claim to a minimum wage but with the proviso that this must be settled on a local basis by agreement or government arbitration. The coal owners were divided on this. The miners accepted on condition that the minimum wage should not be less than five shillings a shift for an adult miner anywhere in the country. However, the Coal Mines Minimum Wage Act 1912 recognized only the principle of a minimum wage and did not fix specific wages in different coalfields or specify the minimum.[60] This was rejected by a majority of miners but the Miners' Federation considered this majority insufficient and ordered a return to work. Unrest mounted at this decision in large mining areas, notably Northumberland and Durham, which had voted overwhelmingly against a return to work, and this was the source of much organized resistance to the return and a widespread anti-leadership crusade.[61] In spite of this the strike faded after five weeks and Minimum Wage Boards were established in all the coalfields. The Boards had no power to fix wages but only to protect the position of miners working in 'abnormal places' or prevented in some other way from earning the current district wage.[62]

In the opinion of the Chief Industrial Commissioner, this would not be the end of the matter in the coal industry; three factors made the continuation of widespread industrial conflict likely. Firstly, 'organized unions and disorganized masses of workers have become more or less organized, they have felt their strength and discovered that their strength is greatly increased by united action.'

Secondly, 'the causes of the industrial conflict in 1910–11, particularly the cost of living, are unlikely to be minimized in the near future. Owing to the coal strike, the importation of foreign food, meat and corn will be greatly hampered by the delays and so on in sailing and freights of ships due to the lack of coal and the certainty that it will be some time before coal supplies are back to normal. The scarcity of food means that the advantages of any gains made by workers in 1911 will be diminished.' Lastly, employers might attempt to get back concessions made as a result of strikes and this might provoke 'very stern resistance by the workers.'[63]

Askwith warned that the country would suffer very badly from any further large-scale strikes in coal, railways and transport, the industries in which workers' leverage was greatest.

For Askwith, however, industrial disputes might well continue but the organization which had underpinned industrial conflict need not. He explained that the continuation of industrial conflict was subject to diverse influences and circumstances, such as the amount of trade union funds and support from other industries, the selection of a time which would be most damaging for employers, the government's policy towards industrial conflict and its arrangements with other countries and finally, fortuitous events – luck. The settlement of industrial disputes however was the province of the Labour Department of the BOT. It was an area where 'careful administration may possibly tend gradually to disintegrate the wonderful combination of last year'.[64] The unions in key sectors pursued their claims individually, the conciliation boards settled them individually and at different times and the impact of these settlements on workers within and between these industries was uneven. Conciliation procedures presented an opportunity to undermine the cohesiveness of worker organization in essential industries. So, for Askwith, 'the form of the agitation will depend upon the claims remaining after the Joint District Boards have done their work.'[65]

Measures had already been taken to weaken the organization which had made the industrial conflict so threatening. In the coal industry, 'the firm and consistent attitude of the government' throughout the proceedings surrounding the Coal Mines (Minimum Wage) Bill 'has for the moment upset the calculations of the militant leaders.' Conciliation machinery had been set up in the coal industry and on the railways. In the coal industry, it was noted, workers' future action would depend on the outcome of the Joint District Board meetings. Askwith pointed out that 'the decisions of the Boards or Chairmen will in all likelihood fall short of the hopes with which the strike was entered upon' ... [nevertheless] ... 'if the main grievances such as 'abnormal places' and 'low paid men' are removed a period of comparative quiet will follow.' It was acknowledged that 'Scotland may present difficulties when its agreement expires in July' but this was not thought significant because 'a stoppage in Scotland or any other isolated district will not raise serious alarm.'[66] In Wales, however, miners' new leaders were essentially agitators and 'even if they wished for a little respite, the discontent they have encouraged drives them on.' Also 'the syndicalist policy is to make no agreements and if they are made, break them and act at a moment's notice if the time is propitious'. Nevertheless, it was concluded that

> 'notwithstanding some agitation in districts where the awards are disappointing and uncertainty and fear consequent upon the new condition of affairs under the Act, the mining difficulty may be taken as out of the way as far as the national danger is concerned.'[67]

On the railways, no immediate difficulties were expected from workers because

> 'their new Boards have been formed, they have been heavily hit by the miners' strike and have had to pay out large sums in unemployment benefit. With railwaymen as contrary to miners, the grade system on the railways and the power in the hands of the companies of lightermen . . . the danger from railways does not in fact rest so much within the ranks of railwaymen themselves as it does in the possibility of their organization being stampeded by other allied sections'.

For Askwith the danger lay particularly in the close connection of the railwaymen with the transport workers and 'it would not be wise to ignore this possibility of action and even greater danger of united action.'[68] Askwith went on to review the options available for counteracting this threat. The first option, of doing nothing and allowing the situation to run its course, was rejected on the grounds that this would mean a constant war between the parties growing bigger until it would reach something approaching a civil war. Secondly, things could be left as they were and matters allowed to take their course. This would involve the state intervening and attempting to mediate difficulties as they arose in the usual way. It was emphasized that this policy had been vindicated by its results on the railways and in the mines but that further action of this type in these industries would be difficult and premature – 'this policy takes time to show its full effects.' Askwith acknowledged that calls for immediate government action 'to relieve the harassment of industry are not silenced by this policy.' Given this, he considered other courses of action which could be undertaken by the government. He rejected 'the many suggestions put forward by uninformed people' such as compulsory arbitration, the extension of trade boards, the doctrine of the Canadian act, enforcement of collective bargaining. He rejected legislation, saying 'it would not address the situation as outlined above or convince the country that panic legislation had not been undertaken'. Because of the power of the 'new force'' in trade unionism, 'stringent action' would not have the desired effect:

'it is certain that in the present temper of labour and capital any crude proposals of this nature would be bitterly resisted by organized labour. The difficulty in this matter is the difficulty of enforcing them, especially on the men. Men cannot be made to work if they will not work and they cannot be imprisoned (a million miners for instance) for striking. Apart from 'conspiracy to defeat the law', under which the leaders in Australia might be prosecuted, a pecuniary penalty is the only alternative. A penalty not easy to impose or to enforce.'[69]

Without any acknowledgement of the existence of the Industrial Council, Askwith weighed the merits of a 'careful inquiry', then rejected this option, too, on the grounds that there were limits to the usefulness of commissions and bodies set up to address the question of trade disputes and combinations.[70] Although he accepted that they bought time, collected a mass of valuable evidence and sometimes revealed hidden grievances, 'we do not think they offer the solution of existing problems.'[71]

The President of the BOT added a postcript advising the Cabinet to do nothing. It was true, he said, that strikes in the coal, rail and transport industries, especially when the workers acted wholly or partially in combination, had a very serious effect on the country and justified very strong precautionary and prohibitory measures. However, in addition to aggravating unrest, Buxton warned the Cabinet of another danger which would result from taking away or diminishing the right to strike in these sectors. Prohibition of strike action would give the workers 'an unanswerable case for demanding from the state that they should be secured an adequately progressive wage and proper conditions of labour.' Buxton concluded that

'the whole question of industrial unrest is obviously one abounding in difficulties of all sorts. It appears clear that the government cannot wholly or effectively move in the direction of legislation or even administrative action without much fuller information than they have at their disposal and after much greater consideration of the question than they have yet been able to give.'[72]

THE LONDON TRANSPORT WORKERS' STRIKE, 1912

The London Transport Workers struck in June and July 1912. This strike began as official union action and was called as a result of trade unionists' attempt to extend the gains of 1911 [for example, on the question of union control over the employment of casual labour, employers' resistance to any further union demands and refusal to recognize the NTWF]. BOT intervention failed and a general strike was called, which attracted support from London workers and their families and included huge demonstrations involving up to one thousand people. The strike was characterized by widespread violent conflict between strikers, blacklegs and police. There were several gun battles, notably on the steamship *City of Columbo* in Victoria Docks at the end of July, and similar conflicts erupted at the Royal Albert, West India, Surrey Commercial and Tilbury Docks. However employers proved intractable and the strike did not attract significant sympathetic action from outside London, since most transport workers had achieved higher wages and union bargaining rights as a result of the 1911 strikes and no common set of grievances existed to unite transport workers nationally. Also, the strike leadership did not make practical preparations for national action – they assumed that 1911 would be repeated.[73] London strikers were thus isolated, food and money dwindled and they were starved into submission. Leaders called for a return to work and the strike was called off on 27th July 1912, although many workers initially refused to return to work.

Askwith's approach was vindicated. Although the number of disputes in 1913 was more than double the average of the preceding twenty years, there were no strikes on the same scale as those in 1910–12.[74] However, on 23rd April 1914 the Executive Committee of the Miners' Federation, empowered by a resolution from South Wales, set up the Triple Alliance of miners, railwaymen and transport workers' unions.[75] This event has been taken to mean that, but for the outbreak of war, Britain would have been transformed by a revolutionary general strike.[76] Askwith himself predicted that 'within a very short time there may be movements coming to a head of which recent events have been a small foreshadowing.'[77]

CONCLUSION

The reports of the BOT highlight the concerns of the state in managing the industrial conflict and offer some valuable insights on the role of trade unions. They emphasize that in the years immediately preceding 1910 'the capitalist had been able to secure a larger reward',[78] whilst the living standards of the working class had fallen. Buxton of the BOT chided particularly intransigent employers and concluded in 1912 that 'looking back over the last twelve months, probably no one, least of all any reasonable employer, would deny that, taking into account the prosperity of the country, the expansion of trade and the increased cost of living, the increased remuneration thus wrung from employers was fully justified.'[79] Although the exploitation of the working class was emphasized, the aim of the Labour Department's activities in the field of conciliation was not to redress the balance in favour of the working class in industrial bargaining. Officials of the Labour Department were primarily concerned to manage the resulting industrial conflict through the established trade unions and prevent the development of forms of worker organization which could dislocate the country.

In 1910–12 the conservatism which made trade union leaders valuable in regulating wages and defusing industrial conflict became its focus. They lagged behind new developments in industry and new ideas for working-class organization, with the result that their members began to perceive them as a brake on their aspirations. Because some trade union leaders refused to embark on sympathetic strikes in an effort to protect their union funds and existence, they came to be seen as collaborators with the state and employers rather than representatives of what their members saw as their interests. The aims of the majority of organized workers were not revolutionary in the sense that there was no coherent radical agenda. Different groups of workers struck for different reasons. They wanted wage increases, to be included in conciliation arrangements, minimum wages, reduced working hours or changes in working conditions. Employers resisted and many official trade union leaders continued to promote workers' claims in traditional ways, with one eye on the long-term interests of the union and the other on their own long-term interests. Newer, more radical leaders offered versions of syndicalism and industrial unionism as an alternative vision and fighting policy. Workers readily subscribed to the methods of syndicalism, 'direct action' and the critique of trade unionism at the heart of industrial unionism rather than the aims of these movements. Direct action was very effective. Success gave workers a new confidence and their organizations gained a new coherence and scale. Leaders of the established trade unions lost power over their members, and even some of the newer more radical leaders felt threatened by the success of the movement they helped to engender.

It was found that trade union leaders' authority (and that of the Labour Party) was fragile and dependent on successfully gauging and meeting workers' mood and aspirations. The prosecution of Tom Mann clearly illustrated the dilemmas facing trade union leaders at the height of the conflict. Many leaders were left with a stark choice: to become more radical or lose their positions. Their response to this leadership crisis varied. Many abdicated responsibility, some put their own material interests before 'the national interest' or the interests of their members, some tended to yield to the greatest threat to their position. Others turned to the state and fuelled workers' distrust of their leaders and the belief that the BOT was biased in favour of employers. This seriously hampered BOT attempts to defuse industrial conflict.

The scale and character of worker organization, trade union leaders' diminished control in key industries and distrust of the BOT combined to produce a potential 'national danger'. It was believed that this could be realized through ill-considered action on the part of the state. The more forcefully the state intervened, the more likely it was to produce the situation it aimed at preventing, and yet to do nothing could have the same result: 'a constant war between parties growing bigger until it would reach something approaching a civil war'.[80]

The state's response was firstly to set up the Industrial Council which addressed public and employers' concern, facilitated the reorganization of the Labour Department of the BOT in an attempt to silence claims of political bias, and bought time during which existing conciliation machinery for curtailing disputes could be strengthened and directed with increased vigour towards disorganizing the 'wonderful combination' which underpinned the threat. This meant exploiting existing divisions in worker organization by manipulating pay settlements and internal rivalries, and was successful. The formation of the Triple Alliance was a collective attempt by leaders of the unions centrally concerned in the 'Great Unrest' to regain and expand their control and safeguard their positions. For Askwith, however, this coalition was a threat to the divisive strategy deployed by the BOT, because each member union could be 'stampeded by other allied sections' into mass strike action. This would compel the intervention of the state and leave the BOT strategy for the management of industrial conflict in ruins. Coming just at this time, the outbreak of war looked like one of Askwith's hoped-for 'fortuitous events'.[81] The next chapter will show, however, that 'the new ideas . . . and new organizations among workers had not disappeared'.[82]

NOTES

1. Evans, 1911; Page Arnot, 1967; Jones, 1973.
2. Jones, 1973.
3. Holton, 1976.
4. Page Arnot, 1967, p. 26.
5. Rees was checkweighman at the Cambrian colliery and secretary of the Cambrian Lodge of the SWMF.
6. Page Arnot, 1967, p. 219.
7. Dangerfield, 1936 p. 203.
8. PRO HO/45/10645/210615/9.
9. Quoted in Dangerfield, 1936, p. 166.
10. Cole, 1948, p. 330.
11. Holton, 1976.
12. Kendall, 1969, p. 27.
13. Cole, 1948, p. 335
14. PRO CAB 37/107/70.1911. Report by President of the Board of Trade to the Cabinet, 25th July 1911.
15. Ibid.
16. Ibid.
17. Ibid.
18. Ibid.
19. PRO CAB, 37/107/70, July 1911.
20. Ibid.
21. Ibid.
22. Ibid.
23. Ibid.
24. In 1907, when unrest was threatened on the railways, George Askwith KC, who had played the role of arbitrator for the Labour Department. since the passing of the Conciliation Act, was appointed full-time conciliator for the BOT by LLoyd George then president of the BOT. In 1909 Askwith was made Comptroller-General of the Commercial, Labour and Statistical Departments of the BOT. See Davidson, 1985.
25. PRO CAB, 37/107 9th Aug. 1911, Buxton.
26. Charles, 1973, p. 38.
27. Ibid., p. 5
28. Ibid., p. 3.
29. Ibid.
30. Charles, 1973, p. 38.
31. Ibid.

32. Ibid., p. 4.
33. Ibid.
34. Ibid., p. 8.
35. Quoted by Charles, 1973, p. 58.
36. Ibid., p. 60
37. PRO CAB, 37/110/63, Report by the Board of Trade to the Cabinet 14th April 1912.
38. See Bagwell, 1963.
39. PRO CAB, 37/110/63.
40. Ibid.
41. PRO CAB, 37/110/62, Buxton, President of the Board of Trade, April 1912.
42. Ibid.
43. PRO CAB, 37/110/62, Buxton, April 1912.
44. White, 1991, p. 181.
45. Quoted in White, 1991, p. 180. Mann called on the police to 'come and get him'; see Holton, 1976, p. 116.
46. PRO CAB/37/110/62.
47. Ibid.
48. Ibid.
49. Michels, 1915.
50. DeLeon, ND.
51. Gilbert, 1992, p. 79.
52. The Miners' Next Step, 1973, pp. 17–20.
53. Ibid., p. 32.
54. Ibid., p. 30.
55. Ibid., p. 24, p. 30.
56. Merfyn Jones, 1973, p. 6.
57. Paynter, 1971, p. 69, cited in Gilbert 1992. TW Paynter 'The Fed' in G.A. Hughes, *Men of No Property*', Caerwys, 1971.
58. Merfyn Jones, 1973, p. 7.
59. Page Arnot, 1967, p. 327.
60. Cole, 1948, p. 340.
61. Holton, 1976, p. 117.
62. Cole, 1948, p. 341.
63. PRO CAB, 37/110/63, Askwith, April 1912.
64. Ibid.
65. Ibid.
66. Coal Mines (Minimum Wage) Act, 1912.
67. PRO CAB, 37/110/63.
68. Ibid.
69. Ibid.
70. Ibid.
71. Ibid.
72. PRO CAB, 37/110/62 (Buxton), April 1912.
73. Holton, 1976, p. 125.
74. PRO CAB/37/118/, No 19, p. 11. Memorandum from the Board of Trade on the conditions of labour and trade at the beginning of 1914.
75. Page Arnot, 1967, p. 376.

76. See Phillips, 1971.
77. Askwith, 1920, p. 849.
78. PRO CAB, 37/107/70.
79. PRO CAB, 37/110/62.
80. Ibid.
81. PRO CAB, 37/110/63, April 1912.
82. PRO LAB, 2/697, February 1920.

5 The Munitions of War Act

There were one hundred strikes in progress when war was declared on 4th August 1914.[1] On 25th of August a joint meeting took place of the Parliamentary Committee of the TUC, the management committee of the General Federation of Trade Unions and the Executive Committee of the Labour Party. At this meeting the co-operation of the labour movement was pledged to the war effort and it was resolved 'that an immediate effort be made to terminate all existing trade disputes, whether strikes or lockouts, and whenever difficulties arise during the war period, a serious attempt should be made by all concerned to reach an amicable settlement before resorting to a strike or lockout.'[2] By the end of August the number of strikes had been reduced to twenty.[3] It seemed that workers' patriotism had triumphed over their conflict with employers.

However, the growing need for recruits to the armed services quickly produced a shortage of labour, especially skilled labour in the engineering trades, and a shortage of munitions.[4] By October 1914 the engineering trades had lost 12.2 per cent of their pre-war male workers.[5] The worsening labour situation led to the Shell Conference on 21st December 1914, at which the BOT proposed, in addition to the no-strike agreement, that trade union rules and practices which restricted output should be temporarily suspended for the duration of the war to allow for dilution. Trade union conditions were to be restored after the war and standard wages preserved on all jobs.

Askwith of the BOT outlined these proposals in a letter to both the engineering employers and the Amalgamated Society of Engineers in January 1915 and asked that they now resolve the labour shortage on this basis. The engineering unions rejected this proposal, mainly because the Engineering Employers' Federation could not bind unfederated engineering employers to this pledge.[6]

On 4th February 1915, still with no agreement reached, the Prime Minister (Asquith) appointed a committee chaired by George Askwith. This committee was called the Committee on Production in Engineering and Shipbuilding and its brief was to obtain the agreement of the engineering and shipbuilding workers to the above proposals.[7] The Committee's intervention resulted in the Shells and Fuses Agreement in March 1915, which provided for the introduction of unskilled labour, including women, on jobs reserved for skilled men in the engineering industry.[8] Women who took over men's jobs were to get the rate for the job (to protect the male rate at the end of the war – not to establish the rate for the job, regardless of sex, as a basic principle). The agreement was to last for the war only and women would be the first to be discharged when the labour shortage was over.[9]

Labour unrest began to escalate.[10] The Committee on Production recommended that the government take action to prevent all strikes and lockouts on war work and to have disputes where parties could not reach a settlement referred to an independent tribunal for arbitration. This recommendation was accepted and the next day (21st February 1915) the Committee on Production became the arbitration tribunal.[11]

Trade union leaders and the state had agreed on the need to implement labour controls, but workers proved less amenable. In January 1915 only ten disputes were known to the Labour Department. By March there were 74 fresh disputes. There had been a 24 per cent increase in the cost of living but wages had lagged behind. Employers resisted demands for wage increases, they increased working hours in order to take full advantage of government contracts and they successfully pressured the government to relax the provisions of the Factory Acts.[12]

In March 1915 trade union leaders in munitions asked the state to help them secure their members' acceptance of the proposed labour controls and a conference was called to discuss the issue.[13] Another agreement was reached between the Chancellor of the Exchequer (Lloyd George), the Parliamentary Committee of the TUC and the leaders of the 36 unions involved in war production that trade union restrictive practices would be abandoned, dilution would be introduced and strikes would be avoided by means of arbitration. This agreement, called the Treasury Agreement, was reached in exchange for the pledge that trade union practices would be restored after the war, that employers' profits would be restricted during the war and was based on the Shells and Fuses Agreement.

The miners' leaders were not party to this agreement and the Amalgamated Society of Engineers held out for better terms.[14] Without the ASE the agreement had little value and a week later a Supplementary Treasury Agreement was drawn up which was more acceptable to the ASE. It contained additional clauses stating that trade practices were only to be relaxed for the war period and protection for skilled workers 'in the case of the introduction of new inventions which were not in existence in the pre-war period the class of workmen to be employed on this work shall be determined according to the practice prevailing before the war in the case of the class of work most nearly analogous.'[15]

The agreement still did not eliminate unofficial strikes which began to proliferate after it was signed. In the three months following the agreement strikes increased, affecting more than 84,000 workers and involving the loss of over 525,000 working days.[16] These strikes were concentrated on the Clyde where industrial unrest had begun to mount even before the Treasury agreement was signed or discussed with the trade unions. On 16th February 1915 events had crystallized in a general strike among Clyde engineers over a wage issue. The strike ended on 4th March after a Government ultimatum to the strikers and the Committee on Production stepped in as arbitrator in advance of its official role as arbitration committee – the strikers were given half of their original wage demand.

The Clyde dispute centred on whether workers were to be allowed to take advantage of their strong bargaining position to improve their wages. The Clyde engineers claimed two pence an hour as a permanent increase in the standard rate. The Committee on Production awarded one penny an hour, not as an addition to the standard rate but as a 'war bonus'. This became the precedent for all subsequent arbitration awards. They were to be temporary and only in very exceptional circumstances would the Committee on Production allow any permanent alteration in standard rates. This prevented any wage increases which workers would normally have received and any increases under consideration before the war.[17] This policy was undermined by employers and substantial wage increases were obtained by skilled workers in key industries owing to competition for scarce labour between employers in the booming munitions industries.

When the cost of living began to rise during 1915, employers began to grant wage increases of varying amounts, on different bases in different trades and in different parts of the country. Wage anarchy set in as employers with and without government contracts began to bid against each other in offering higher wages to attract and keep skilled workers. Officials of the BOT emphasized to the government that the success of the war effort depended on keeping skilled workers on government munitions work.[18]

Dilution was another fertile source of dispute. The Treasury Agreement laid down that 'dilutees' were to be paid identical wages to workers previously employed on the same work. However, much work performed in munitions workshops after the war started was work of a new type and existing jobs were changed by the introduction of machinery and by the fragmentation of jobs previously performed by skilled workers. Employers therefore had considerable scope for avoiding the payment of identical wage rates. Moreover, increasing numbers of dilutees were women and it quickly became clear that the government did not intend that women should receive equal time rates with men and that employers had no intention of even paying the same piece rates to women.[19]

The dilution issue was brought into sharp relief in a dispute over dilution at the Elswick works of Armstrong Whitworth and Co., where management had brought in workers (including women) from depressed textile areas to perform previously skilled jobs. So opposed were Elswick workers that they actually suggested 'that before dilution was permitted they should be allowed to go to the Front and ascertain whether the guns alleged to be required were really needed'.[20]

Reports from the BOT had already indicated to the government that patriotism had lost to self-interest and both workers and employers were taking advantage of the war situation. The shortage of labour was an increasingly serious problem which directly delayed production, but it was emphasized that it had effects 'perhaps even more serious'. The situation was that 'practically any workman of any pretensions to skill at all in the engineering and shipbuilding trades has so little difficulty in finding work the moment he wants it that he has little economic motive left for remaining with his employer, if he is in any way dissatisfied, whether with good reason or without'. Employers played a key part in this. They were

'constantly urged by the Government to increase their output . . . [but they] . . . do not feel themselves really in a position to bargain with the men, and have indeed, in many cases owing to the terms of their contracts, little incentive to do so. The ordinary economic control of the individual workman has practically broken down.'

The situation was further compounded by

'the increase in prices, the rumour of large profits made by those who were regarded as enemies of the working class and the distrust of established authorities which survived the excitement of war – all this had developed into a movement opposing the generally accepted policy of the Government and the officials of the trade unions . . .

The result is that to a very considerable extent the men are out of the control of both employers and their own leaders'.[21]

The attempt to prevent strikes and implement dilution by voluntary agreement had failed. These had been agreed to in theory, but strikes had broken out and dilution was still the subject of protracted negotiations between all parties. Llewellyn Smith, Permanent Secretary to the BOT, put the matter succinctly to the Cabinet:

'the difficulty . . . is that the workmen, though engaged in armaments work, still feel themselves to be working essentially for private employers with whom they have only a 'cash nexus' and that in the present circumstances a cash nexus is quite inadequate to secure control.'[22]

Llewellyn Smith pressed for compulsion. In a report circulated to the War Office at the beginning of June, he urged:

'my considered judgment is in favour of immediate legislation, as I am convinced that any further attempt on merely voluntary lines unsupported by legislative enactment will only break down and lose valuable time. I am glad to find that these views are shared by Sir George Askwith and Mr Mitchell of the Chief Industrial Commissioner's Department.'[23]

Llewellyn Smith proposed that the government put a stop to wage anarchy and labour mobility, firstly by strengthening the Defence of the Realm Regulation prohibiting employers from holding out inducements to workmen to change their employment.[24] Secondly, he proposed that no new employer should take on workers engaged on government work within a certain period of their leaving such employment without either a certificate from the previous employer or a certificate from some tribunal such as a Court of Referees that this refusal was unreasonably withheld.[25]

Llewellyn Smith emphasized that if workers in munitions were to accept these new demands it was necessary to appeal to their patriotism – to substitute 'a motive not of a purely economic character'.[26] He suggested that patriotism might be encouraged and the shortage of skilled labour eased by 'the raising by voluntary enrolment of an 'Industrial Army' of munition workers with some such title as the King's Munitions Corps.'[27]

Officials of the War Office expressed themselves largely in favour of these initiatives 'as a penultimate measure in the hope of avoiding industrial conscription,' but, they argued, they would not address the problem of recruitment or increased arms production. Trade union leaders were the main obstacle to further recruitment and increased industrial production. They should be bought off for the duration of the war and replaced by factory managements.[28] For the Labour Department of the BOT, however, the goodwill of trade union leaders was indispensable. Llewellyn Smith had earlier warned the government that 'nothing but disaster would attend any attempt to rush the position by a frontal attack on union policy, or by any Government action which would give the unions the impression that the Government in this matter were acting as the mouthpiece of the employers.'[29] Of the industrialists at the War Office he noted that 'on labour matters . . . Girouard and Booth are amateurs . . . I doubt if either has any idea of the pitfalls in any 'new labour policy'.'[30] In any case, as employers their primary objective was not the national interest but competition with each other in search of individual profit.[31]

THE MUNITIONS OF WAR ACT

The Ministry of Munitions was set up, headed by Lloyd George, on 9th June 1915.[32] The Ministry was organized in separate sections, including a Labour Department whose personnel and policy were transplanted from the BOT.[33] Immediately after the formation of the Ministry of Munitions, Lloyd George held talks with the unions which had signed the Treasury Agreement about giving statutory effect to the latter. The unions agreed and the Munitions of War Act was passed on 2nd July 1915.

The Munitions of War Act went much farther than the Treasury Agreement. The Act gave the state extensive powers over workers in controlled industries. Their mobility, pay and conditions of work were now controlled by the state. The Act provided that for a period of six weeks no employment was to be given to a worker who left work in munitions without a leaving certificate from his employer. This made it difficult for workers to increase their wages by moving to employers offering higher rates. Strikes and lockouts in all industries engaged in war work became illegal and all disputes were to be referred to the Committee on Production for arbitration. Since there was now a boom in the munitions industry and employers had no use for the lockout, workers bore the brunt of this regulation and now had no way of improving their wages except through the long process of a tribunal. The Act did not forbid incitement to strike, but under the Defence of the Realm Acts (regulation 42), amended in November 1915, it was an offence 'to impede, delay, or restrict the production, repair or transport of war material or any other work necessary for the successful prosecution of the war'.[34]

Under the Act, 6,000 Controlled Establishments were ultimately created and Munitions Tribunals were established as the agency of enforcement of the Act. In addition, it provided for the control of employers' profits so that the restriction of trade union liberties should benefit the state and not employers.[35]

The Munitions Act met worker resistance almost immediately. Thirteen days after it was passed, 200,000 miners stopped work in South Wales. An agreement between miners and coal owners had expired and negotiations for a new one had broken down. The BOT had been conducting negotiations, but the miners had rejected the peace formula suggested. On 13th July a Royal Proclamation was issued under the MOW Act, making it an offence to take part in a strike in the South Wales coalfields, and a General Munitions Tribunal was set up in that area. This exacerbated the strike, and on 20th July the Minister of Munitions and the President of the BOT (Lloyd George and Walter Runciman) went to Cardiff and ended the strike by granting practically all the strikers' claims.[36]

The storm centre of industrial unrest in 1914–16, however, was the Clyde Valley, where the Munitions Act was known as the 'Slavery Act' because it removed the right to strike, rendered trade union officials impotent and suspended trade union customs and practices. This created resentment, suspicion and distrust of the trade union leaders who had agreed to it and a shift of allegiance to local shop stewards.[37] Munitions production was concentrated on the Clyde and from the outbreak of war, workers found themselves under increasing pressure to accept dilution. On 25th July 1915, coppersmiths at Fairfield's shipyard struck. In early July the management of Fairfield's had applied for and was granted permission from the Glasgow and West of Scotland Armaments Committee to substitute plumbers on work usually done by coppersmiths. The coppersmiths' union had been reluctant to approve of this move but was told by management that since the firm was a controlled establishment it would do it anyway. After the annual works holiday, the coppersmiths struck over the initiative but were subsequently fined only a very small amount by a Munitions Tribunal and the coppersmiths' union showed its support by paying the fines.[38]

On 26th August Fairfield's workers struck again over the dismissal of two shipwrights for slacking. The latter had been sent on their way with leaving certificates which bore the inscription 'not attending to work.'[39] After a meeting the shipyard director had reluctantly agreed to remove the offending phrase but not to reinstate the workers, and 426 shipwrights struck. The Ministry of Munitions was informed and a week later 26 of the strikers were prosecuted (mostly shop stewards). Shortly after the coppersmiths' hearing Lloyd George had told the shipbuilding employers that the Ministry would consider prosecuting 'in suitable cases . . . where we could make sure we could make a real example.'[40] At the shipwrights' hearing fifteen men pleaded guilty to contravening the MOW Act and two of those who pleaded not guilty were convicted and fined ten pounds, each with 21 days to pay. Three of the men refused to pay and were imprisoned; this provoked a swell of unrest among Clyde workers and threats of a general strike.

It should be noted that unrest on the Clyde predated the MOW Act and there had been considerable trouble over swingeing rent increases imposed by landlords taking advantage of the housing shortage, made worse by the influx of munitions workers into the region. In the summer of 1915 the Clyde Workers' Committee had been formed out of the strike committee which had co-ordinated the February 1915 strike over wages and the attempt to introduce Taylorism in engineering on the Clyde. This strike marked a new stage in the history of shop stewards: it was the first occasion on which the shop stewards took decisive and effective action apart from and in opposition to the official trade union leadership. It gave birth to the Shop Stewards' and Workers' Committee movement, which was later to spread across the country. The whole district was divided into sections, each controlled by a local committee which sent representatives to a central committee. This movement grew out of the engineering workshop which was organized around shop stewards and their committees. For some years the Amalgamated Society of Engineers had organized its membership in disparate factories through a system of shop stewards appointed by, and responsible to, District Committees (also known as Vigilance Committees) of the union. In the years leading up to the First World War, however, a rift developed between the District Committees and the shop stewards such that they became semi-independent of the former and were appointed by the rank and file.[41] However, it was only during the war that an independent shop stewards' movement developed outside the existing trade union organization and evolved its own policy, based on the theory of class struggle, the abolition of capitalism, the reorganization of trade unionism and workers' control of industry.[42]

The Clyde Workers' Committee leadership was dominated by members of the influential Socialist Labour Party. The SLP had the most consistently revolutionary outlook of any political party active on Clydeside at that time. Members of the SLP were adherents of Daniel DeLeon's industrial unionism.[43] The influence of the SLP was expressed among the leadership of the CWC in its awareness of the need for one union in each industry and for political action.

This was the backdrop to industrial unrest on the Clyde and the leaders of some of the strikes, with the exception of the rent strikes and the strike at Lang's of Johnstone (see below), were members of the CWC. The CWC was not against dilution per se, believing that it was an inevitable step in the evolution of capitalism. Given this, the leaders of the Amalgamated Society of Engineers were wrong to believe that the pre-war situation of labour could be restored. In adhering to industrial unionism the CWC was, theoretically, against barriers of craft, sex and race and sought workers' control of industry as the only way workers' interests could be protected. Of all the agreements negotiated concerning dilution on war work, the Clyde Workers' Agreement, negotiated by the CWC, won the best terms (equal pay or the rate for the job) for dilutees who were largely women. There is no evidence, however, that this was done for women workers but to ensure that women could not be used to undercut men.[44]

The Cabinet became concerned on receiving reports on the situation from the Labour Department of the Ministry of Munitions. Lord Balfour of Burleigh and Lynden Macassey were appointed 'to enquire into the causes and circumstances of the apprehended differences affecting munitions workers in the Clyde district.'[45] Balfour and Macassey had no authority to release the imprisoned workers, and union leaders of the Clyde engineering and shipbuilding industry sent a telegram to the Ministry of Munitions demanding the release of the workers and a reply within three days. The union leaders met Lloyd George and it was decided that the men would be released and the unions could pay the fines.

The state of mind of Clyde workers was characterized by Macassey as 'universal irritation, unveiled hostility to the Act and corroding suspicion of every clause under the Act. From this mental disposition, all the present unrest is begotten' and is not 'the spontaneous product of the workmen's own cogitation' but the work of 'two or three local trade union officials who deliberately and for their own purposes, circulated only too effectively, untrue statements as to the origin of the Act and garbled, misleading versions of its effect.' These officials did this for their own advancement (the prize was the General Secretary-ship of the ASE) and did not expect such a powerful response from their members.[46] The officials lost control and were swept along by the tide of resentment, and 'soon the crowd overtook their local leaders. Now these particular officials, to justify their existence, are forced to inflate and paint as crowning tyrannies of the Act, every pettifogging complaint that in peacetime would not have secured report by a shop steward to his union local branch.'[47]

STALEMATE

Towards the end of 1915, information received from controlled establishments led officials of the Labour Department to conclude that the Munitions Act had so far failed to achieve the results anticipated. Although the suspension of restrictions and the dilution of labour was taking place, it was happening too slowly for the necessities of the situation. There were several reasons for this. Some firms were making changes but many more were not. In explanation, these employers asserted that they did not need to abolish trade union restrictions (they had managed to increase output in other ways) and had therefore not attempted to do so. A number were willing to make changes but the threat of worker resistance prevented them. Some unions (notably the Boilermakers) would not work with non-unionists.[48]

There was a great deal of conservatism among both employers and workers, and the introduction of women workers was practically a guarantee of resistance and unrest, with the result that some employers avoided attempting to implement change. Other employers resisted change, however, simply because they shared workers' attitude towards the introduction of women workers. When challenged on the issue, one employer had pointed out that 'it is no use proposing dilution of labour when competent unskilled male labour cannot be obtained for work which would be unsuitable for women.'[49]

The appeal to workers' patriotism (or the attempt to substitute a motive not of a purely economic character), in the shape of the War Munitions Volunteer scheme,[50] 'had failed to live up to expectations and the total number of skilled men transferred from private work to munitions was only 12,000 [51]. It was decided that this laid to rest the theory (favoured by the trade unions) that the absolute shortage of skilled men could be met by shifting skilled men from one shop to another. The policy of releasing skilled men from the army had also proved disappointing, as had the importation of skilled men from the Dominions and other countries.[52] As early as December 1914 the Board of Trade had been considering importing labour from outside Britain.[53] Although some trade unions had suggested this, in practice it had proved problematic, not least because trade unionists would not work with imported labour while their own workmates were recruited to fight in the trenches.[54] Of the bid to introduce 'coloured' labour, it was noted that 'the trade unions constantly and successfully set their faces against the attempt.'[55] The Ministry of Munitions did not press the unions on this issue and opted for segregation by setting up separate establishments staffed exclusively by foreign labour – as at Birtley in Durham, which consisted exclusively of Belgian workers.[56]

In July 1915 a National Registration Act had been passed and on 15th August 1915 a census was taken to provide information as to the size and skills of the maximum possible workforce in Britain. From this exercise it was concluded that no more skilled labour could be recruited, that Britain could not expect to produce munitions with male labour while maintaining an army of continental size, and without dilution it would be impossible to raise the 1,500,000 men thought necessary for the 1916 campaign.[57]

This evidence persuaded the Minister of Munitions that a higher degree of coercion was necessary. Lloyd George addressed a conference of the executives of the engineering unions in September 1915 and told them that since all other expedients had failed, only dilution could prevent labour conscription or the destruction of the nation.[58] He assured the engineering unions that their interests would be safeguarded if dilution was accepted and suggested the appointment of a committee of trade union representatives, engineering employers and representatives of the Ministry of Munitions to help implement dilution. This committee was to draw up a comprehensive scheme for dilution which would increase the scope and numbers of women employed in a way acceptable to men and women workers.

The Central Labour Supply Committee was duly formed and at its first meeting on 22nd September 1915 it dutifully agreed that dilution was the only solution to the labour shortage and a directive known as CE 1 was issued to all controlled establishments, instructing them to implement dilution on 13th October 1915.[59] This directive laid down that no worker in munitions production was to be employed on any work requiring less skill than he possessed. Where there was a shortage of manpower, invalid soldiers, army rejects ·and women and children were to be introduced, and the substitution of unskilled for skilled workers was to be achieved by the introduction of automatic machines and the subdivision of skilled tasks into their simplest processes.[60] Following this directive the 'L' Circulars were issued – a series of five circulars dealing with wages and general policies with regard to the implementation of dilution in controlled establishments. These circulars included recommendations on which jobs were 'within the limits of women's capabilities,' on health and welfare and minimum wages for women. Circulars L2 and L3 respectively recommended a £1 minimum wage for women workers and a minimum for substituted male labour.[61] They recommended also that dilution be implemented only after consultation with the workers and following clear explanation by management of the proposed changes. The adoption of these recommendations was, however, optional, and although they were implemented in munitions factories directly controlled by the government they were ignored by employers who subcontracted work from the government, as well as by some government departments, notably the Admiralty.[62]

In advance of a proposed visit to the Tyne and the Clyde by the Minister of Munitions to expedite dilution, Lynden Macassey (arbitrator for the Labour Department) visited the Tyne in early December 1915. His aim was to meet the District Committee of the ASE 'to force the issue as to whether or not the men of the district would accept the scheme of dilution agreed upon by the government.' On arrival, however, he found the atmosphere such that 'it was inadvisable to force any issue, especially as I felt that by delaying matters for a few days and by careful handling the question could be satisfactorily settled.' In spite of 'careful handling' Macassey found that workers on the Tyne remained unconvinced of the need to increase the output of munitions. For Macassey, this was 'merely an excuse not to give up their restrictions . . . there was no question that the munitions were necessary and 'every workshop must be diluted to the full.' For Macassey, this was necessary not only to increase the flow of munitions but also to discipline skilled workers in the engineering works, who had such power that the government, their employers and their own leaders were careful not to upset them. Macassey pointed to 'the lamentable and disgraceful timekeeping which takes place in these works. I believe I am right in saying that between thirty per cent and sixty per cent of the men in many cases do not turn up on Monday at all . . . The men are better off than they have ever been, and whether they are fully employed or underemployed, the wages they are receiving now are higher than they have ever received before.' In Macassey's view, 'dilution should be put into operation with all possible speed and force since [the workers] do not have a leg to stand on . . . the way the government have met their point of view is far more generous than might have been expected when compared with the great national crisis.' Macassey's experience led him to conclude that, while Lloyd George's proposed visit could be beneficial, it would be insufficient to implement dilution. Macassey had been informed by the workers' leaders that although they were convinced that dilution was necessary the workers would not believe them, so that 'definite and strong measures will have to be taken in any case where the men object to their restrictions for the moment being done away with.'[63]

Similarly, on the Clyde, Paterson (the Chief Labour Officer) reported that in spite of the MOW Act, 'trade union restrictions were being as firmly insisted upon as ever they were and it was hopeless to expect employers to take any action in the direction suggested (in CE1) until the Ministry of Munitions had brought the necessary pressure to bear on trade unions to secure the waiving in practice – and not merely on paper – of their restrictions.'[64] Employers on the Clyde were convinced that the Ministry of Munitions knew the hollowness and insincerity of trade union action but was unwilling to pressure the unions, preferring to let individual employers take the brunt of union opposition. Employers were determined not to be used in this way by the Ministry. It was emphasized that, as far as Clyde employers were concerned, the Ministry's position had been amply demonstrated at Lang's of Johnstone, where 'the Ministry allowed the ASE to dictate the terms of settlement and this had resulted in the evaporation of all interest in the question of the dilution of labour.'[65] Paterson emphasized that he had not discussed the employers' views or the great scope for dilution in works across the Clyde with the local officials of the trade unions because 'I am sure that no purpose could be served by consultation with the local officials of trade unions. The matter would merely be referred to the central executives of various unions and much valuable time would be lost.' Like the report on the situation with regard to dilution on the Tyne, this report was intended to acquaint the Minister of Munitions with the position before he went to Glasgow to meet the shop stewards with a view to expediting the implementation of dilution there.

Paterson concluded his report with the opinion that no appreciable increase in dilution would be achieved by Lloyd George meeting the Glasgow shop stewards. This was because 'the atmosphere which is essential to permit of such a movement yielding any result does not exist, and the chances of any movement might well be likened to an effort to advance and sustain an advance against a wall of poisoned gas.'[66]

This assessment of the situation proved accurate. In his report on the visit, the Ministry of Munitions Intelligence officer in Glasgow chose a quotation from *The Vanguard* (which had been suppressed) instead of further comment on Lloyd George's reception on the Clyde. It read: 'seldom has a prominent politician, a leading representative of the Government class been treated with so little respect by a meeting of workers. It is evidenced that the feeling of servility towards their masters no longer holds first place in the minds of the workers, but that very much to the contrary they hate their masters, and understand thoroughly the difference between capitalists and working-class interests'.[67]

Shortly after this humiliation J.W. Muir of the CWC made its position clear and at the same time enumerated the reasons for Lloyd George's failure. Firstly he pointed out that the focus of the campaign on the Clyde was not official trade union leaders but the government itself. Trade union leaders were the servants and not the masters of the rank and file. At times they needed prompting 'to move on the path the rank-and-file desire them to tread' but the CWC existed to prevent the dissipation of rank-and-file efforts through lack of organization. Secondly, the CWC aimed at co-ordinating the forces of labour and were not susceptible to attempts to 'divide and conquer' by diverting their attack away from the government towards trade union officials. The policy of the CWC was to back trade union leaders 'with all the power and influence at our disposal when they act rightly and when they fail to act rightly, to make the pace ourselves'. Thirdly, he emphasized that the CWC would vigorously defend workers' interests on issues such as dilution, high food prices, conscription and the endless demand for new sacrifices. Lastly, the CWC rejected Lloyd George's claim that the only alternative to military discipline in the workshops was the Munitions Act. They demanded 'another policy which was not coercive and consequently was free from any taint of slavery and which would promote the harmony and efficiency which is absolutely essential to get the increased output asked for by him'. This was the takeover by government of all the industries and national resources to be partly managed in all departments by organized labour.[68]

THE STATE'S RESPONSE

On 31st December 1915, at a meeting between a deputation from the ASE, the Prime Minister and the Minister of Munitions, the Minister of Munitions challenged the ASE on its resistance to some aspects of dilution, especially the provisions surrounding the employment of women workers, saying:

'you see, we have had an agreement since March and it really has not been carried out. You will all admit that. We simply cannot produce the stuff unless you do it . . . It has not arisen through the Executive's fault. You have played the game right through, but you have men behind you who put forward fresh demands. They say "we are not going to do it unless you do so and so" and then we are confronted with another difficulty . . . We never seem to get to a firm agreement. It makes such a difference when one is considering whether to make a concession or not. Is it really a firm agreement?'[69]

The Prime Minister felt that the solution to the dilution problem lay in the hands of the union leaders, whose duty was to exert 'all their force to remove these suspicions and to encourage the men, and indeed, I will not say coerce, but bring every influence they can to bear upon them.' The Minister of Munitions professed himself sympathetic to the Executive's point of view: 'I know your reasons and you know you are getting very big concessions for your people' but concluded with a barely concealed threat:

'what I am afraid of is that you will say, "Yes, we will accept this" and then your men begin again. They do not like dilution and therefore they are always trying to find some sort of objection to it. They will find another and we shall be no nearer the end. If so I shall have to put another proposal before the Prime Minister to deal with the situation. That is a ghastly thing to contemplate.'[70]

Trade union leaders had agreed to co-operate, but it was recognized that their insistence on consultation and agreement at both local and national level meant that they either would not co-operate actively in order to retain credibility with their members or that they could not deliver their members' co-operation because power had shifted to local leaders. In the original draft of the Munitions of War Act the provision requiring notice to the workmen concerned and local consultation over the introduction of changes was omitted, it had been reinserted after talks with union leaders. This was now seen as a mistake which stood in the way of further dilution, because asking workers whether women workers could be introduced or whether other changes could be introduced 'practically means inviting them to raise difficulties, and this they do. It also means inviting them to ask for evidence that the change proposed is necessary'.[71] Events at Armstrong Whitworth & Co., at Lang's of Johnstone and Smith's of Coventry, where large concessions had to be made to secure any co-operation from the ASE, were cited to support the Ministry of Munitions case.[72]

It was concluded that in practice consultation usually meant stalemate since 'consultation unfortunately means, as a rule, consulting both the local workmen and trade union leaders and it sometimes happens that when one is favourable the other is unfavourable, and vice versa.'[73]

Since it was now obvious that dilution could not be implemented through the trade unions, the Ministry of Munitions assumed responsibility for the implementation of dilution at the beginning of 1916 and mounted a campaign to enforce dilution, firstly on the Clyde. Responsibility for the implementation of dilution was centralized in 1916 with the formation of the Dilution Section of the Labour Department of the Ministry of Munitions, which was to replace the Central Munitions Labour Supply Committee, now seen as slow and cumbersome.[74] Lloyd George spearheaded the campaign on the Clyde but only succeeded in aggravating unrest and hardening resistance when *The Forward* was supressed under DORA Reg. 51 on 4th January 1916 for attempting to print a report of his Christmas Day speech thought likely to impede the progress of dilution.

On 17th January a letter was sent by the Chief Labour Officer of the Ministry of Munitions to Ministry headquarters in London which acknowledged that, while there was no evidence of their direct obstruction of dilution (they were willing to negotiate), the shop stewards focused public attention on them and this obscured the underlying problem, which was the refusal of skilled workers generally to co-operate in dilution. They had been able to hide behind the more public activities of the shop stewards. If progress was to be made, this buffer would have to be removed – but only after care had been taken not to escalate the situation or present the government in a bad light. The Chief Labour Officer thought that the removal of Kirkwood, Gallacher, Messer, Muir, McManus, Clark, McLean, and Petroff would go a long way towards helping production. But he cautioned that the removal of almost any one of these men (with the possible exception of McLean and Petroff) would at once cause a big strike. He advised that when the strike did take place 'the Government should have the best case possible to present to the public. Ultimately it will be forced to give some reasons for the removal of these men, and it would have to be disclosed that action had been taken on general statements, unsupported by real evidence of a convincing nature. A very much cleaner issue would be a strike against the enforcement of the dilution of labour, as the Government then would be in a position of asking the skilled men of the country to allow their skill to be used to the best advantage, and the public opinion would be overwhelmingly against the men. If therefore, definite orders for the dilution of labour are to be given, I think it would be better to delay consideration of the question of removing the men out of the district.'[75]

On 22nd January the Clyde Dilution Commission was appointed to introduce dilution on the Clyde. Shortly after its arrival in Glasgow on 29th January there was a strike of 2000 munitions workers in a number of CWC-controlled factories over the suppression of *The Worker* (the organ of the CWC) for an article entitled 'Should the Workers Arm?' The article concluded that they should not. Nevertheless, on 7th February William Gallacher and John Muir (leaders of the CWC) and Walter Bell (the printer of their journal) were arrested on sedition charges. The strikes ended when the men were released on bail (it was not until 14th April that the men were tried and imprisoned).

A memorandum from the Clyde to the Ministry of Munitions on 9th February however, reported fresh activity from the CWC and the increasing weakness of the trade unions. The tentacles of the CWC

'are now fairly widespread and are growing. However, the committee has not effective control over the workers in more than five or six shops. The outstanding feature of the position is that the Official Trade Unions in the district are in many works now wholly unable to speak for their members. Agreements arrived at between the Commissioners and the local Trade Union officials or even the shop stewards in the works are promptly repudiated by the instigation of the emissaries of the Clyde Workers' Committee. The authority of the official trade unions in the Clyde district is being steadily undermined and will be inevitably ruined unless the Unions quickly rise to an intelligent appreciation of their position and exert themselves to recover their waning control over their members.'[76]

In March 1916 David Kirkwood, convenor of shop stewards at

Parkhead Forge, resigned as convenor after the management refused him access to a new department in which women were at work under the dilution scheme. The Parkhead workers struck and were soon joined by workers in other factories. Kirkwood and four shop stewards, James Haggerty, Samuel Shields, Robert Wainwright and James Messer, were deported on 24th March 1916 and a further three stewards on 28th March under the Defence of the Realm Act. Under the threat of fines and further deportations and in the absence of its leadership, the strike was broken.

The CWC rightly challenged the state's justifications for its actions by pointing out that, as convenor, Kirkwood had the customary right to enter any shop in which a dispute was in progress, that there was no elaborate plot to stop work on any type of gun vitally needed for the army, that the CWC had not embarked on any definite 'policy to hold up the production of the most important munitions of war' and that the CWC had no deliberate policy of calling men out on strike and had not called them out in the above case.[77]

The CWC drew the fire of the Ministry of Munitions because it was recognized as a danger to the war effort and to the maintenance of social stability in its own right.[78] Through organization at shop floor level, engineers reclaimed the right to strike which had been given up by union leaders and proscribed by law. This enabled them to focus the state's attention on local grievances. The trade unions had abdicated their traditional responsibilities and at the same time freed unofficial action from national discipline. Jobs were easy to find, the state intervened to settle disputes, unions had agreed to suspend strike action – there were thus no effective sanctions against unconstitutional behaviour. In short, 'the forces that before the war had kept rank and file protest relatively routine and circumscribed were thus suspended.'[79]

The development of unofficial organization also provided opportunities for militants from Amalgamation Committees, the Socialist Labour Party and the Industrial Workers of the World to further their aims. They saw works committees as the basis of all grades organization and therefore the key to ousting craft unionism and achieving the democratic control of industry. Their radical influence was plain among the leadership of the SSM, and although most shop stewards and most rank-and-file engineers were committed trade unionists, the SSM's programmes were effective and therefore attractive when sectional unions seemed no longer able to defend their interests.

The ASE did have an intelligent appreciation of its position. Aware of the state's predicament, its dependence on official trade unionism to exert its authority over workers, the need to implement dilution and its own fragile position with its members, the ASE became less 'responsible' and thought nothing of holding the country to ransom. The outcome was that

'the nation is being held up by a single union ... the negotiations with this union appear to be interminable, and no sooner is one agreement arrived at than it is broken, and new blackmailing conditions are imposed.'[80]

It was not until February 1916 that the ASE, on condition that the state made circulars L2 and L3 legal and mandatory, agreed to accept the scheme of dilution 'and co-operate actively therein.'[81] By July 1916 the number of women employed in munitions establishments had risen from 2.6 per cent in 1914 to 26 per cent. Even so, in December 1916 it was noted that the extent to which processes performed by these women were identical or even similar to those done by men prior to the war was very limited – and in the case of skilled work it was almost non-existent. Also, a considerable amount of semi-skilled work was being done by women, but this was under the supervision of men and largely confined to repetitive activity. The new and highly automatic machinery which had been introduced into munitions factories (to enable the introduction of women on work that had previously been the province of skilled men) had largely resulted in the operation of the machines, too, being the province of skilled men.[82]

The need to introduce women workers was successfully exploited by skilled workers' leaders in their campaign against dilution.[83] It was difficult for Llewelyn Smith to disentangle whether resistance to the introduction of women was tactical or principled, but, unlike wages or calls for a new social order, their campaign evoked support across class barriers and contributed to the skilled workers' success in modifying the impact of dilution. Officials of the Labour Department themselves saw resistance to women workers, because they were women, as understandable and concessions were made to compensate:

'every argument was used that could possibly be thought of to persuade the men to allow the introduction of female labour without causing trouble'[84]

The introduction of women was clearly presented as an unavoidable temporary expedient; work areas were rigidly defined as 'men's work' or 'women's work'; women were to be paid men's wages when employed on men's work (although this became contentious when the Minister of Munitions moved the goal posts by regrading jobs).[85] In February 1916 the Labour Department conceded victory to the ASE:

'the Amalgamated Society of Engineers have pledged themselves at intervals from March onwards to cooperate with the Government in the dilution of labour and the prevention of strikes on munitions work. They have continually gone back on their agreements at a moment's notice, that is to say have themselves gone on strike.'[86]

On 27th January 1916 the Military Service Act had been introduced. Initially it affected single men but was extended to include married men on 25th May 1916. Until mid-1916 the munitions industries had not been greatly affected by the introduction of conscription because the problem of munitions supply was as great as the shortage of men for the army. The TUC and the Labour movement generally were against conscription but assisted the voluntary recruiting of men not classed as skilled. There were many disputes over whether this or that worker was skilled. Employers classed men who were paid unskilled rates as 'skilled' in order to keep them. Trade unions would then demand skilled rates for these men.[87] Sometimes the army would recruit a skilled man and negotiations would ensue: sometimes the army won and sometimes the unions. As dilution spread, however, the conditions of exemption tightened. The Ministry of Munitions was largely dependent on information from employers for nominees for exemption. This gave employers opportunities for victimization. Also, recruiting officers were as anxious to enlist men as the Ministry of Munitions was to exempt them 'and the consequent clash of influences was not conducive to equality of sacrifice.'[88]

On 22nd July 1916 skilled workers' trade unions sent a deputation to the Government protesting against the recruitment of skilled men. On 9th November 1916 a Sheffield engineer was wrongfully enlisted and an unofficial strike followed which spread across many munitions centres. The strike lasted until 17th November, when the ASE called a National Conference after which the ASE and the Government came to an agreement known as the Trade Card Scheme, whereby the ASE took over the administration of exemption certificates. Other skilled unions demanded the same power, however, and this was granted – whereupon the general unions demanded equal treatment on the grounds that no clear demarcation line existed between their members and the craft unions.[89] The ASE dismissed this claim, saying that skilled men should not be in general unions, and the government refused to extend the scheme to general unions.

Control over recruitment was given to the unions in the belief that it would engender a sense of responsibility and enable them to appreciate not only the short-term interests of their members but the long-term interests of the country as a whole. The bid to persuade the craft unions to put the 'national interest' first had failed. They used the Trade Card Scheme for the benefit of their own members and there was 'little doubt that the Trade Card system had opened a door through which very many passed in the hope of escaping active service thereby.'[90]

CONCLUSION

After an initial lull at the beginning of the war, industrial conflict began to rise significantly in response to the state's attempts to increase production and at the same time prevent workers taking advantage of the shortage of skilled labour. The success of these initiatives relied on the trade unions' ability and willingness to deliver their members' voluntary agreement to restrictions on wages and mobility, dilution and the suspension of the right to strike. However, attempts to manage industrial conflict and obtain workers' co-operation through the trade unions failed. It was concluded that workers were out of the control of both employers and their own leaders, that they pursued ever higher wages without regard to the national interest, and that this made legislation the only option.[91]

The Ministry of Munitions was set up and the MOW Act was passed. It immediately came up against both active and passive resistance from other state agencies, from employers and from workers. The MOW Act suffered from the conflicting priorities and friction between the Ministry of Munitions and the Ministries whose functions it supplanted or duplicated.[92]

Employers resisted this legislation. They pursued profits without regard to the national interest and many engineering employers were criticized for their obstructiveness, incompetence or conservatism. Some employers resisted change to keep their skilled workers and avoid disputes. Others defied the MOW Act simply because they shared workers' attitude towards the introduction of women workers.

The Act removed the right to strike, rendered trade union officials impotent and suspended trade union customs and practices. This created resentment among workers, suspicion and distrust of the trade union leaders who had agreed to it and a shift of allegiance to local shop stewards.[93] Active resistance came from the highly organized shop stewards.[94]

As Hinton has shown, the first priority of the state in passing this legislation was to break through the purely craft resistance to dilution typified by the workers at Lang's and the ASE executive.[95] As this chapter has shown, the implementation of dilution was frustrated at every stage by the response of the official trade unions, in particular the ASE, whose passive resistance proved more difficult for officials of the Ministry of Munitions to understand and deal with. The ASE was the largest and most powerful trade union at this time. It represented a great number of skilled workers in the munitions industries with which the state was primarily concerned.[96] Because of this centrality the co-operation of its leaders was sought in the implementation of labour policy from the beginning of the war. The Executive of the ASE readily agreed to co-operate, and yet dilution was impeded and the management of industrial conflict became a confused mixture of coercion, conciliation and concession.[97] The leaders of the ASE persistently dragged their feet over dilution. The dilution campaign had begun with the Treasury Agreement in March 1915, but the introduction of women did not begin in earnest until January 1916. This delay was seen to be due in large part to 'the remarkably successful rearguard action fought by the Executive of the ASE against the dilution to which it was nominally pledged.'[98] Intelligence reports revealed that resistance to the MOW Act on the Clyde was encouraged by local trade union officials for their own advancement. On the Tyne the District Committee of the ASE professed themselves committed to dilution but helpless in the face of workers' objections. The National Executive of the ASE could not be pinned down by either the Prime Minister or the Minister of Munitions to a firm agreement on dilution. It was concluded that 'trade union restrictions were being as firmly insisted upon as ever they were and it was hopeless to expect employers to take any action until the Ministry of Munitions had brought the necessary pressure to bear on trade unions to secure the waiving in practice – and not merely on paper – of their restrictions.'[99]

Reports to the Ministry of Munitions from the centres of munitions production encouraged the view that progress in dilution could only be made if the CWC was removed and the ASE publicly revealed as responsible. The CWC drew resources and public attention but for officials of the Ministry of Munitions this focus obscured the fact that it was the leaders of the ASE and not the CWC who had embarked on a deliberate policy to hold up munitions production. It seemed that they did have an 'intelligent appreciation of their position':[100] they understood its strengths and weaknesses. The bargaining position of official trade unionism (embodied by the ASE) was significantly strengthened by the challenge offered by the CWC to the state. The leaders of the ASE were aware of the state's dependence on official trade unionism, on 'the authority of sectional unions and the constraints of industrial relations rules and procedures' for the containment of industrial conflict in Britain.[101] They were acutely aware, too, of their own fragile position with their members.

As a result, the country was held to ransom: 'the nation is being held up by a single union?'[102] To a large extent this ransom was paid. Virtually no attempt was made to legally enforce dilution during 1914–16. Even where the Munitions Acts gave power to do so, and even though it was recognized that consultation with workers' representatives meant modification, unrest and delay, dilution proceeded mainly through conferences and agreements with the official trade unions. There were practically no occasions when the Munitions of War Act was used during unrest on the Clyde to enforce dilution. The Ministry of Munitions claimed that dilution could only proceed peacefully if labour's consent and co-operation were secured. In all cases dilution agreements included clauses to safeguard the standard wage rate and to restore male workers' places and trade union rules after the war.[103] By December 1916, in spite of 'very big concessions' which later included control over army recruitment, skilled workers' control over production had not been sufficiently weakened and industrial conflict continued unabated.[104]

Against this background 'hasty changes in government machinery' took place early in 1917, including the setting-up of the Ministry of Labour.[105] The next chapter analyses the crisis in the state's management of industrial conflict from the perspective of the new Ministry which saw the responses of workers and unions to restrictions and the erosion of skilled workers' status and privilege as the entirely predictable consequences of the inept interventions of the Ministry of Munitions.

NOTES

1. Sharp, 1950, p. 304.
2. Twelfth Report of Proceedings under the Conciliation Act 1896, 1914–18. (1919).
3. Ibid.
4. Ibid.
5. Amulree, 1929.
6. Dobb, 1940.
7. Chang, 1968, p. 67.
8. Pelling, 1963, p. 151.
9. Boston, 1980, pp. 102–112.
10. Twelfth Report of Proceedings under the Conciliation Act.
11. Sharp, 1950, p. 307.
12. The Board of Trade Index of Food Prices March 1915 cited in Dobb, 1941, p. 6.
13. Orton, 1921, p. 41.
14. Amulree, 1929, p. 126.
15. Cole, 1923.
16. Sharp, 1950, p. 309.
17. Both the Clyde engineers and the railwaymen had been preparing to negotiate increases prior to the outbreak of war. See Dobb, 1940.
18. PRO MUN 5/73/324/15/2, December 1915.
19. Dobb, 1940, pp. 11–12.
20. PRO MUN/5/73/324/15/2, December 1915.
21. PRO MUN 5/9/180/, 3rd Jan.1915.
22. PRO MUN 5/57/320/1, June 1915.
23. PRO MUN 5/20/221/1/17, 4th June 1915: Llewellyn Smith's preliminary note on required changes in labour policy.
24. PRO MUN 5/10/180/22. D.O.R. regulation on labour stealing, 1915.
25. Ibid.
26. Ibid.
27. PRO MUN 5/20/221/17, 4th June 1915.
28. Ibid.
29. PRO MUN 5/92/346/15, 23rd January 1915.
30. PRO MUN 5/20/220.1/17, 4th June 1915.
31. Percy Girouard – a director of Armstrong Whitworth & Co., member of Armaments Output Committee and Munitions of War Committee and Director General of Munitions Supply Committee until July 1915. G.M. Booth was an industrialist on the same committees.
32. Wrigley, 1982, p. 32.
33. Davidson, 1974, pp. 320.
34. Chang, 1968, p. 74.
35. Sharp, 1950, p. 315.
36. Cole, 1948.
37. LAB/2/697 ND
38. Rubin, 1987, p. 75.
39. The leaving certificate rule was increasingly used by Clyde employers to discipline workers. By threatening to dismiss workers without leaving

certificates, which would effectively mean they would be unemployed for at least six weeks, employers could force workers to take on dirty, low-paid and unpopular work and keep skilled labour, regardless of the availability of work elsewhere. See McLean, 1972.

40. PRO MUN 5/48/300/9
41. Hyman, 1982.
42. Cole, 1973.
43. See Chapter 2.
44. Boston, 1980, p. 112.
45. Official History of the Ministry of Munitions 1V,ii,56.
46. McLean (1972) notes the longstanding tension between militant members and the Executive Council of the ASE on the 'machine question', where leading members were ousted in favour of new men pledged to take more vigorous action to protect the craftsman's position against erosion.
47. PRO MUN 5/73/324/15/2, December 1915.
48. PRO MUN 5/49/300/15, November 1915.
49. PRO MUN 5/73/324/15/2, 18th Dec. 1915.
50. Formerly The King's Munitions Corps.
51. Adams, 1978, p. 93.
52. PRO MUN 5/57/320/3, June 1915.
53. PRO MUN 5/69/323/6, Late 1915.
54. PRO MUN 5/342/170/2/1/A, December 1915
55. Cole, 1923, p. 8.
56. PRO MUN 5/78/327/13.(14,15) Board of Trade, May 1915.
57. PRO MUN 5/65/322/131, 6th & 31st August 1915.
58. PRO MUN 5/57/320/4, September 1915.
59. PRO MUN 5/348/324/1, October 1915.
60. PRO MUN 5/72/324/11/9, Labour Department, October 1915.
61. The word 'minimum' was subsequently changed to 'standard' under pressure from employers.
62. Boston, 1980, p. 109. It was not until February 1916 that these circulars were made mandatory under pressure from the ASE.
63. PRO MUN 5/73/324/15/2, (Macassey) December 1915.
64. PRO MUN 5/73/324/15/2, (Paterson) December 1915.
65. Ibid.
66. Ibid.
67. MUN 5/70/324/18, January 1916.
68. Ibid.
69. PRO MUN 5/73/324/15/8, 31st December 1915. Minutes of proceedings of a Deputation from the Amalgamated Society of Engineers to the Prime Minister and the Minister of Munitions.
70. Ibid.
71. Ibid.
72. Re Armstrong Whitworth, see p. 3 of this chapter. At Lang's of Johnstone, a major machine-tool manufacturer, notice was given of the intention to introduce female labour at the end of August 1915. This was made impossible until November because of lengthy negotiations with the central and local officials of the ASE. This led to a protracted dispute with the ASE which eventually resulted in a heavily qualified agreement and

the introduction of only a few women. At Smith's in Coventry and Manchester, after consultation failed, the Ministry instructed the firm to introduce women, and it did so, whereupon the men struck in defiance of their union. The union managed to get the men back to work and the women stayed at work, but there was still opposition to women in other Manchester machine shops.

73. PRO MUN 5/73/324/15/8, December 1915.
74. MacLean, 1972.
75. PRO MUN 5/49/300/23, (Paterson to MIN MUN) 17th January 1916.
76. PRO MUN 5 /73 Memorandum on the Industrial Situation on the Clyde, 9th February 1916.
77. Statement by W.Gallacher & J.Muir. *Glasgow Herald*, 30th March 1916.
78. Hinton, 1973, p. 140.
79. Ibid, p. 145.
80. PRO MUN 5/70 (notes for the Prime Minister on deputation from ASE by Llewellyn Smith. 31st December 1915).
81. Ibid.
82. PRO MUN 5/70/324/10, Ministry Order 885, 24th December 1916.
83. PRO MUN 5/73/324/15/2, December 1915.
84. Ibid.
85. Boston, 1980, p. 110.
86. PRO MUN 5/324/15/8 1916, 11th February 1916.
87. Cole, 1923, p. 131.
88. PRO LAB 2/254/13, Memorandum on the Strike of Engineers in May 1917 (September 1917).
89. Cole, 1923, p. 133.
90. PRO LAB 2/254/13, 18th December 1917.
91. PRO MUN 5/9/180/, 3rd Jan.1915.
92. See Chapter 5.
93. LAB/2/697 ND.
94. Haydu, 1988.
95. Hinton, 1973.
96. Cronin, 1982.
97. Ibid, p. 76.
98. McLean, 1972, pp. 3–25.
99. PRO MUN 5/73/324/15/2, (Paterson) December 1915.
100. PRO MUN 5/73, February 1916.
101. Haydu, 1988, p. 206.
102. PRO/MUN/ 5/70, 31st December 1915.
103. Andrews & Hobbs, 1921, p. 55. Rubin, 1987.
104. PRO MUN 5/73/324/15/8, December 1915.
105. Middlemas, 1979, p. 99.

6 The Ministry of Labour

The Ministry of Labour (MOL) was formed on 11th January 1917 and given responsibility for the management of industrial conflict. The decision to set up the Ministry was taken by Lloyd George 'after a few minutes' consideration' in December 1916.[1] Until 1916 various government ministries had had a hand in labour matters. The new government sought to co-ordinate its labour activities and also to secure the allegiance of labour leaders and invited members of the Labour movement to participate. There was to be a seat in the Cabinet and two new Ministries headed by Labour (MOL and the Ministry of Pensions). The Minister of Labour acquired the role of labour adviser to the government. The Ministry of Labour was given responsibility for conciliation and arbitration. It was to administer the Conciliation Act 1896, the Labour Exchanges Act 1909, the Trade Boards Act 1909, the National Insurance (Unemployment) Acts 1911–1916 and Part 1 of the Munitions of War Act (concerning arbitration). The implementation of much of this legislation was previously the province of the Labour Department of the Board of Trade. The Ministry also acquired responsibility for the implementation of the Whitley Report, which proposed offering a measure of control over the running of industry to workers.[2]

However, much of the work which the new Ministry took over from other departments had arisen out of the war and was temporary, and not all of the activities of other Ministries which fell within the scope of the MOL were transferred to it.[3] This made the management of industrial conflict so difficult that George Askwith felt compelled to report to the Prime Minister that 'the Ministry of Munitions has established a Disputes Department, the Admiralty has at least two. There is nothing to prevent the Board of Agriculture, the Shipping Controller or the Controller of Mines following the same course and the Ministry of Labour is itself divided'. The number of overlapping departments was causing 'uncertainty and confusion' and 'is seriously impairing the relations and responsibility of actual employers and workpeople to settle their own differences'. It was causing unrest in the ranks of labour, weakening the authority of trade union leaders, spreading bureaucracy throughout the country and pitting one Department against another.[4] Askwith's protests appeared to fall on deaf ears and 'internecine struggles' between the MOL and the Ministry of Munitions, in particular, 'continued

125

on such a scale that the two Ministries prepared entirely different versions of the May 1917 engineering strike for the Official History of the war'.[5]

The version compiled by officials of the MOL focused on the part played by the Ministry of Munitions in the May strikes in order to demonstrate that officials of the MOM were guilty of such a degree of incompetence that the stability of the country was jeopardized. The May strikes were seen to be the clearest example of labour mismanagement on the part of Ministry of Munitions personnel. Their action in connection with the strikes had 'provoked a reaction from munitions workers which turned a non-revolutionary situation into a potentially revolutionary situation' and against this background 'the account prepared in the Intelligence and Record Section of the Ministry of Munitions . . . appears to some extent to have been framed as an apologia for, and an explanation of the action of the Ministry.'[6]

The seriousness of the industrial situation which the MOL had inherited, the extent to which the approach adopted by the Ministry of Munitions towards the shop stewards had contributed to it, and the responsibility conferred on the MOL for the management of industrial conflict made a 'fuller and more accurate record' necessary and so 'the point of view adopted in our history is of course different'.[7] Events leading up to the 'potentially revolutionary' situation are set out below.

THE MAY STRIKES

On 3rd April 1917 the Trade Card Scheme was abolished on the grounds that insufficient numbers of men were volunteering for the army. It was replaced by the Schedule of Protected Occupations, making exemptions the prerogative of the National Service Department which then narrowed the grounds for the exemption of skilled workers.

The extension of conscription increased the shortage of skilled labour and on 29th April 1917 a Bill was introduced to spread dilution to private work. This broke an agreement made with the unions at the Treasury Conference. Skilled workers had agreed only to dilution on war work protected by legislative safeguards and ministerial promises; 'now they fancied that they saw the cloven hoof.'[8]

On 3rd May there was a strike arising out of these new proposals at Tweedale & Smalley, near Rochdale, which anticipated the passage of the Bill. The firm instructed workers to teach and supervize women on work previously done by skilled men. The workers refused and were dismissed. The firm tried again with other workers, who also refused and were dismissed. A strike ensued. The military authorities called up some of the strikers for the army. The strike threatened to escalate as the firm was fined under the Munitions Acts. This strike triggered a succession of strikes after 10th May. These strikes were all unofficial and were all led by shop stewards. They were not directed from any one centre; they involved both skilled and unskilled workers and different grievances, such as the spread of dilution to private work in Lancashire, the operation of the Military Service Acts and the Munitions of War Act and the abolition of the Trade Card Scheme. The strikes spread to Coventry, Sheffield, Luton, Derby, Birkenhead, Liverpool, Bristol, Southampton and London. Many of the leaders were arrested under the DORA. Within a fortnight there was a general return to work on an undertaking given by the government that outstanding grievances would be dealt with by negotiation with official trade union leaders. On 12th June 1917 eight Commissions on Industrial Unrest covering the whole country were appointed to ascertain the causes of unrest.

The Minister of Munitions began to bargain with the unions. Initially, in exchange for the extension of dilution to private work, it was proposed that the Leaving Certificate provisions of the MOW Act be amended to permit labour mobility in cases where real hardship would be caused by denying a leaving certificate. The unions rejected this plan. Addison, the Minister of Munitions, then decided to abolish the Leaving Certificate (against the advice of employers, his own Labour Department and the Ministry of Labour) on the grounds that it was a major cause of unrest. At the same time, the wages of skilled workers were fixed by Order and it was decided to bow to union pressure and provide a 12.5 per cent bonus on skilled workers' wages.

One of the restrictions on output which the Treasury Agreement was designed to remove was the resistance to piecework. Its removal was implicitly directed by Section 4(3) and Section 4(5) of the MOW Act. Many employers had interpreted the Act to mean that workers had to accept payment by results or be penalized by the Act. The resulting opposition to piecework proved 'as fundamental as the objection to dilution' and its implementation made very slow headway.[9] It was not that objection to piecework was universal in the munitions industries, but in some sections it was strongly opposed − because of craft pride and the belief that piecework led to unemployment, but mostly because of the conviction that whenever remunerative piecework rates had been fixed they were cut by employers. On 13th September 1915 the Ministry of Munitions had pledged that this would be prevented under the provisions of the MOW Act, which laid down that no changes in wage rates could be made without reference to the Ministry (they could not be increased or decreased). This pledge was to result in further complications as more and more firms received government contracts for shell production. These firms based their price list for production on pre-war production of shells and when these prices were applied to war production, wages on less skilled work more than trebled. Employers put the additional cost due to wage advances onto the charges they made to government contracting departments.[10] The resulting high wages earned by less skilled workers with the help of automatic machines became a source of grievance for skilled workers, who could find themselves with lower wages than semi-skilled and unskilled workers.

To prevent a repeat of the wage anarchy which characterized the earlier part of the war, this bonus was delayed by Churchill, who succeeded Addison as Minister of Munitions, until the possible consequences of these measures were clarified and means of counteracting them were put in place. The Hills Committee was appointed on 27th August 1917 to report on the effect of the removal of the Leaving Certificate on skilled workers' time rates. The Committee was made up of representatives of the trade unions, employers' associations and the state. The employers wanted to exclude from the bonus any workers who had been given the opportunity of working on the payment by results system and had refused. Union representatives would not consider this and were backed by the Minister of Munitions. The union representatives asked for a general advance to time workers and piece workers not on repetition work. The employers' representatives, the Ministry of Labour and the Committee on Production were opposed to the bonus on the grounds that it would disturb existing wage relations and provoke further demands and unrest. No agreement was reached. Ultimately the War Cabinet ordered that a flat bonus of 12.5 per cent should be paid to those classes of workers covered by the Hills Committee. This order was made on 13th October 1917 and immediately drew claims of eligibility from other skilled and semi-skilled workers. The bonus was extended to all adult male workers in munitions, which left the differentials between skilled workers and others and the grievance substantially unchanged.[11] On the day after the bonus was conceded the Leaving Certificate was abolished. Its removal deprived the Ministry of Munitions of much of its power to refuse wage demands.

The Ministry of Munitions continued to press its case for dilution on private work by sending circulars to unions in munitions which read:

'dilution is the only means by which private industries can be maintained in such a state that they can recover after the war and compete against foreign trade. During the war foreign countries have been organizing to capture industries from this country and unless dilution is introduced to carry private trades over the war period, there is a danger of serious loss of trade after the war.'[12]

A ballot of its members by the ASE decisively rejected dilution on private work. The repeal of the Leaving Certificate had already been agreed and could not now be withheld. Churchill concluded that the dilution clause of the Bill

'was only valid in so far as it was accompanied by agreement between the parties concerned.' He found it 'impossible to force the question through . . . [because] . . . any attempt to do so would have led to friction by which more would be lost than would have been gained by dilution . . . happily however, in this matter, as in the matter of exemption from military service, the thoroughness of American assistance diminished embarrassments which would otherwise have been grave . . . they had gained a complete victory by the use of unconstitutional methods. The presumption is strong that these methods will again be adopted when the occasion presents itself.'[13]

An agreement was reached between the Minister of Munitions, the ASE and the unofficial strike committee confirming the withdrawal of the Trade Card Scheme, the suspension of the MOW Bill and the release of strike leaders.

THE VIEW FROM THE MINISTRY OF LABOUR

The Ministry of Labour condemned the implementation of the recommendations of the Hills Committee on the grounds that it was a recipe for industrial conflict and pointed out that

'the Cabinet was not primarily or continuously a wage-fixing authority; it did not understand, or if it did, could not be relied upon to bear in mind, the reactions which an isolated decision might have on wage demands that were not before it; it was influenced by considerations of political expediency rather than considerations of consistency in economic policy. Its decisions therefore were frequently illogical and inconsistent with one another and represented rather concessions to the strength of the group demanding them than a recognition of the reasonableness of their claims.'[14]

The MOL went on to consider the Reports of the Commissions on Industrial Unrest which concluded that unrest was due to a variety of causes, including high food prices in relation to wages, restrictions on individual freedom, narrowing wage differentials between the skilled and unskilled as a result of the MOW Acts, a feeling that government did not intend to honour pledges to restore trade union practices, delay in settling disputes, the Military Service Acts, housing shortages and restrictions on alcohol. The Commissions found that unrest was due to conditions arising out of the war and was not revolutionary: 'a comparison of the Reports shows that there is a strong feeling of patriotism on the part of employers and employed throughout the country and they are determined to help the state in the present crisis. Feelings of a revolutionary character are not entertained by the bulk of the men.'[15]

The Commissioners' recommendations included an immediate reduction in the price of food (to be subsidized by the government) and better distribution, the adoption of the proposals of the Whitley Committee, a change in employers' attitudes such that workers should be regarded as partners and not servants in industry, wider publicity concerning the abolition of leaving certificates, government affirmation of its intention to restore pledges, the publication of policy with regard to housing formulated by the Ministry of Reconstruction, a bonus for skilled workers and other workers on day rates, and the encouragement of closer contact between employers and employed. A system of food rationing was being set up and reassurance on pledges was being given. The Leaving Certificate was to be abolished and a 12.5 per cent bonus was to be added to skilled workers' wages.[16]

When the Commissions on Industrial Unrest reported, most of the causes of industrial unrest identified by them had already been addressed, with the exception of the implementation of the Whitley Scheme.

The Ministry of Labour noted that the features of the Commissions' reports which most impressed the workers were the evidence of government incompetence, the exemption from blame for industrial unrest of the workers themselves, the government policy which made profiteering possible and even encouraged it, the necessity for decentralization of control, government determination to increase tax on workers' wages and the deliberate depreciation of the workers' views in the press. The reports lent weight to the charges already brought against the Government by labour and socialist writers, namely that the Tyne and Barrow strikes, the strike at Tweedale and Smalley, and the Engineers' strikes in May were 'due to the dilatory methods of the Ministry of Munitions where the interests of the workers were concerned.' The MOL seized on this last finding of the Commissions to emphasize that once the strikes had broken out, the action of the Ministry of Munitions provoked a reaction from munitions workers which turned a non-revolutionary situation into a potentially revolutionary one.[17]

It was noted in the Ministry's favour that the shop stewards' organization had proved very troublesome in connection with previous conflicts on the Clyde and elsewhere, and that it had, through some of its more prominent members, suspicious associations with both syndicalism and pacifism. It was acknowledged that the Ministry of Munitions 'had some reason to apprehend that it was in the presence of deliberate sedition – a deliberate attempt to exploit the prevalent unrest for ulterior purposes.'[18] Officials of the Ministry of Munitions saw two options. They could recognize and negotiate with the shop stewards (men in rebellion against the heads of their own organization) or they could arrest and prosecute the leaders of the agitation, whether shop stewards or not, under the Defence of the Realm Act, for impeding the supply of munitions. The Ministry chose the second option and the War Cabinet concurred, although the information on which this decision was based did not amount to legal proof and 'this was a direct challenge to a trial of strength and it was promptly taken up.'[19]

For the MOL, this was an error of judgment. Firstly, 'before the challenge was thrown down, a tendency towards the resumption of work had been discernible. It was not a very pronounced tendency, but there were reasons for expecting that it would soon be accentuated . . . work would be resumed while the negotiations with the trade union leaders continued.'[20]

Secondly, although the Ministry of Munitions believed its position to be a strong one, it soon became evident that it 'had little prospect of maintaining the output of munitions at a satisfactory level as long as the arrested men remained in prison, and that it must either settle its dispute by discussion with the shop stewards or fail to attain a settlement.'[21] In this situation a rigid attitude could not be maintained and eventually the Ministry was forced to recognize the shop stewards. The modus operandi decided upon was as follows. The shop stewards became 'the unofficial strike committee'. The Executive Council of the Amalgamated Society of Engineers agreed to introduce them and the Ministry agreed to receive them under that designation.[22]

Thirdly, the measures taken by the MOM, although aimed at quelling unrest and safeguarding the production of munitions, were inappropriate. This was because it was not clear that the shop stewards acted in opposition to the official trade union leaders. In attacking the shop stewards, the Ministry of Munitions was also attacking the trade unions. It was emphasized that, although the shop stewards had taken the reins from official union leaders, this did not necessarily mean that union leaders had been discredited. It meant that in negotiations, union executives were fighting without the one effective weapon in their armoury – the strike. If the men were dissatisfied with the result of negotiations with the Committee on Production, they took the matter into their own hands and struck. The MOL clarified this point, saying

'it is impossible to fight entirely unofficered and it is just here that the unofficial shop stewards' committee, being the only organization in a position to conduct negotiations, steps in and captures the strike . . . [this] . . . does not mean that the Labour World has been revolutionary but that the normal channels through which it acts have been changed by war legislation.'[23]

The MOL thought it probable that the shop stewards' strength and persistence owed more to the support unofficially given to the shop stewards by the official trade unions and less to their associations with syndicalism and pacifism. The MOL pointed out that 'it is now fairly clear that however much the executives of the Unions objected to the methods pursued by the strikers their sympathies were entirely with the objects of the strike.'[24] The MOM did not investigate the situation thoroughly before acting, even though

'there is a wealth of valuable detail as to the activities of the local workers' committees which has not been recorded. Their action locally and their liaison system both deserve and require record . . . though an exploration of the facts would probably be a matter of some difficulty, the relations of the ASE executive to the Unofficial Strike Committee call for some examination. . . . It may well be questioned whether relations between them and the unofficial strike committee were non-existent. If the Executive is in any way representative and is in any sort of touch with local organizations, it is incredible that no consultations should have taken place'.[25]

Further,

'it is rumoured that of those members of the strike committee for whom warrants were issued, but who were not arrested, one was in hiding under the aegis of a permanent official of the Executive. The strike was not official, for no strike in a controlled industry can be official, but it is safe to conclude that at least a considerable section of the Executive of the Society is in accord with its main objects.'[26]

It was acknowledged that the immediate causes of the strike were the proposed amendment of the Munitions of War Act to legalize dilution on private work and the withdrawal of the Trade Card Scheme. However, for the MOL the matter could not be allowed to rest there: 'it is however necessary to insist still further on the unofficial agency which managed the strike. This was composed of committees of shop stewards, and the strike is peculiarly important as a demonstration of the growing power of these committees.' The shop stewards had a more important agenda and the strike enabled them to pursue it.[27]

A clear understanding of the strike turned on a clear understanding of the development of the Shop Stewards' Movement in England. When the movement developed in Sheffield in the summer of 1916, shop stewards had been appointed on a large scale by the ASE and were led by J.T. Murphy, who had been elected as convenor of shop stewards. Murphy founded the Sheffield Engineering Shop Stewards' Committee which later became known as the Sheffield Workers' Committee. In July 1916 Murphy and other shop stewards influenced by the CWC founded a group advocating the control of industry by the workers. This was a turning point when

'to the original advocacy of particular grievances in opposition to trade union officials a new principle was added and the Shop Stewards' Movement became connected with a large industrial policy; but even in Sheffield the main body of the shop stewards do not appear to have been moved by a large view of policy.'[28]

The first success of the Sheffield Workers' Committee, it was noted, was in November 1916 when its activities secured the release of the engineer Hargreaves from the army. This enhanced the Committee's prestige and power with the rank and file. During 1917 the SSM spread to Coventry, London and Liverpool and the organization of the movement on a national scale was achieved. This was accompanied by a modification in the character of the movement such that, in addition to the organization of workers on the basis of the workshop, its stated aims included 'a larger policy of revolt against the whole of the accepted system of industry'. On the other hand, this was offset by the fact that 'the mere growth of the movement had a steadying effect.' Moreover, although increasing numbers of skilled men supported the movement and for some time it was possible to identify the rank-and-file movement with the Shop Stewards' Movement even then the rank and file 'were not keenly interested in far reaching industrial and political programmes. They might accept these as desirable and yet they were not willing to act unless for quite definite and immediate ends.'[29]

In April 1917 during the strike at Coventry a Shop Stewards' Committee appeared for the first time. This movement added to the SSM a theory and practice in regard to amalgamation of all workers irrespective of craft or grade. It was true that 'in all of the May strikes, independent as they were of official trade union authority, the Shop Stewards gained prominence.' On the other hand, the strikes were not engineered by the shop stewards and the general disturbance was not in any sense primarily due to the shop stewards. The strikes were not organized by the shop stewards but were the result of sporadic discontent among the men. The strikes expressed no policy except opposition to dilution. The shop stewards were used by the men but the Shop Stewards' *Movement* had little effect on the situation. The action taken by the Ministry of Munitions was fortuitous for the shop stewards, since it 'appears to have made the situation still more difficult, for the rank and file took it as a challenge to their right to elect their own representatives.' The result was that

'the Shop Stewards' Movement in its extreme form, as well as in its permanently constructive policy, was thus much assisted by this situation . . . the widespread strike had now produced a tendency to the organization of shop stewards on a national scale and this organization imperils the established official organization of the trade unions.'[30]

It was clear to officials of the MOL that from the beginning of the engineers' agitation in May, the shop stewards' committees were determined to use the strike to improve their own position. Before this their position was irregular, ill defined and unconstitutional. They aimed 'to compel recognition of the shop stewards . . . [and] . . . to improvise a national bond between committees in the various localities'. Recognition of the Shop Stewards' Committee as a definite authority in matters of dispute, whether between labour and capital or between labour and the government, had not been achieved. It was obvious to 'the more far-seeing' that these were their real aims. In the first of these aims

'they were actually successful, though their success is not admitted. The interview between the Minister and the Unofficial Strike Committee, even though facilitated by the presence of the ASE Executive, in fact amounted to recognition of the former to speak for the men. In the latter aim, the shop stewards were also successful, though in a minor degree. The Unofficial Strike Committee was composed of representatives of the districts affected. That a permanent National Council of shop stewards, representative of all areas where shop stewards' committees exist, has not as yet been constituted, is beside the point. The principle of national as distinct from local action was enforced, and it is probable that, in future, whenever any question of more than local importance is agitated attempts will be made to ensure that it will be dealt with on the side of labour by a national body in some form representative of the shop stewards' committees. Of this there is an instance in the action taken recently in connection with the Coventry agitation. It is only a question of time for a National Council of shop stewards to enter the arena as a permanent factor in Labour politics. It appears advisable that some workshop authority representative of the workmen should be recognized at an early date.'[31]

Finally and most importantly, it was emphasized that this outburst of industrial unrest was significant not just because of its size, its widespread nature and the danger to the nation from the interruption to the supply of munitions of war: 'its chief importance . . . lies in other directions.' It was a threat to the state itself, precipitated by the ill-judged intervention of the Ministry of Munitions. In the first place, it was a conclusive demonstration of contempt of lawful authority. Every one of the strikers was guilty of a breach of the law and knew it, but the knowledge had no restraining influence. Any restraint was due, not to fear of a breach of the law, but to loyalty to the unions (whom it was felt that the shop stewards were attacking) and to patriotism, to which the Joint Engineering Trades Committee appealed in Coventry with great success. The Engineers' strike

'differed from the majority of strikes occurring at any period in the fact that it was not primarily directed against the employers of labour. The local strike which brought the dispute to a head was indeed so directed, but the more general strike which eventually developed was a strike of protest and resistance against certain items of policy of the government.'[32]

Much of this need not have happened. That it did was evidence of the miscalculation of the Ministry of Munitions which issued statements prejudicial to the workers and to the impotence of the MOW Act. The shop stewards were not having much success in interesting workers in fighting for a new industrial policy. The workers used them to lead their fight for immediate ends because the official unions could not. It was the action of the Ministry of Munitions which escalated the strike. At the beginning of the strike, certain clear-minded and un-prejudiced critics 'advocated a policy of trusting the workers; abolishing all wartime restriction on their independence of action – a procedure which would of course have restored their right to strike.' This was ignored but was vindicated in retrospect because

'this strike proved clearly that the penal provisions of the Munitions Act are powerless in any case in which a general grievance is involved. Further the strike was important as a revelation of that weakness of official trade unionism to which reference has been made above. The officials of the unions officially deplored the strike, officially called upon the members to return to work. Their official deploration and invitations were disregarded . . . Lastly . . . the strike was important both as an indication of the power of the rank and file movement and as a stimulant to its activity.'[33]

It was concluded that 'the Munitions Acts have throttled above-board Trade Union action and forced the workers to subterranean methods . . . Trade Union leaders are summoned not to argue or bargain or indeed do anything directly representative of Labour. They are called together and confronted with a fait accompli.'[34] To restore the authority of the official trade unions, the shop stewards' committee must be recognized. With this in mind the Ministry of Labour emphasized:

'it is necessary that in recognizing the Shop Stewards' Committee that organization must be constitutionalized. It cannot be recognized as a body detached from the unions whose members it represents. To this end it is essential, not only that the Trade Union officials should be brigaded with the Government and the employers in recognising Shop Stewards' Committees but also that the Trade Unions should undertake the responsibility of overhauling their own machinery so as to assimilate those Committees.'[35]

On 26th November 1917 a strike broke out at Coventry Ordnance (White & Poppe) works over the disparity between skilled workers' and others' pay, the employment of Belgian workers in place of discharged men and the recognition of shop stewards. Representatives of the War Cabinet (G.N. Barnes and G.H. Roberts) met a deputation from Coventry and the strike ended on 4th December, when it was agreed that the Employers' Federation and the Trade Unions would discuss the status to be accorded to shop stewards. The resulting agreement recognized that trade unionists in the shops should have the right to elect shop stewards. The trade unions accepted the new status of shop stewards and the employers accepted the policy of negotiation with elected representatives of the rank and file in the shops. The ASE was not a party to this agreement, however, partly because works committees of shop stewards from different unions cut across the distinction between unions and undermined the authority of the ASE.

THE EMBARGO CONFLICT

In July 1918 Coventry engineers struck again over an order issued by the Ministry of Munitions preventing three Coventry engineering firms from hiring additional skilled men, except discharged servicemen, without permission.[36] The Coventry employers took skilled men to mean those in receipt of standard wages. Coventry shop stewards interpreted this as an attempt to reintroduce the leaving certificate, to wipe out distinctions of skill and introduce industrial conscription, which boded ill for the restoration of trade union practices after the war. 10,000 men struck in Coventry and were soon joined by 12,000 in Birmingham. Lloyd George issued a statement to the effect that continuation of the strike would mean conscription for the strikers and the strike collapsed.[37]

The industrial unrest led to the formation of a Commission of Inquiry known as the Committee on Labour Embargoes or the McCardie Committee after its chairman. In September 1918 this Committee found that unrest was caused by the Government's slowness in redeeming pledges given with regard to the restoration of trade union practices, the fact that skilled workers' wages had in many cases been overtaken by others, and the promises given regarding women's wages (they were paid less than agreed) and the recruitment of skilled men had not been kept. Nevertheless it was pointed out that 'the Munitions Acts had been passed after full consultation with organized Labour and with the full approval of the community . . . A large measure of freedom was left to the worker, and such a degree only of regulation was made as was necessarily required by the national interest.'[38] The Committee approved the principle of the embargo and recommended more effective means of consultation between employers and workers.

Commenting on the strike and its handling by the Ministry of Munitions, the Ministry of Labour again emphasized that the movement emanated from workers and not their leaders and that workers' response to Ministry of Munitions initiatives should have come as no surprise. It was pointed out

'that the embargo scheme should be disliked by the workers of this country was perhaps natural; that its object should be misrepresented by agitators was inevitable; that it should be made the occasion of a sudden and widespread strike proves the indiscipline of our industrial forces.'[39]

The MOL found that the munition makers had a plausible but not unanswerable case which could have been put before the Government with favourable results,

'but a large body of munition makers have preferred war to negotiation and have sought to extort concessions from the Government rather than support it in safeguarding the national interests. The people who have made this choice are the engineers and toolmakers of Coventry . . . a hotbed of unrest during the last two years . . . While the present strike may be regarded from one point of view as concerned with wages, from another as concerned with dilution and from a third as concerned with a worker's freedom to choose his employment, it is nevertheless probable that the real source of trouble is the demand of the workers for a share of responsible functions in the conduct of industry.'

This was not a demand pressed by the official representatives of the engineering unions; nevertheless, 'their inaction has led to the rise of a second and third party within the ranks of labour who are prepared to push such claims by the exercise of the strike weapon.' The first of these were the unofficial shop stewards and local Workers' Committees, now organized nationally by a National Administrative Council meeting generally in Manchester and Sheffield, 'whose aim is revolutionary [i.e.] the assumption of responsible functions by direct representatives of the men in the workshops.'[40] An intermediate position was occupied by the local officials of the engineering trade unions, organized in Joint Committees in a dozen districts or more. Their object was to secure a share of local control for trade union representatives, organized at the time through branches and districts of each union and associated in Joint Committees of allied unions.

Again, the Ministry of Labour emphasized that the full significance of the embargo conflict could only be appreciated in the light of the development and spread of the unofficial movement for control since May 1917. At that time the rank-and-file party, consisting mainly of young and aggressive workers in skilled crafts who were unhappy with the conservatism of trade union executives in London, came to the fore. They believed firstly that the trade union movement was over-centralized and that officials had ceased to understand and sympathize with the views of the men in the workshops. Secondly, they believed that craft union officials were narrowly concerned with craft interests and not sufficiently alive to the necessity for solidarity and common action by all crafts working in the same industry and for the same group of employers. Thirdly, the trade union leaders who had been selected by the Government to advise it were thought to have neither the power nor the inclination to enforce conditions on the determination of Government policy or to secure a share of control in carrying it out. This movement aimed therefore at decentralization, inter-union solidarity and control in the conduct of industry for the workers.

An attempt was made to deal with the first problem by the creation of unofficial shop stewards, the extension of the function of all shop stewards and the formation of local Workers'Committees based on the unofficial shop stewards organization. In this movement the leadership had definitely fallen into the hands of the Sheffield and Glasgow groups, notably of J.T. Murphy and E.T. Lismer 'who have displayed considerable constructive ability and have maintained a fairly reasonable attitude during the crisis of the war.'[41] Simultaneously, it was noted, endeavours were made to secure inter-union solidarity and combined action through the unofficial 'Amalgamation Committee' organized by W.F. Watson of London. Among Watson's followers at Coventry were T.W. Dingley and J. Read. Watson sought to achieve his ends, not through the normal constitutional authorities of the unions, but by revolutionary means – by referenda to the rank and file.

At Coventry a shorter cut was devised – putting pressure on the existing local officials of the craft unions and infiltrating existing Joint Committees of Allied Trades. In October it was reported at a conference of Watson's 'Amalgamation Committee' that his Coventry followers had gone over in body to the Engineering Joint Committee. This body acted as a co-ordinating link for the official shop stewards of more than a dozen unions of skilled workers and as it came under the control of the revolutionary party, it assumed in November the responsibility for the conduct of a large-scale strike to secure the recognition of shop stewards as direct representatives of the workers in each shop.

Officials of the MOL predicted that the next stage was to provide the means for common action by the Joint Committees of Allied Trades in the several centres in which they sympathized with the 'advanced policy'. A national conference met at Leeds on 1st September 1917 to consider the question of food control; another was held on 22nd October when a National Emergency Committee was appointed, with Leonard Mason of Leeds as secretary. On 20th January the Joint Committee again assembled at Leeds to deliver an ultimatum to the Government on the subject of manpower and the summoning of an international labour conference.

In the early part of 1918 the two rank-and-file movements united. They had behind them the prestige of the successful strike of May 1917, but their lack of standing in the existing organization of trade unionism was a considerable handicap. On the other hand, the semi-official Joint Committees, which were for some purposes 'recognized' trade union authorities, had still to win their spurs as champions of the liberty of the workers. They found their opportunity in the embargo scheme and the circumstances of its introduction – an industrial issue much more convenient than either food prices or the Manpower Bill. The strike policy is in direct defiance of the Government and the motive is workers' control over industry. Strike leaders have not 'been slow to seize upon the incongruity of recruiting skilled men for the army and then announcing that there is a shortage of these men for providing necessary munitions' and misrepresenting it as the revival of the leaving certificate, an attack on the status of the skilled worker by promoting dilution and an expedient for reducing wages.'[42]

The MOL concluded that the strike leaders had consistently and successfully exploited the fundamental weakness of wartime labour policy, which was the selection by the Government of conservative officials who did not constitute 'an adequate representation of the mind of the men and women in the workshops' to act in a purely advisory capacity in London. In consequence,

> 'labour has come to regard itself as having no real responsibility either for policy or for administration of the industrial matters which concern it. At the same time the exigencies of war place in the hands of labour unprecedented opportunities for showing its power to thwart a policy and hamper administration. The strike is the natural outcome of the concentration in inexperienced hands of power without responsibility.'[43]

In this context officials of the MOL now considered what they saw as the only option remaining for the management of industrial conflict: the Whitley proposals.

THE WHITLEY COMMITTEE

The recommendations of the Whitley Committee (set up in 1916) were widely believed to offer the solution to industrial conflict by offering a measure of control over the running of industry to workers. Although it used 'the phraseology of far-reaching reform', however, the Whitley Committee 'confined its actual proposals to conservative modifications of the existing practice of industrial negotiation.' It proposed to extend the existing machinery for conciliation and arbitration so that it would be available at works, district and national level to 'materially reduce the number of occasions on which, in the view of either employers and employed, it is necessary to contemplate recourse to a stoppage of work.'[44]

The committee claimed that these recommendations had 'the effect of conferring on the Joint Industrial Councils, and through them upon the several industries, a large measure of self-government.' Indeed, this report was popularly taken to have conceded industrial self-government. In fact it conceded nothing and placed 'no obligation on anybody to do anything.' Even those officials of trade unions and employers' associations who were on the Committee ignored it. Those trade unions and employers who did co-operate on industrial councils found their rights and powers exactly the same as before.[45] However, the rhetoric of the Whitley Report had caught the public imagination which 'was unfortunate, since it tended both to raise hopes that were certain to be disappointed and to divert attention from the need and possibilities for improving the machinery of industrial conciliation to which the practical proposals pointed.'[46] Although officials of the MOL acknowledged that 'in certain places a successful method is in vogue in the constitution of Joint Trade Committees consisting of union officials and dealing on the one hand with the unions and on the other with the shop stewards', it was concluded that 'no solution of the problem created by the strikes could be obtained without acknowledging the power of the shop stewards as representing the rank and file.'[47] This the Whitley Scheme did not do. Even if it had done so, it was emphasized that 'it would be absurd to minimize the great difficulties which will have to be overcome.'[48]

The MOL outlined the difficulties. Firstly, employers objected strongly to any further extension of collective bargaining, especially if it involved further recognition of the unions by giving them some status in relation to works committees. Secondly, there was the danger that other employers, equally opposed to an extension of trade union recognition but more politic in their methods, would attempt to use works committees to 'dish' the unions and stop the mouths of agitators, without conceding any real devolution of authority and responsibility. Whitleyism was not welcomed either by the ASE or the Triple Alliance, and it was recognized that the Shop Stewards' Movement saw works committees as an employers' dodge' which had been started in order to take the wind out of the sails of the Shop Stewards, and 'were not intended to improve the position of the workers.'[49]

Although the Whitley scheme was embraced by general workers' unions and in poorly organized trades, many of the well-organized and established trade unions were fiercely protective of their independence and of their sectional interests. They suspected the scheme variously of being a device for marginalizing trade unions, for avoiding honouring the pledge to restore trade union practices, for substituting the concept of workers' participation for workers' control, and such 'executive powers' as works committees were to have – for example, the maintenance of discipline, timekeeping and so on – were seen as largely in the interests of employers.[50] So trade union reaction seemed to bear out the prediction made in another MOL internal memorandum on works committees:

'inevitably sooner or later (they will) rouse the opposition of the keener trade unionists, who could hardly be blamed if they were to regard it as a mere bogus scheme. Hollow reforms are not merely useless; they are dangerous, for they cannot fail to be used to point the argument that the government is not sincere in its treatment of labour.'[51]

The situation had been limited and temporarily defused, in the MOL's view, not by the authorities concerned or by the promise of the Whitley Scheme but mainly by a surge of patriotism engendered by the German offensive which had begun on 21st March 1918 and lasted until October 1918. This

> 'changed the whole industrial situation. The Government was enabled to pursue its policy without fear of serious opposition and the political aims of the leaders in the shop stewards' movement became ineffective so far as popular feeling was concerned even in their immediate entourage.'[52]

CONCLUSION

The climate created by the MOW Act and the handling by the Ministry of Munitions of industrial unrest during the war had rendered the MOL's task, the management of industrial conflict through conciliation, extremely difficult. The MOL found that the measures taken by officials of the Ministry of Munitions in respect of industrial unrest had been ill-considered and inappropriate. In particular, they seemed oblivious to their part in the changed relationship between the official trade unions, the shop stewards and the rank-and-file and changes within the shop stewards' movement. The MOL believed that there was no longer any clear opposition between the official and the unofficial movement – that the latter had the practical support of the former. Although the shop stewards' aims were radical, the aims of the rank and file were not. The workers used the shop stewards to represent their interests not because they supported their aims but because they had little choice. The workers had interpreted the intervention of the Ministry of Munitions as a challenge to their right to elect their own leaders and the state became a clear focus for workers' discontent. This was fortuitous for the shop stewards, who were able to strengthen their own organization, but dangerous for the state which now had few options left for maintaining control. One widely favoured solution was the Whitley Scheme. However, even though the MOL believed that its continued existence and authority was to a large extent tied up with the implementation of the Whitley scheme and the status and functions given to structures set up under it by the state, it was at pains to point out its shortcomings as a solution to industrial conflict. The Minister of Labour had earlier advised the Cabinet that if the war ended before these concerns had been addressed, 'the outlook for the future of industry is by no means bright.'[53] However, as Middlemas records, the Cabinet had contingency plans and 'made one further essay in search of an industrial concordat' in the shape of the National Industrial Conference.[54] In the next chapter the National Industrial Conference will provide the backdrop for an examination of the state's management of the resurgence of industrial conflict at the end of the war.

NOTES

1. Askwith cited in Allen, 1960, p. 57.
2. Allen, 1960.
3. Ibid.
4. Askwith, cited in Allen, 1960, p. 57.
5. Middlemas, 1979, p. 99.
6. PRO LAB 2/254/13 September 1917.
7. The Ministry of Labour took over the task of reporting on the labour situation from the Ministry of Munitions in 1917.
8. PRO LAB 2/253/13, September 1917.
9. Wolfe, 1923, p. 246.
10. Clay, 1929, p. 202.
11. Ibid., p. 273.
12. Cole, 1923, p. 147.
13. PRO LAB 2/254/13, September 1917.
14. Clay, 1929, p. 163.
15. Summary of the Reports of the Commissions on Industrial Unrest London, HMSO.1917.Cd 8696.
16. Wolfe, 1923, p. 262.
17. PRO MUN 5/56, Review of Government Policy and Administration (Intelligence and Record Section), August 1917.
18. PRO LAB 2/254/13, Attitude of the Ministry of Munitions to the Demands of the Shop Stewards. September 1917.
19. Ibid.
20. Ibid., p. 129.
21. Ibid., p. 134.
22. Ibid, p. 135.
23. Ibid.
24. PRO LAB 2/254/13, Memorandum on the strike of Engineers in May 1917. (September 1917)
25. PRO LAB 2/254/13, September 1917 (a handwritten supplementary note

attached to this document stated that it had proved impossible to obtain any details of negotiations between the ASE executive and the shop stewards).

26. PRO LAB 2/254/13, September 1917.
27. Ibid.
28. Ibid.
29. Ibid.
30. Ibid.
31. Ibid.
32. Ibid.
33. Ibid.
34. Ibid.
35. Ibid.
36. This was known as the Embargo Scheme – a Ministry of Munitions attempt to ration skilled labour.
37. Clegg, 1985, p. 190.
38. Wolfe, 1923, p. 147.
39. PRO MUN 5/55, (Intelligence and Statistics Department), 26th July 1918.
40. Ibid.
41. Ibid.
42. Ibid.
43. Ibid.
44. Ibid., p. 327.
45. PRO LAB 2/212/11, Memorandum On The Interim Report of the Reconstruction Sub-Committee on the Relations between Employers and Employed, 28th June 1917.
46. Clay, 1929, p. 153.
47. Ibid., p. 11.
48. PRO LAB 2/254/12, (The Establishment of Works Committees in Controlled Engineering Establishments), August 1917.
49. PRO LAB 2/254/12, 1918.
50. Ibid.
51. PRO LAB 2/254/12, (Comments on the Ministry of Munitions Memorandum, 1917).
52. PRO LAB 2/697, February 1920.
53. PRO LAB 2/212/18, (Internal Memorandum signed by the Minister of Labour), 29th May 1917.
54. Middlemas, 1979, p. 139.

7 Towards the General Strike

In November 1918, less than three weeks after the Armistice, the Scottish Trade Union Congress (STUC) called a conference on demobilization problems and passed a resolution calling for the immediate reduction of working hours to a maximum of forty per week. Failing government action, the Conference voted to 'devise such methods of industrial action as will enforce this demand.'[1] The Parliamentary Committee of the STUC prevaricated, caught between pressure from the factories and shipyards led by the shop stewards' movement, and criticism from some trade union officials who had been trying unsuccessfully to put the brakes on the mass movement led by the shop stewards. The shop stewards met on 19th January and prepared a strike manifesto. A general strike was to be called on 27th January and a Joint Strike Committee was appointed, chaired by Emmanuel Shinwell, councillor and chairman of the Glasgow Trades and Labour Council. There was widespread support for this move and offers of sympathetic action came from Tyneside and Belfast, as well as most other Clyde factories and yards. The ASE, however, had already negotiated a 47-hour week with engineering employers (without meal breaks or loss of production, which was not a great improvement on the previous 54-hour week with meal breaks) and was opposed to further struggle. Nevertheless, the strike went ahead and spread rapidly: 40,000 men were out by the second day. Harland and Wolff's shipyards closed down and the city was without gas or electricity.[2]

In a Cabinet meeting called to discuss this dispute, the Minister of Labour, Sir Robert Horne, stressed that the strike was in direct contravention of an agreement reached by the accredited representatives of the employers and workers. In a bid to reinforce the trade unions' authority the Minister sent a telegram to the Lord Provost of Glasgow with a message to be conveyed to the strikers' leaders, which read:

'the government are unable to entertain requests for intervention made by local members of unions if representatives are acting for them in conference with employers. Such action on the part of the government could only undermine the authority of those who have been chosen by the men to represent them and would destroy the cooperation between employers and employed on which the hope of industrial peace depends.'[3]

146

This message was ignored. By 29th January 70,000 men were out and sympathy strikes began in Edinburgh and Leith. John Brown's shipyards came to a standstill under the weight of massive picketing. Power stations were closed in Glasgow. By 31st January 100,000 men were on strike and all main factories were idle.[4]

The Cabinet was close to panic because of the industrial unrest and uncertainty as to whether the armed services would remain loyal in the face of a general strike.[5] Plans had already been made to break a general strike of the Triple Alliance. During the war a central mechanism had been established to secure the supply of essential goods and services under the auspices of the Committee on Industrial Unrest (1917), which later became the Supply and Transport Organization, and this had set a precedent for a similar apparatus in peacetime.[6]

Plans were made by the War Cabinet to concentrate sufficient force in Glasgow to prevent disorder and protect volunteers or others available to take over the operation of the generating stations and municipal services.[7] Members of the Cabinet agreed that the situation in Glasgow had been brewing for a long time, that the disaffected were in the minority and that there would have to be a conflict to clear the air. Winston Churchill advised caution, however, saying 'we should be careful to have plenty of provocation before taking strong measures. By going gently at first we should get the support of the nation and then troops could be used more effectively – the moment for their use has not yet arrived'. For Churchill an appropriate moment to act was when

'the revolt advanced over the line of a pure wage dispute and the strikers were guilty of a serious breach of the law; in the meantime the Defence of the Realm Act is still in force and some of the leaders of the revolt should be seized.'[8]

The moment arrived on 31st January with a mass demonstration of strikers marked by outbreaks of violence in George Square.[9] The demonstration was broken up with baton charges by mounted policemen. Overnight, troops and tanks were moved into the city and machine-gun posts set up. The strike leaders were arrested and by 3rd February the leaderless strikers began to drift back to work. The forty hours demand was abandoned and the STUC accepted 47 hours in the engineering trades.[10]

In the coal industry in 1919 more than 6,600,000 working days were lost through disputes.[11] Early in 1919 miners demanded an increase of thirty per cent on existing wages less war wage; full discharge of demobilized miners; a six-hour day and the nationalization and democratic control of the mining industry. During the war, production and working conditions had vastly improved, national wage agreements (including a 'war wage' of three shillings a day) had been instituted and no other industry had received comparable wage increases.[12]

The miners' demands were rejected and they were offered a flat rate of one shilling a day. The miners declined this offer and a national strike threatened. A national ballot showed a large majority of miners in favour of industrial action and notices of a national strike went out for 21st February 1919. Lloyd George called the Executive of the MFGB to meet him and offered participation in a Commission of Inquiry into the situation if the strike notices were postponed. The MFGB executive had great difficulty in persuading miners to accept this offer.[13] Eventually it was accepted and the Commission (known as the Sankey Commission) was instructed to present an Interim Report by 31st March 1919.[14] The Government agreed to adopt its findings 'in the letter and in the spirit.'[15]

The Interim Report of the Sankey Commission was produced on 20th March 1919. Evidence to the Commission had disclosed the huge profits made by the coal industry during the war, the inefficient organization and chaotic structure of the industry and the grim living conditions of the miners. The Report recommended wage increases, reduced working hours, a minimum-wage Commission and a committee to look into removing the coal industry from private ownership. This report helped miners' leaders to keep their members in check. Meanwhile 'Lloyd George was presented with some crucial evidence as to the temper of the labour movement and its leaders'.[16]

At this time there was widespread industrial unrest in Britain aside from that in the mining industry, on the Clyde and in Belfast. Workers in many industries, notably the railways, threatened strike action. The railwaymen, like the miners, presented a programme of demands to the Railway Executive Committee in March 1919. The 'Leicester Programme' had been drafted by the NUR in 1917 and included demands for equal representation, both locally and nationally, for the NUR in the management of all UK railways; standardized conditions of service for all railwaymen; an eight-hour day, and the conversion of war wages to permanent wages. Negotiations between the BOT and the Association of Locomotivemen Engineers and Firemen (ASLEF) had taken place in August 1917 and a promise was made by the BOT on behalf of the government that the question of reducing working hours would be considered by the War Cabinet when the war was over.

In November 1918 a meeting had been called to discuss unrest on the railways. Sir Albert Stanley, President of the BOT, agreed that the government had promised to consider the railwaymen's demands on the cessation of hostilities. He emphasized, however, that the government had not promised to settle it within a few days or weeks of the cessation. In his view the issue was being forced by members of ASLEF because they 'wished to score off their rival union' (the National Union of Railwaymen – NUR).[17] About half of the enginemen were members of the NUR and in any negotiations both unions would have to be dealt with. Mr Bromley of ASLEF had, however, sent a written ultimatum to the BOT which declared that if the eight hours demand was not conceded within the next few days there must be a trial of strength. The War Cabinet authorized the President of the BOT to inform the leaders of the unions concerned that there would be a government statement on the matter in the next week.[18]

On 4th December 1918 the President of the BOT informed the War Cabinet that talks were under way with the leaders of the railway unions about postponing the issue of shorter hours until after the General Election. The talks failed and the Cabinet reconvened on 6th December to hear the Prime Minister announce that the country was again confronted by the danger of a serious strike rising out of the old quarrel between ASLEF and the NUR. J.H. Thomas of the NUR had promised Lloyd George that he would support the government and postpone the dispute until after the General Election. Thomas now appeared to have gone back on his word and had joined forces with Bromley of ASLEF in demanding that the matter be settled immediately.[19]

Lloyd George felt that the demand for shorter hours would be very difficult to resist, because the railwaymen had public opinion on their side and there was a general feeling that the working class should be entitled to the same sort of leisure as the middle class. The President of the BOT (Sir Albert Stanley) dismissed this interpretation and insisted that there were more concrete reasons for granting the railwaymen's demands: firstly, the railway leaders had every right to expect the government to fulfil its pledge on the eight hours issue, and secondly the matter could not be allowed to become the ground for a general strike. The problem was that it would cost too much. The cost of conceding the eight hours principle would be about 20–25 million pounds and the issue was bound up with the larger issue of the nationalization of the railways. In normal conditions (when the railways were not under state control) the railway companies would never have conceded the eight-hour day because they could not afford it. Stanley advised the Cabinet to concede the general principle of the eight-hour day but to exclude as many classes of railwaymen as possible. The exceptions could include those railwaymen in outlying parts of the country where there was very little traffic. These workers amounted to about one fifth of all railwaymen and this would mean a substantial saving – but care would have to be taken to avoid provoking sympathetic action in support of the excluded workers. Stanley's plan was accepted by the Cabinet, which instructed him to announce the setting-up of a committee to look into these matters after the General Election.[20]

The General Election took place on 4th December 1918 and Lloyd George formed a new Cabinet on 10th January 1919.[21] The eight-hour day came into operation on the railways on 1st February 1919 but as intended this was very partial victory for the railwaymen. On the same day notices were posted in railway stations notifying railwaymen that the five-minute break at 6 a.m. and 1 p.m., which had been the custom for forty years, was cancelled. The manager of London Tube Railways refused to include mealtimes in the eight hours and the NUR called a tube strike on 3rd February. This strike was called off on 7th February after the President of the BOT elicited an undertaking from the railway companies that they would meet 'the ordinary physical needs of the men under the new conditions of service.'[22] Disputes continued with the Railway Executive and the Board of Trade 'pursuing the usual policy of haggling over every point, trying to make the smallest possible concession and grudgingly giving way by degrees.'[23] There was growing unrest among railwaymen at the delay and the resistance to their demands and on 20th March the NUR voted to ask for Triple Alliance support in calling a strike. The Triple Alliance was against a strike at that time, but government negotiations with the miners were at a delicate stage and the government feared the escalation of conflict. Railway leaders were summoned by Lloyd George and informed of the dangers inherent in a confrontation with the state. The NUR was given an undertaking that wages would be 'standardized upwards'. The Executive Committee of the NUR then found that 'differences between the demands embodied in the Leicester programme and the achievement of the negotiating committee were insufficient to warrant calling a strike.'[24] The leaders of the Triple Alliance confirmed that an attack on the state was not their intention. The NUR called off the strike pending negotiations.[25]

PROSPECTS FOR A GENERAL STRIKE

In reports of the situation to the Cabinet throughout May and June 1919 the Ministry of Labour singled out the movement towards 'direct action' – syndicalism – as 'the most disturbing feature of the current wave of industrial unrest'.[26] The Ministry emphasized that in Britain 'syndicalism has always been in existence' but that it had gathered great impetus in recent years due to stronger, more widespread and sophisticated worker organization, the reaction against political action among workers which began about 1910 and 'the teachings of the school whose motto is that industrial action precedes political action and controls the strength of it'. Syndicalism, it was concluded, 'may roughly be said to be the key-note of the whole labour situation since that time.'[27] This development was less threatening than it seemed, however, because of the timidity of workers' leaders and 'even the most extreme upholders of the syndicalist view in Britain had never recommended the general strike except as a last resort'. This was where British syndicalists differed from and were less dangerous than the French syndicalists, for whom the strike was an end in itself. Instead

'our more prosaic and philosophical pioneers tread more slowly and carefully. They firstly recommend organization so as to make the threat of a serious strike a real danger to the community. Secondly they make full use of the threat to strike and lastly, and only if absolutely necessary, mount the strike itself. In short, for the English revolutionary socialist a great parade of industrial power, even if there is nothing behind it, is of immense importance.'[28]

This was most clearly demonstrated by the formation and development of the Triple Alliance, created quite definitely as a weapon for industrial action in 1915. The formation of the Triple Alliance showed that in the more highly organized trades, especially the coal industry, the first aim – strong and sophisticated worker organization – had already practically been accomplished and that fulfilment of the second aim – the full use of the threat of the strike – was perhaps reaching its zenith 'and it is here that the practical importance of these considerations emerges.'[29] The mere threat of a general strike had proved to be a powerful weapon.

The miners had secured the Coal Commission through the strike threat and 'it is impossible to conceive of an ill-organized industry playing the part the Miners' Federation did in the negotiations which led to the Coal Commission and equally impossible to conceive of their producing such an outcome.' Nevertheless, it was believed that the Coal Commission, whatever its findings, would not placate the miners and

'it would be a mistake to suppose as many people do, that the more extreme miners' leaders or even the more level-headed look upon the Coal Commission as an impartial tribunal appointed as the best means of settling the future of the industry. They look upon it as a means to certain ends envisaged even before it was set up and if it does not attain those ends, other means will have to be found for doing so.'[30]

While it had its disadvantages for those miners who thought they did not need the Coal Commission and could achieve their aims through industrial power alone, the MOL pointed out the advantages of the Coal Commission for the state and for the miners. The Commission

'has thrown a great deal of light where it was needed. It has spent a considerable amount of time, during which hot feeling may have had time to cool, and whatever decision it comes to will have the backing of that portion of public opinion in the country, even among the miners themselves, which looks upon it as an impartial tribunal and this is a very real force with which the Miners' Federation has to reckon.'[31]

The MOL believed that the miners' leaders had taken the wiser course because they knew that 'organization is never so strong as it looks and the strike possessed disadvantages as great, if not greater than, the disadvantages of the Commission'.[32]

Nevertheless, given the fact that for the miners the Commission was a means to preconceived ends, it was likely to provide only a temporary respite, and the MOL again predicted that if the miners failed to get what they wanted from the Commission they would attempt to get it otherwise if they thought they were strong enough. Even if they did get what they wanted from the Commission, the MOL believed that it would be a mistake to suppose that that would be the end of the matter, because 'industrial power, like any other power, grows with success and use. It is moreover, a versatile thing which can be used in all sorts of ways, apart from actually embarking on a general strike.[33]

The versatility of the strike threat was demonstrated by 'a number of experiments with a view to substituting it (industrial might) for older political methods'. For example, a movement had been started to deflect the government's policy in foreign affairs with industrial muscle. The miners had coupled their acceptance of the Interim Report of the Coal Commission with a threatening resolution on the question of the withdrawal of troops to Russia and subsequently further action was taken in conjunction with the Triple Alliance, which, however, 'as was anticipated, appears not to have come to very much.' A similar resolution with regard to conscription was passed at the same time and 'again the miners of South Wales – led, it is to be noticed, by two of their political leaders, members of the House of Commons – have just resolved to refuse to pay further income tax on the present basis and called on the MFGB as a whole to take similar action. The Northumberland miners, in addition to appealing to the MFGB on this matter, have resolved to lay the case before the Triple Alliance with a view to taking industrial action.'[34]

The miners were the clearest example of the trend away from constitutional methods, as 'theirs is the boldest and most progressive organization in the field, but there are other examples to be found.' The railwaymen were in the same position as the miners. They too had gained their recent settlement by the threat of industrial action and would not be easily diverted by delaying tactics. The reason for this was that the

'... settlement was not final, and when a final settlement is attempted, as it will have to be sooner or later, no doubt the railwaymen will repeat the same tactics, perhaps with some new devices which by that time will have been discovered to be effective. The same tendency can be seen too in a more general form in the large crop of Commissions and Committees recently appointed to settle definite industrial problems.'[35]

It was concluded that a shift in power had taken place and that

'the increased industrial power of labour – and it must be added here of employers, too – has made the ordinary legislative procedure inadequate, with the result that a sort of devolution into the industrial sphere has taken place and with it has gone a certain amount of power from the supreme legislative assembly, which in industrial matters becomes merely a body for registering decisions arrived at outside itself.'

These political ambitions, harboured both by organized labour and employers, had taken shape in

'. . . a supreme Joint Industrial Council with the aim of settling industrial conditions largely without reference to Parliament in future. This aim is undoubtedly held by strong personalities both on the employers' and on the workers' side, and is clearly reflected in the Report of the Provisional Joint Committee.'

For the MOL this was a consequence of the temporary increase in power of both sides of industry due to the temporary economic boom at the end of the war, which had created novel and artificial conditions.[36]

Fox has pinpointed certain issues central to the nature of British industrial relations and political systems which had been left dangerously unresolved after the war. During the war the state had actively intervened in the control and operation of industry and the line between the industrial and political areas became blurred. 'Political' was what governments did and 'industrial' was what industry did.[38] For the state the trade unions' role was industrial, to bargain with employers over wages, hours and working conditions. Industrial action after the war increasingly challenged the state's authority in political matters and illustrated the need to publicly redefine the industrial role of the trade unions. The calling of the National Industrial Conference (NIC) in February 1919 was intended to serve this purpose. In the event, however, the Provisional Joint Committee, appointed to address the causes of industrial unrest, did not include representatives of the most powerful unions, called for wages and hours to be regulated by the state and entertained notions of a sovereign national industrial council, an industrial parliament with legislative powers.[39] For the Minister of Labour there was no question of the government 'handing over to any body of people, however eminent,' its responsibilities in the matter of legislation.[40] It was precisely because workers' and employers' organizations began to see themselves as governing institutions that the NIC failed. The Joint Industrial Council, brought into being by the National Industrial Conference, aimed 'to settle industrial conditions largely without reference to Parliament in future.'[41]

WHAT WAS TO BE DONE?

In June 1919 officials of the MOL advised the Cabinet that in the short term the best solution to the rapid growth of industrial power was 'to give way before the concentration of industrial and social power' but 'to give way as little and as gradually as possible.'[42] In the long term, however the only adequate solution lay in meeting the workers' demand for control in some form or other. A decision would have to be made about 'what form and what amount of control, for control is a very vague term'. Enough control must be given to labour

'. . . to develop such a sense of responsibility as will enable labour representatives, when considering demands to be put forward, to appreciate their possible results, not only from the individual workman's point of view in the short period but from the wider point of view of the general welfare, which is the individual's point of view in the long run.'[43]

The extent of control envisaged by the Whitley Report was so vague that 'it leaves in the mind the assumption that things in this sphere will remain more or less as they are.' The situation had developed since the Whitley Report was written. Now it was not just on control but on 'how much' control that the big organizations were concentrating all their industrial power and they were forcing this issue into the foreground as a matter of immediate concern. This opened up a vast area of consideration left untouched by the Whitley recommendations. It was for this reason that

'the Unions most conscious of their industrial powers, i.e. the miners, the railwaymen and the engineers, together with the advocates of State or Guild Socialism, have exhibited little sympathy with the Whitley Report. Yet even a minimum of control, without going so far as any of these recommend, would involve a transformation which may be likened to the transformation from secret to open diplomacy and involves similar difficulties to those encountered in that process.'[44]

To meet the threat, officials of the MOL advised that

'an absolute minimum necessary would appear to be throughout the whole field of industry the throwing open to examination of the workpeople or their representatives all the commercial and financial processes of business and, incidentally, in the words of the Report on Trusts, "the institution of machinery for the investigation of the operation of monopolies, trusts and combines."'

The MOL acknowledged that this was a step regarded as drastic and even impossible by the majority of employers. On the workers' side it was rigidly held that shorter hours with unaltered earnings and simple time rates without any appeal to extra exertion in the way of bonuses did not have an adverse effect on output. The fact was, however, that

'workpeople being after all human, this is simply not true . . . evidence is accumulating which goes to show that inflated industrial power coupled with lack of responsibility for any results of action taken are already having adverse effects on production. But it is difficult to see how such an unpleasant and unpopular fact can be adequately driven home by demonstration alone and it may be the wiser and, in the long run, the only stable solution of the difficulty to concede something to the demands made by labour itself along another line, that of control, and leave the truth to demonstrate itself by the visible and obvious working of cause and effect. Certain organized bodies of workpeople are in a position to force certain results. It is only a question whether they shall or shall not be exempted from responsibility for the consequences both before and after the fact. If they are not exempted then the gain will be immeasurable in steadying not only their aggressive action before but also their resentment after, even though such a course is one of very great difficulty owing to the commercial considerations involved, to which labour is not accustomed.'

The only logical alternative to this course in the Ministry's view was 'boldly to deny that these labour organizations are as strong as they appear to be and prepare to shatter them in industrial conflict. This course must sooner or later lead to a struggle which can only be disastrous, whatever its upshot.'[45]

The MOL ruled out legislation because it was not as effective as 'trade union discipline and control' and could be counter-productive. Recent experience showed that workers might not abide by legislation and this would drive a wedge between union leaders, local leaders and the rank and file.[46] The MOL concluded that 'organized industrial power is a thing which cannot be abolished, any more than a physical force can be abolished, but can only be dealt with by being turned in the right direction and harnessed through the superposition of corresponding responsibility.'[47] Trade union leaders must be the focus of future strategy and future strategy must be based on restricting the opportunities available for exercising it to those who controlled this power. It was emphasized that there was little point in relying on the findings of Commissions, Committees or Conferences, 'as these will carry little weight with the more advanced controllers of industrial power since they look upon them only as so many ways of avoiding a strike.'[48]

For the MOL the focus of strategy had to be the chief organ of industrial power, the Triple Alliance: 'this is exactly the role which its creators foresaw for it and it is bidding fair to vindicate their foresight with extraordinary accuracy.' It was thought difficult to predict what the Triple Alliance might achieve in the future because this depended on outside forces. However, the threat of a general strike of the Triple Alliance had already achieved its leaders' aims. Their organizations had 'become the focus and machine for the use of the industrial weapon'. The Triple Alliance had overshadowed 'all other activities in the same direction' and entirely superseded 'any other organization which might have similar pretensions such as the General Federation of Trade Unions'.[49]

The Ministry advised the government to think ahead and consider the number and importance of the opportunities which forthcoming events were likely to provide to the leaders of the Triple Alliance for the development and accomplishment of their aims. When these were considered it became obvious that there was 'considerably more cause for anxiety than a superficial glance at the state of affairs at the moment might suggest.'[50]

The first of these opportunities was likely to be the Coal Commission Report, due for 20th June. The MOL reiterated

'if this doesn't give the miners' leaders all they think their industrial power entitles them to, they will not be content, especially if other circumstances favour industrial action. While in other circumstances nationalization alone would not be a sufficient plank to obtain solid backing for action or the serious threat of it, any additional issue of a personal nature might entirely alter the situation.'[51]

Another opportunity was likely to arise out of the negotiations with the railwaymen. At the time they were proceeding satisfactorily but 'in view of the somewhat uncertain situation as regards railway control in general . . . they might develop dangerous qualities and in any case the wage problem had only been postponed.'[52]

These were issues in which the Triple Alliance was directly concerned, but there were a number of other issues in which the leaders
were directly involving themselves as a result of the industrial power
which they were in a position to exploit. Conscription, the Blockade,
the question of Russia, the treatment of conscientious objectors and
political prisoners, the income tax limit and finally the military circular with regard to strikes were cited.[53] It was emphasized that 'they
are all being used together and separately to their fullest capacity. In
none of these particular cases has anything of great importance happened, but together, in an atmosphere otherwise troubled, they could
all become effective.' This was because they all contained grievances
and some grievances with quite serious implications. For example, the
income tax and conscription issues

> 'both affect the individual in a way that makes them of some impor-
> tance. The Army circular is just the sort of thing to raise a maxi-
> mum of indignation as results have shown. The questions of the
> Blockade and Russia are closely connected with the question of Peace
> Terms and policy towards enemy countries – which of course, pos-
> sesses considerable potentialities.'[54]

Officials of the MOL turned to another 'quite peculiar' issue with
which the Triple Alliance was reported to be concerning itself. This
was the issue surrounding the Police and Prison Officers' Union which,
they believed, would be certain to be exploited to the utmost by those
who intended to make trouble. The trouble over the Police Union, especially in the light of its reported recruiting successes in Scotland,
could quite easily attract attention in industrial labour circles and provoke sympathetic action.

There were other sources of trouble not directly connected with the
Triple Alliance. Two of these were seen as particularly important. Firstly,
the movement in favour of a 44-hour week was not exhausted. It was
noted that following a conference representing the E & STF, the ASE
and the Workers' Union, a ballot had been taken on this matter and in
the case of the E & STF it was reported to have resulted in a strong
majority in favour of action. In the case of the ASE it was thought
unlikely that the Executive would be allowed to let matters rest even
if they wanted to. The National Union of General Workers, the cotton
trade unions and even a number of smaller organizations were also
moving in this direction and

'here again is an issue with very personal implications and one in which public opinion has already gained considerable momentum which the 48-Hour Bill will do little to allay and may even aggravate.'[55]

Then there was 'the large and vague question of unemployment' which had an aggravating effect on all these other issues. Also, certain industrial settlements already made were having adverse commercial effects, both directly, through a diminution in production, and indirectly, in a vaguer and wider sphere, in the lack of confidence which they tended to foster. In short, a movement of this kind was cumulative and tended to invade every sphere of social activity with corresponding direct reactions in the industrial world which was its source. So that

'if the attitude and position of controllers of industrial power, outlined at the outset, be now recalled, it will be seen that the situation is hardly one in which all difficulties can be considered to have been overcome. It is probably not entirely accidental that all these issues may be expected to come more or less to a head at about one and the same time not very far off.'[56]

In this dangerous situation it was recommended that the government, for the moment, adopt the tactics employed successfully by the German government in dealing with similar situations. The German government was in a strong position with labour and socialist organizations generally, because although it took no action, it purported to represent their interests 'as it takes every opportunity for saying, that it does the very thing they are striving for.'[57]

THE SANKEY REPORT

The Sankey Commission finally reported on 23rd June 1919. There were four reports. The reports from the chairman, Sir John Sankey CBE and the six labour representatives recommended nationalization of the mines. The report from employers' representatives recommended no change in ownership. Sir Arthur Duckham recommended a scheme of district unification of the mines under private ownership and some measure of government control.[58]

The government prevaricated and began to engage in a series of actions, including increasing the price of coal and issuing an order preventing any increase in piece rates in excess of ten per cent while negotiations over working hours were in progress. This last led to a bitter strike in the Yorkshire coalfields which lasted for a month. Troops were sent to the coalfield and naval ratings manned the pumps.[59]

On 18th August Lloyd George announced that the government would not accept nationalization and pointed to the Yorkshire strikes as evidence that nationalization would not bring industrial harmony.[60]

Redmayne, who was assessor to Sankey and sat with him throughout the Commission, felt that this *volte face* was justified and the government had no choice but to play for time and agree to adopt the Interim Report 'to relieve the tension . . . there can be little doubt that had any other course been followed the country would have been plunged into a national coal strike, the end of which no one could foresee.'[61] However, the evidence favoured Miliband, who argued that 'the challenge to the miners was unmistakeable. The question was whether labour would use its industrial power to coerce the government'.[62] By late July 1919 divisions had begun to appear within the ranks of labour and weaknesses within the leadership of the Triple Alliance and the labour movement generally were exposed, which allowed the state to step back and revise its estimation of the impact of the inevitable struggle.

THE GENERAL STRIKE POSTPONED

A combination of factors persuaded the MOL that there would be no general strike. Firstly, the miners' leaders were divided. Events at the Miners' Federation Conference at Keswick on 15th July were analysed in support of this belief.[63] At this Conference it was decided that the government's offer to defer the proposed increase in the price of coal for three months, if the Labour Party would guarantee no strikes or stoppages and the miners agreed to increase output, be rejected. No ballot of the members had been taken on this issue. The Conference believed that this offer was not final and that the situation was still subject to negotiation. Some miners' leaders had faith in the government but others believed that the Prime Minister's offer was an attempt to postpone a Cabinet decision on nationalization. The Conference decided that if the Prime Minister would give an undertaking that the Government would decide the question within a limited time and couple this with an exhortation to the miners not to strike and to increase output, this would be put to the miners by ballot and conference and an agreement reached. This initiative betrayed a lack of appreciation of the situation by miners' leaders – a certain naivety. The prospect of an amicable agreement was remote in view of the extent to which the miners' strikes in Yorkshire had gone and the Government's action in connection with them.[64] The question of nationalization had been settled long before. The final reports of the Sankey Commission had been presented to the Government on 20th June. The Commission was split on the question of nationalization. The Yorkshire miners' strike and the decline in the output of coal were to be the Government's reasons for its decision to reject nationalization. The announcement of this decision had been delayed.[65]

Secondly, the rank and file of the MFGB were unwilling to delegate decision-making power to their leaders and the MFGB Executive would not be bound by the decisions of the other sections of the Triple Alliance. At the Conference, an attempt to authorize the Executive Committee of the Federation to declare a strike without taking a ballot of the members was defeated. For officials of the MOL this was 'interesting as an indication that the rank and file are inclined to distrust a policy which gives practically unlimited powers to the Executive.'[66] The proposer of this motion urged that new machinery was needed to meet new circumstances that were going to arise. The Federation had joined the Triple Alliance and it was not desirable in a crisis that they should have to stand peacefully waiting until a ballot had been taken. This motion was opposed on the grounds that it was not democratic but autocratic and W. Brace MP (MFGB Executive) characterized it as reactionary, saying that he objected to being controlled by an 'oligarchy of his own class.'[67] The proposal was rejected by a large majority. The MOL noted that in recent years extremists had made several unsuccessful attempts to give the Executive or a National Conference power to call a national strike, and that the latest effort was not unconnected with the fact that the National Union of Railwaymen had the power to call a strike without a ballot and to put into immediate effect any decision of the Triple Alliance with regard to direct action.

Thirdly, some miners would not be bound by agreements reached by the MFGB Executive. The Conference displayed considerable anxiety over the disciplinary aspect of unofficial strikes. Vernon Hartshorn MP and Smillie (both of the MFGB Executive) expressed regret at the action of South Wales surfacemen who had struck against the hours of work fixed by the Sankey award. Smillie called on the men to go back to work, saying, 'to have men striking against conditions accepted by a ballot vote of all the members would destroy the Federation.'[68] Intelligence sources reported to the MOL that many of the miners' leaders

viewed with alarm the prevalence of unofficial strikes and freely admitted that the men were in some cases getting out of hand.

Fourthly, by August the MOL was convinced that some influential
leaders of the labour movement were not in favour of direct action.
There were 'signs that the "direct action" issue is leading to a sharp
cleavage of opinion in the Labour world.'[69] The feelings of the rank
and file of the Triple Alliance on the policy of direct action would not
be known until 25th August, when the results of a ballot on the issue
were released. However, the MOL saw as encouraging and influential
on the results the fact that the Labour Party had declined to commit
itself on the matter and that the President of the NUR and the secre-
taries of the MFGB and the Transport Workers' Federation had publicly declared that

> 'the working class in general and the organized workers in particu-
> lar derive more advantage from a clear and unprejudiced presenta-
> tion of their claims and aspirations by and through a Labour daily
> newspaper than by costly strikes and wage movements.'[70]

Much significance was also attached by the MOL to the TUC Conference in Glasgow on 10th September 1919, which had revealed opposing factions within the leadership of the labour movement.[71] Much
publicity had been given to the fact that this Congress was the largest
on record, representing over five million trade unionists – more than
double the membership before the war – and that the Congress now
claimed to speak for a larger body of opinion than any national gathering in the world. Its publicity notwithstanding, the MOL discerned
'much dissatisfaction among the Unions affiliated to it on the grounds
that its actual effective power, when compared with its enormous latent potentialities, is very much less than it ought to be.'[72] The Ministry acknowledged that this criticism was not new, but it was observed
that it had become very prominent in connection with the Triple Alliance demand that the Congress declare its stance on the Government's
policy in regard to Russia, conscription and so on. The TUC stood
accused by the intelligentsia of the Labour movement of being fettered
by its history and of making little attempt to address itself to the task
that urgently awaited it, namely the constitution of a body able to give
shape to the expressed policy of the trade union movement and of a
general staff to co-ordinate the forces of Labour in the industrial field,
especially as regards the problem of industrial and craft unionism. It
was generally believed by its critics that the TUC should devote itself

to an effort in the industrial sphere to link up the sectional efforts and programmes of labour into a common policy and scheme of action. The Triple Alliance found fault with the TUC on the question of direct action. The definite movement in favour of direct action was inaugurated at a Conference of the Alliance at Southport on 16th April. It took the form of a resolution urging the Parliamentary Committee of the TUC to convene a special National Conference to consider whether industrial action should be taken to compel the Government to accede to the abolition of conscription, the withdrawal of British troops from Russia, the raising of the blockade and the release of conscientious objectors. At this time the Alliance was flushed with success at obtaining most of the concessions demanded from the government in the national programmes which two of the constituent bodies formulated on the conclusion of the Armistice. Subsequent events brought the Alliance into sharp conflict with the Parliamentary Committee. Instead of supporting the Alliance, the Parliamentary Committee sent a deputation to the Prime Minister and, in view of his assurances, decided not to call a National Conference. At this all the constituent bodies of the Alliance endorsed the policy of direct action at their annual conferences. At a full delegate conference on 23rd July the Alliance pledged itself to pursue its policy of direct action and recommended a ballot of Triple Alliance members to ascertain whether they were prepared to take industrial action to enforce their demands.

While the whole industrial and political situation was overcast, waiting for the decision of the members of the Triple Alliance on direct action, there was an unsuccessful attempt at co-ordination and exploitation of strikes by extremist elements. Against a favourable background characterized by a general spirit of discontent, the unsettled miners' strike in Yorkshire and the dispute in the baking trade, the police strike erupted. The latter, 'deliberately and secretly organized by agitators in the Police Union, was sprung on the country and was followed by riots in Liverpool and the sympathetic strike by L&SW railwaymen and others.' The MOL believed that

'if the police strike had succeeded, the events which occurred in Liverpool would have taken place elsewhere also and that extremists in various branches of industry might have attempted to call sympathetic strikes on a large scale. It is not intended to maintain that there was a causal connection between all the strikes and events that have been mentioned, but it is probable that their coexistence was not purely fortuitous.'[73]

Fifthly, workers themselves were against direct action. In the wake of this abortive coup the rank and file of the Triple Alliance reacted against the policy of direct action. The MOL concluded that this reaction was not unconnected with the complete failure of the revolutionary policy and sympathetic strikes and that it had exerted a sobering effect on the Alliance. Its executive postponed the ballot and the full delegate conference homologated the decision and agreed to adjourn the whole matter until a meeting of the TUC was convened to consider the issue. It was then possible for the Alliance to claim that the policy of direct action was wrecked by the conservative constitutionalism of the Parliamentary Committee of the TUC – to claim that if it had consented to convene a National Conference in June or July, when the revolutionary elements in labour were at the height of their power, it would not have been impossible that that policy might have been endorsed.[74] For the MOL this enabled the leaders of the Triple Alliance to divert attention from the important part they played in averting a general strike. A clear example of this was to be found in the railway dispute.

THE RAILWAY STRIKE, 1919

A settlement 'unparallelled in the history of British locomotivemen' had been awarded to ASLEF.[75] This settlement was reached on 20th August, the day after the Government rejected coal nationalization. This move was widely seen as 'one way of weakening the railwaymen's forces', i.e. settling the locomotivemen's claims generously so that they might be less inclined to support other grades' claims with strike action. The NUR wanted this 'standardization upwards' to be awarded to all grades to prevent local and sectional strikes. On 19th September the Board of Trade forwarded proposals to the Executive of the NUR which included a list of swingeing wage cuts with the message that they were 'not a basis for negotiation' but 'a definitive offer of the Government'.[76] A national railway strike began on 26th September 1919 which the Prime Minister labelled 'an anarchist conspiracy.'[77] The NUR made no appeal to the Triple Alliance for support.

Emergency arrangements on a huge scale came into operation for the transport and distribution of food and supplies, and 6,000 servicemen and military vehicles were deployed to maintain order and supplies. Civilian volunteers provided a skeleton railway service and were paid the standard rate plus bonuses of 50 per cent of earnings.

In a report on the strike in early October 1919, officials of the MOL advised the Cabinet that the most significant aspect of the strike was the reluctance of those directing it to further extend the area affected by it. It was noted that 'usually it is of advantage from the strikers' point of view so far as possible to extend the area of a strike. Hence the policy of federation and amalgamation and the policy of "sympathetic action."' The reasons why the strike had not been extended were analysed in this report.[78]

The leaders claimed that the extension of the strike was unnecessary 'because the National Union of Railwaymen were by their size and position already able to bring sufficient pressure to enforce any demand that mere pressure can enforce.' This had been well illustrated by their ability to carry matters to the supreme head of the Government whenever they had a mind to. So far, the Triple Alliance had proved to be 'a first-class manoeuvring weapon' but for how long did its leaders believe that the *threat* of a general strike would retain its impact – how far was the 'mere capacity to strike' useful in achieving social transformation? The answer was that, for the railwaymen's leaders at any rate, it was not a vehicle for social transformation. This was an appalling prospect which they strove to avoid. One of the main reasons why the strike had not been extended was that the leaders of the Triple Alliance saw it solely as a bargaining weapon and a boost to their standing with their members, government and the general public. This could be most clearly illustrated through a comparison of the positions of two key figures in the railway dispute, Cramp and Thomas.[79]

Intelligence received by the MOL revealed that Cramp and Thomas had made their positions clear at Carlisle on 25th May. Cramp was reported to have consulted other members of the Triple Alliance over the progress of the strike and presented the situation in revolutionary terms. However, Cramp expressed doubt as to whether the rank and file understood what was happening – revolution. The question for Cramp was

'were the people clear-eyed and conscious of the fact which was involved, because it meant either revolution or defeat? Whenever they said they were ripe for industrial revolution, he was with them, but not for them to enter it merely under the belief that they were out for a trade dispute. Let them approach it with their eyes open and be prepared to carry it through, but do not let them through false pretences, engineer a thing of this kind unless the people they were calling upon to follow them knew what they had to go through.'

Ministry officials dismissed Cramp's justification for his hesitation and reluctance to extend the strike as bluster and fear. He was not a true revolutionary because:

'if he is thinking in terms of revolution and not of a trade dispute, [he] should be all for the extension still farther of the area of the strike. He should want to completely disorganize and finally paralyse the present system of government. For this, no more effective means could be devised than the simultaneous strike of all the members of the Triple Alliance, the Postal Federation and the ETU and the newspaper compositors. In the complete breakdown which would ensue Mr Cramp might have an opportunity of establishing a social order more in consonance with his ideals.'[80]

Although Cramp's attitude appeared more threatening it was Thomas's approach which was more worrying. Thomas was a strong opponent of direct action and an upholder of the ballot-box method of revolution. Thomas hesitated to extend the strike area saying that he had already applied sufficient pressure. He explained his restraint in terms of 'the interests of the community'. This seemed to be 'more on the plane of practical politics'. Thomas's motives did not, however, survive closer inspection 'this may be quite sincere though hardly in the way Mr Thomas suggests'. Thomas's forbearance, according to Ministry analysts, did not so much grow out of his concern for the interests of organized workers as for his position in public life generally. Thomas craved the good opinion of 'the community' and it was this which underpinned his decision not to extend the strike. Thomas mistakenly differentiated between 'the community' and the working class. This endangered his position as a trade union leader which was the source of his authority and his role in public life. The government adopted an approach which appeared to mirror that of Thomas on the grounds that 'no single body can stand against an overwhelmingly hostile community' but the understanding of 'community' and 'public opinion' which guided this policy was quite different:

'since much of this opinion is labour opinion, it has been desirable to do nothing in the course of measures taken in connection with the strike which involves principles to which labour is solidly hostile without making abundantly clear that it was necessary and why. This is why it was desirable to concentrate rather on organising emergency means of transport than a direct attack on the Union, e.g. through its funds, or on forcibly carrying on the railways with soldiers &c. It has also been desirable in appealing for volunteers to be careful that appeals should not be so framed as to appear to be applicable to one social class in the community, as for example, an appeal for all to lend their motor cars. This brings the conception of the class war dangerously into prominence.'[82]

The strike was settled on 5th October on the basis of no wage reductions till 30th September 1921, negotiations about new standard rates, wages tied to the cost of living and repayment of wage arrears. Bagwell (1963) notes that the strike successfully frustrated the attempt to reduce railwaymen's wages but did nothing about the problem of the future organization of the transport industry, and the Railway Act 1921 avoided nationalization by forcing the majority of existing lines into four companies to be privately owned and run for profit.

THE MINERS ISOLATED

Confronted by the continued refusal of the government to nationalize the mines, the MFGB had launched the 'Mines for the Nation' campaign aimed at capturing public support for industrial action to achieve the nationalization of the coal industry. Page Arnot notes, however, that the general public were no longer interested in the miners' cause after the railway strike. Their attention had been diverted by 'foreign and Empire affairs' and the campaign aroused little interest outside the mining areas.[83]

The MFGB Executive asked for a Special Trade Union Congress to be held in February 1920 to consider mounting a general strike on the nationalization issue. The Executive Committee of the TUC (in particular the Rt Hon Charles Bowerman MP) questioned the advisability of an early meeting of the TUC. The Special Congress was held on 11th March 1920. At the Preliminary Conference held on 10th March by the MFGB, the delegates voted for industrial action by a small majority. The miners were divided on the issue of nationalization. On 11th March at the Special Congress there was an overwhelming vote against the general strike and in favour of intensive political propaganda in preparation for the General Election. There was no General Election imminent and so the nationalization issue was effectively shelved.[84]

The MOL reported to the Cabinet that although the decision of the Congress was 'a foregone conclusion', its deliberations were very important since 'its great achievement was to put an end, for the time, to the direct action controversy which has agitated Labour and the country as a whole for the past year'. The report focused on the standpoints of the labour leaders involved in this decision and how they were received. J.H. Thomas presided over the Congress and set the agenda by emphasizing that the Congress had not assembled to discuss the issue of nationalization but 'to decide how best to secure the enactment of a measure which they believed would be in the interests of the community'. Thomas warned the Congress of the great responsibility involved in the right to strike and urged that it should not be exercised lightly or impulsively. He pointed out clearly that the future position of the Labour and trade union movement depended on the decision of the Congress. Instead of a general strike, Thomas urged the Congress to adopt constitutional methods. Political action had not failed, it had not yet been tried and trade unionists had not yet used their power as intelligently as they could and returned the number of members of Parliament which their voting strength warranted.

Frank Hodges (Secretary of the MFGB) rejected this view, arguing that the miners' faith in the existing Parliamentary institution had been shattered. The government had failed to honour its promises, not only to the miners but to the whole working class. Throughout his speech there was an atmosphere of resentment at the failure of the other union leaders to support the miners' claim and Hodges gave voice to this: 'it was easier to wait for political change, it was more comfortable but he called on the working class to sacrifice something to achieve the end which they desired'. If the movement for nationalization did not succeed the miners would be pushed 'back into the vortex of wage claims'. However, Hodges 'had no chance of moving the Congress'.[85]

Tom Shaw MP, leader of the textile workers, 'in a conservative speech' then called on the Congress 'to consider the realities of the situation' and reject direct action. These realities were firstly that, even in the miners' own ranks there was a huge minority against direct action. Secondly, the people of the country were against the miners' policy and if there was a general strike it would be a dangerous experiment which would recoil with tenfold force upon the poor and set the trade union movement back by twenty years. However, what concerned Shaw most of all was 'whether one section of the movement (the miners) could be allowed to dictate to the country'.[86]

J.R. Clynes MP, of the General Workers' Union, 'in a very incisive and lucid speech', expressed his disapproval of direct action, not because it might fail, cause suffering or because it was wrong but because the Prime Minister would welcome a general election on the question of direct action to secure nationalization at a time when the Labour movement was fundamentally divided on the issue.[87]

Then Tom Mann, General Secretary of the ASE, 'in an amusing but unconvincing speech', argued that after such a long campaign in which they had been supported by the whole of the Labour movement the miners had a right to expect Congress to support them.

Finally, Jack Mills of the Shop Stewards' Movement argued that the issue should be put directly to the rank and file, but 'this suggestion did not find favour' with other leaders.[88]

A glance at the general labour situation revealed a continuing pattern of internal fragmentation in trade unions. There was continuing friction between railway unions manifest in efforts to prevent its recurrence. A joint sub-committee of the NUR and ASLEF proposed an agreement for adoption by the two unions of a common policy in all matters affecting railwaymen and an end to situations in which the railwaymen's unions attacked each other. These were to 'be discountenanced by all responsible officers and members of each union'. There was also continuing friction between different types of trade unions and general labourers' unions, and some unions had adopted a decidedly provocative attitude in trying to poach members of other unions. For example, in advertisements in the *Daily Herald* the National Union of General Workers attacked builders labourers' unions for poaching their members. The Workers' Union issued a circular letter refuting the argument that only a union of building workers could represent builders' labourers, only a miners' organization could represent miners, a transport workers' union represent tramwaymen, and so on. From this, officials of the MOL concluded that the growing movement in favour of industrial unionism would be strongly opposed by general labourers' unions.

The Labour and Socialist movements in Britain were also becoming more inward-looking. Ramsay MacDonald of the Independent Labour Party expressed his disappointment in a review of the international socialist position in *Forward*. He saw no prospect of an International which would comprise socialists of all countries. The Socialist Labour Party had begun to concern itself with the formation of a united Communist Party in Britain and its affiliation with the Labour Party. In its paper *The Socialist* the SLP 'roundly declared that the SLP should never sacrifice for a mere tactical advantage, principle, consistency and truth'. Erstwhile members of the SLP – Murphy, Bell, McManus and Paul – were condemned for this, for their association with the Shop

Stewards' and Workers' Committees Movement and especially for their sympathies with the IWW. The SLP insisted on remaining a revolutionary socialist *political* party. For observers in the MOL this insistence on the word 'political' was of great interest in view of the word's recent unpopularity in 'these extreme papers'. If this was the opinion of members of the SLP as a whole, then they concluded that there was 'no immediate prospect of amalgamation between the SLP, clinging as it does with almost religious fervour to the strictest and narrowest formulae of Marxian socialism, the group of opportunists and tacticians represented by *The Call*, and the body of irresponsible firebrands represented by *The Workers' Dreadnought*'.

Socialism in Britain was losing its intensity and widening its scope. *The Call* looked forward to the extremists in French trade unionism regaining the position of authority they held before the war, while *The Forward* congratulated the CGT on extending its membership, accumulating funds and pursuing a practical policy. In the *New Statesman*, 'Herr Bernstein claims that a purely socialist community in Germany is not yet possible of achievement and defends the German Democratic Republic with what he describes as a "Socialist Reform Policy", against the attacks that have been made upon it in this country on various grounds'.

The MOL concluded this report by advising the Cabinet that there was very little criticism of actual government policy in Britain, apart from the decision to reduce the bread subsidy which meant an increase in the price of bread.[89] Agitation for industrial action on a considerable scale to secure political ends was at an end and 'interest has been transferred from schemes for the control of industry to claims for further wage advances.'[90] Subsequent events were to confirm this analysis.

THE MINERS DEFEATED

With no support for nationalization, the miners pushed for wage increases to match the rising cost of living. In July 1920 the cost of living had reached 152 per cent of the pre-war level and was still rising. The miners presented their demands to the government, arguing that since the coal industry had a surplus of about 66 million pounds a year available, it could well afford to increase wages.[91]

The government rejected the miners' claims, arguing that they had not based their calculations on existing wages plus the Sankey increases. In addition, the government held that the British coal consumer was, even after the increase in coal prices, paying much less than the world price; that any differentiation between domestic and industrial prices would mean more state control and higher administration prices; that the surplus made from the coal industry was excess profits, which ought to go to the state to reduce taxes; and that coal price increases were necessary to place coal-producing districts and individual collieries on a profit-making basis. The miners argued that this last was being done as a prelude to the imminent decontrolling of the coal industry. The government rejected this and offered to negotiate higher wages in exchange for higher productivity. This proposal was not accepted by the miners. Negotiations reached deadlock and on 31st August 1920 the miners voted overwhelmingly for strike action.

Simultaneously, a conference of the Executives of the Triple Alliance agreed to give all possible support to the miners. Cole points out that this did not amount to a definite declaration in favour of a sympathetic strike. The Transport Workers' Executive took the view that they had no power to call a strike and could only recommend their affiliated unions to take action. The Railwaymen's Executive did have the power to call an immediate strike but they wanted to re-open negotiations with the government on behalf of the Triple Alliance to avert the strike. The positive action of the Triple Alliance was, then, limited to the establishment of a joint Publicity Committee to take charge of propaganda and to an expression of faith in the justice of the miners' cause.[92]

On 2nd September 1920 the Miners' National Conference called a national strike for 25th September. The government responded with a productivity deal which the miners rejected, pointing out that the ability to increase output was not theirs but the coal owners'. The government suggested that the miners' leaders meet the coal owners to thrash out a solution and suspend strike notices meanwhile. The miners' Executive agreed, but talks with the coal owners rapidly broke down as the latter argued that miners' wages had increased by 157 per cent compared with pre-war wages and the cost of living had increased by only 152 per cent.[93]

The miners struck on 16th October. On 28th October the government intervened with a provisional settlement. This settled none of the outstanding issues and included arrangements which tied wages to output. It proposed the establishment of a National Wages Board to formulate standard rates of wages in spite of the fact that there were regional differences in the difficulty of coal extraction, working practices, the division of labour, payment systems and wide variations in the profitability of coal seams, not to mention swings in trade.

The MFGB recommended these proposals to the miners and a ballot was taken in which the miners rejected the scheme by a majority of 8,459. Nevertheless, the strike was called off because of a Federation rule which required a two-thirds majority in favour of a strike, and work resumed on 3rd November.

In February 1921 the Mines Department announced that the coal industry was to be decontrolled on the 31st of March 1921. The MFGB was informed that all agreements made under state control, including wage increases, would no longer be binding. At the same time a state of emergency was declared under the Emergency Powers Act of November 1920.[94] The MFGB protested and asked for state financial control of the coal industry to be continued until 31st August, as originally intended. Coal owners also opposed decontrol, since this would put them in the position of having to reduce wages which had been increased by the state. Cole advances two important reasons which may have precipitated decontrol in the coal industry. Firstly, there had been a rapid downturn in the coal trade. The state had counted on the continued prosperity of 1920, which was dependent on the inflated prices charged for coal exported to Europe. However, American coal had become a powerful competitor (which had filled the gap during the 1920 coal dispute in Britain) and reparations from Germany in the form of cheap coal exports brought world coal prices down. France bought cheap coal or accepted free coal from Germany. It looked as though the guaranteed profits instituted by the state might have to be met by the state. Secondly, the dates originally fixed for the decontrol of the railways and the mines coincided. The early decontrol of the coal industry was financially expedient and reduced the likelihood of sympathetic action.[95]

By late March 1920 there were irreconcilable differences between miners and coal owners arising out of the attempt to devise a scheme in respect of wages in the coal industry as agreed after the 1920 strike. The differences centred around a national settlement of wages and a national pool of profits. The miners wanted the establishment of a national pool with which the surpluses of one coalfield could be used to maintain wages in another at a level fixed by a National Wages Board.[96]

A fall in trade at the end of March prompted coal owners to decrease wages and notices of termination of existing contracts were distributed to all grades. This was a lockout which made a million miners idle. The MFGB ordered that all notices be allowed to expire regardless of occupation. This included safety men who had not previously been affected by stoppages in the mining industry. It had been the policy of the MFGB to instruct safety men to remain at work to stop pits flooding, keep them workable and avoid permanent damage.[97] Both the government and the press seized on this and public sympathy for the miners' cause was reduced.

On 30th March the MFGB called for Triple Alliance support and on 8th April the Executives of the Triple Alliance issued a strike order to take effect at midnight on 12th April. Troops were moved into the coalfields. On 9th April a deputation from the NUR and the Transport Workers Federation met the Prime Minister. It was agreed that the miners should allow the safety men to go back to work in exchange for the reopening of negotiations. Negotiations resumed with the government, the coal owners and miners on 11th April but none of the participants changed their positions, with the exception of the miners who agreed to a reduction of wages proportionate to any fall in the cost of living. Negotiations continued into the next day and the strike was postponed for the outcome of the discussions. Lloyd George put forward proposals which were substantially the same as before, and still without the national pool, but with the offer of a temporary subsidy to mitigate wage reductions. The miners rejected this proposal. On 13th April the Triple Alliance reassembled and fixed a strike date for 15th April. Frank Hodges, Secretary of the MFGB, made a speech which seemed to imply that wage reductions not below the cost of living would stop the strike. The Prime Minister offered to negotiate on this basis. The miners' executive replied that the only basis on which a temporary settlement could be arrived at would be the concession of a National Wages Board and a National Pool.[98] The other sections of the Triple Alliance refused to support the miners and the strike for Friday 15th April was cancelled.

CONCLUSION

This chapter has focused on the state's actions in response to the threat of a general strike. In this period it seemed that the moment for a general strike had finally arrived. This was 'the old dream of using the mass power of organized labour as a means of exerting direct pressure on government for what Establishment figures, including most leading union officials, defined as political ends'.[99] For the state, 'the issue was not revolution and socialism but direct industrial action for limited and specific purposes.'[100]

In the short term appeasement was favoured. The MOL advised the government to give way in the face of powerful worker organization but to concede as little as possible as gradually as possible. At the same time care was taken to restrict the opportunities available to the Triple Alliance for exercising its industrial muscle. As time passed, however, deep divisions within the ranks of labour showed that worker organization was not as strong as it looked and that this was no longer necessary.

By late September 1919 it had become apparent to the MOL that the threat of direct action had receded, that the labour movement as a whole was fragmented and that a strike of the Triple Alliance would not take place. All the indications were that the state had nothing to fear from the labour and socialist movements in Britain. The trade unions were characterized by fragmentation, sectionalism, leader dominance and parliamentarianism, all of which were encouraged and reinforced in state policy. Within the socialist movement there was no consensus over tactics and strategy in the struggle for socialism. Against this background it was felt that the state could safely withdraw and let worker organizations, notably the miners, 'shatter themselves in industrial conflict'. The success of this policy owed much to the structure and leadership of the Triple Alliance.

The Triple Alliance magnified the defects which made trade unions unsuitable vehicles for revolutionary transformation and made the management of industrial conflict easier. It was not designed for rapid responses to sudden crises, either internal or external. There were disagreements among the leaders as to whether the activities of the Triple Alliance were to be controlled by all three Executives acting as one or whether there were to be parallel movements controlled separately by each union. There was no procedure by which a joint strike could actually be begun, organized or resolved. The three organizations followed different practices in taking strike decisions. At best this made mounting combined strikes complicated and time-consuming, and the delay caused by long negotiations impaired the effectiveness of mass action and 'enabled the country to be prepared.'[101] In any case, the Alliance was not primarily intended to undertake sympathetic strikes in support of the sectional claims of its constituents. Many of its founders saw it as a means of averting stoppages, not of enlarging them – and even those leaders who did envisage the general strike thought that the constituents of the Triple Alliance should have time to strengthen their organization and increase their membership before launching a general strike.[102]

As Phillips makes clear, the Triple Alliance was in no sense 'a victory for the syndicalist idea'. He cites the trade union leaders centrally concerned to show that it was formed to control and discipline rank and file militancy and prevent small sections of striking workers dragging everybody else in 'willy-nilly'. One aim of this co-operation was to avoid a recurrence of the embarrassing circumstances of 1911–12 when railwaymen, transport workers and miners struck in isolation, careless of the damaging repercussions of their stoppages for unions in ancillary or dependent industries.[103] Another was to synchronize the wage claims of its members, to arrange for their agreements to expire simultaneously.[104] It was believed that the bargaining advantage afforded by the simultaneous conduct of negotiations, reinforced by the threat of combined action, would usually be sufficient to achieve the desired outcome. Even if it did not and employers proved intractable, the spectre of mass strike action would bring the government into the situation 'more or less as a protagonist of labour' as in 1911–12. For its leaders, an important consideration in the formation of the Triple Alliance was the effect that its potential bargaining power would have on other unions rather than employers and the government. Unions in competition with those of the Alliance would want to share the benefits of this improved organizational power. They would be more willing to consider mergers (which was to be the only means by which they would be allowed to associate themselves) and so the membership, resources and control of the three constituent unions over related organizations could be increased.[105] But perhaps the most important aim of the leaders concerned in setting up the Alliance was to pool their resources as leaders against challenges to their leadership from below.[106] They sought to regain the confidence of the rank and file of their respective organizations, and the power that went with it, by signalling their willingness to actively engage in direct action.

NOTES

1. PRO CAB 23/9, WC 522 30/1/1919.
2. Ibid.
3. Ibid.
4. Middlemas, 1979, p. 93.
5. Ward, 1973; Clegg, 1985, p. 276.
6. Jeffery & Hennessy, 1983, p. 3.
7. PRO CAB 23/9, WC522 30th January 1919.

8. Ibid.
9. Chewter, 1966.
10. Ibid.
11. Butler & Butler, 1986.
12. Cole, 1923.
13. Miliband, 1972, p. 66.
14. Ibid.
15. Redmayne, 1923, p. 218.
16. Fox, 1985, p. 301.
17. PRO CAB 23/9, War Cabinet Memo 508, 28th November 1918.
18. Ibid.
19. PRO CAB/28, War Cabinet Memo 510, 6th December 1918.
20. Ibid.
21. Mowat, 1968, Chapter 1.
22. Bagwell, 1963, pp. 370–371.
23. *The Times*, 18th March 1919.
24. Ibid., p. 379.
25. Ibid.
26. PRO CAB 24/90, (Report on the Labour Situation by the Ministry of Labour), 21st May 1919.
27. This refers to Industrial Unionism see Chapter 3.
28. PRO CAB 24/90, 21st May 1919.
29. Ibid.
30. Ibid.
31. Ibid.
32. Ibid.
33. Ibid.
34. Ibid.
35. Ibid.
36. Ibid.
38. Fox, 1985, p. 302.
39. The Triple Alliance and the ASE abstained from participation in the Joint Committee and leaders of the NUR took the view that 'no useful purpose is served by collusion with the employers through the Government to maintain the existing order of society'. See *Railway Review*, 27th June 1919.
40. PRO LAB 2/556/WA 7809, September 1919.
41. Ibid.
42. PRO CAB 24/81, (Report on the Labour Situation from the Ministry of Labour), 4th June 1919.
43. Ibid.
44. Ibid.
45. Ibid.
46. PRO LAB 2/254/13 December 1917.
47. PRO CAB 24/80, (Report on the Labour Situation by the Ministry of Labour), 28th May 1919.
48. Ibid.
49. Ibid.
50. Ibid.

51. Ibid.
52. Ibid.
53. See Allen, 1960, pp. 147–167.
54. PRO CAB 24/80, 28th May 1919.
55. Ibid.
56. Ibid.
57. Ibid.
58. Cole, 1960, p. 392.
59. Ibid.
60. Ibid.
61. Redmayne, 1923, p. 218.
62. Miliband, 1972, p. 67.
63. PRO MUN 5/55 (Report from the Ministry of Labour), 23rd July 1919.
64. PRO CAB 23/15 WC 595A, 21st July 1919. An unofficial strike of York-shire miners erupted on 17th July over the Government's interpretation of the recommendations of the interim report of the Sankey Commission on higher wages and the seven-hour day. The Government increased the price of coal and issued an order preventing any increase in piece rates in excess of ten per cent while negotiations over working hours were in progress. This strike provoked alarm in the Cabinet and was described as 'practical Bolshevism'. Troops were sent to the coalfield and naval ratings manned the pumps.
65. PRO CAB 23/15 WC 607A, 7th August 1919.
66. PRO MUN 5/55 (Report from the Ministry of Labour), 23rd July 1919.
67. Ibid.
68. Ibid.
69. PRO MUN 5/55 (Ministry of Labour Report on the Labour Situation), 20th August 1919.
70. Ibid.
71. PRO MUN 5/55 (Report from the Ministry of Labour), 10th September 1919.
72. Ibid.
73. Ibid.
74. Ibid.
75. McKillop, 1950, p. 122.
76. Bagwell, 1963, p. 383.
77. *The Times*, 29th September 1919.
78. PRO MUN 5/55 (Report from the Ministry of Labour), 1st October 1919.
79. Ibid.
80. Ibid.
81. Ibid.
82. Ibid.
83. Page Arnot, 1953, p. 217.
84. Ibid., p. 218.
85. PRO LAB 2/758/2 (Report from the Ministry of Labour), 17th March 1920.
86. Ibid.
87. Ibid.
88. Ibid.

89. Ibid.
90. Ibid.
91. Cole, 1923, pp. 141–146.
92. Ibid., p. 144.
93. Ibid., Chapter 8.
94. Cole, 1960, p. 399.
95. Ibid.
96. Redmayne, 1923, p. 244.
97. Page Arnot, 1953.
98. Cole, 1960, p. 212.
99. Fox, 1985, p. 300.
100. Miliband, 1972, p. 66.
101. CAB/37/63 Askwith, 1912.
102. Phillips, 1971.
103. Report of the Triple Alliance Joint Executive Council, 23rd April 1914, cited in Phillips, 1971.
104. Phillips, 1971.
105. Ibid.
106. Hinton, 1973, p. 282.

8 Conclusion: Trade Unions and the Management of Industrial Conflict

The understanding of trade unions, trade union leaders and industrial conflict which underpinned state industrial relations policy at the beginning of the period covered by the study corresponds to a large extent with rank-and-filist premises. It was believed, firstly, that workers had a reservoir of latent power which was contained by well-organized and responsibly led trade unions; secondly, that a clear line of demarcation could be drawn between the leadership of trade unions, activists and the rank and file; and thirdly, that trade union officialdom was synonymous with moderation and defused the radical aspirations of the rank and file. The structural and hierarchical features of trade unions and the particular concerns of their leaders made them a valuable mechanism for the management of industrial conflict. The architects of this initiative were in no doubt, however, that this policy could not eradicate industrial conflict. At best it could only achieve 'peaceable relations to ensure the highest amount of prosperity'. This was because trade unions arose out of the conflict of interest between capital and labour and the interests of capital and labour could never be identical.[1]

TRADE UNIONS

Early research by the Labour Correspondent of the BOT revealed that trade unions were not related to the mediæval guilds but were creatures of capitalism. They were workers' response to the decline of the guilds and to the fact that in capitalism no mutuality of interests existed between employers and workers. These unions had their roots in the time-lag between the decline of the guilds and the rise of trade unions. In this transitional period the state attempted to regulate the terms of the relationship between capital and labour but 'a state of social anarchy' existed in Britain and the condition of the mass of workers was miserable in the extreme. Combinations of workers were illegal, but workers resisted their immiseration by forming themselves into clandestine unions and engaging in a guerrilla war against their employers. This situation persisted into the 1820s, when it was realized that some worker organizations (notably those in the engineering, shipbuilding and printing trades) had evolved beyond this typically anarchic pattern and become trade unions managed by individuals who displayed executive ability of a very high order, who were not 'industrial incendiaries' or 'social disturbers' but 'cautious and moderate in the extreme'. The structure of these organizations reduced industrial conflict. Although agitation for strike action generally came from workers, the decision to strike was subject to deliberation by lodges and committees on its way to the central executives of these unions, and the executive committees of all of the chief unions were to a very large extent hostile to strike action. In this process many potentially serious disputes lost their momentum or were curtailed. It was not that union officials did not share their members' concerns, but that as leaders they had to put the good of the whole union before the claims of any part of the union. These unions also addressed the immiseration of the working class which fuelled the guerrilla war against employers. They offered welfare benefits which kept a great body of workers out of pauperism. Repressive legislation and employers' oppressive practices aggravated industrial unrest and blocked the development of well-organized trade unions like these which were 'plainly useful both to capitalists and to the community'.[2] The Trade Union Act 1871 made these trade unions lawful.

By the late 1880s and early 1890s this rank-and-filist conception of trade unions, trade union leaders and their members had been refined and tested by the experience of large-scale industrial conflict. Removing the legal obstacles to responsible unionism had not been enough. Analyses of unrest in these years showed that the scarcity of this type of trade union, the reluctance of the rank and file of the established trade unions to cede decision-making power to their leaders, the rise of unskilled unions, the refusal of many employers to recognize trade unions and the reluctance of the established unions to recruit unskilled workers had combined to reduce the effectiveness of this initiative. The solution was seen to lie in state intervention to actively foster trade union recognition and collective bargaining and the Conciliation Act 1896 was passed.

The experience of industrial conflict in the years from 1910 to 1921, however, forced further revisions in state labour policy. Industrial unrest in this period revealed that the chief obstacle to the attempt to permanently manage industrial conflict through responsible trade unionism was workers themselves.

INDUSTRIAL CONFLICT

State analyses of industrial conflict throughout 1910–21 found that workers could not be persuaded to subscribe in any consistent or informed way to any 'ism'. In common with the advocates of socialism, syndicalism and industrial unionism, the state found that the mass of workers were fickle and unpredictable and confounded any attempt 'to substitute a motive not of a purely economic character'.[3] In this view the mass of workers had no vested interest in the capitalist order and their exploitation in the workplace periodically led them to struggle against managerial authority and the trade union structures and collective bargaining procedures which stifled autonomous action.[4] Workers were primarily interested in wage issues and allied themselves to leaders who proved their usefulness in this respect, regardless of political orientation. At the beginning of the period younger and more militant leaders devised strategies composed of elements of syndicalism and industrial unionism to displace established union leaders, to reorganize key unions and make them more efficient fighting organizations, and so consolidate their leadership. These organizations, notably the miners, the railwaymen and the transport workers, surpassed their leaders' expectations and began to manifest features defined by the state as a threat to the national interest. Strike movements generally were increasingly characterized by the potential for concerted action on a large scale which threatened economic and civil disturbance, a disregard of the methods of moderate trade unionism, widespread support among the working class and indifference to the law.

Hobsbawm rightly suggests that at best syndicalism was 'a slogan of the struggle and not a programme for social transformation' but wrongly concludes that there was no revolutionary threat at this time.[5] Newer, more radical leaders offered versions of syndicalism and industrial unionism as an alternative vision and fighting policy. Workers readily subscribed to the methods of syndicalism, especially 'direct action' against employers and the critique of established trade unionism at the heart of industrial unionism rather than the aims of these movements. Direct action was very effective. Success gave workers a new confidence and their organizations gained a new coherence and scale. Leaders of the established trade unions lost power over their members and even some of the newer more radical leaders felt threatened by the success of the movement they helped to engender.

Workers were enamoured of this 'new policy' as long as gains were achieved by it and the stock of leaders who subscribed to it rose and fell accordingly. Leaders, both radical and moderate, were carried along on the wave. For the state and for the trade union officials concerned, from 1910 onwards, the strategies and tactics of syndicalism and industrial unionism added a new and threatening dimension to worker organization because of their emphasis on empowering the rank and file of trade unionism rather than its officials. This was 'power without responsibility' – a potentially disastrous combination.[6] It constituted a 'national danger' which forced the state to intervene but limited the forms which intervention could take. The state could intervene by means of legislation, but this further diminished the power of official trade unionism and there was the possibility that workers would not comply. The stability of the state itself was challenged.

TRADE UNION LEADERS

State analyses of industrial conflict found that at these moments of great tension the 'responsibility' of trade union leaders was variable. The dilemmas facing trade union leaders in this period were most clearly illustrated during the prosecution of Tom Mann at the height of the 'Great Unrest', by the response of the Executive of the ASE to dilution during the war and by C.T. Cramp and J.H. Thomas in the postwar period. Many leaders were left with a stark choice: to become more radical or lose their positions. Their responses to pressure varied. Many abdicated responsibility, some put their own material interests before 'the national interest' or the interests of their members, some tended to yield to whatever appeared to be the greatest threat to their position. Others turned to the state and fuelled an increasingly popular view (among workers) of trade union leaders as collaborators with the state and employers rather than representatives of what their members saw as their interests. The issue of whose side the state was on seriously hampered BOT attempts to defuse industrial conflict and continued to dog the footsteps of state officials in subsequent attempts to mediate in disputes.

It was recognized that officials had to respond to mass sentiment to retain their position and 'the problem for the leaders is, on the one hand, to get their followers to do what may be necessary from the

national point of view, without on the other either alienating their loyalty and jeopardizing their interests.'[7] This was why officials did not
always favour conservatism at the expense of industrial action and 'it
is not generally realized what a delicate and difficult problem this is
for such men in their official capacity to handle.'[8] Rank-and-file trade
union members were not always prepared to fight militant struggles,
but neither were they always passive or in awe of their leaders (pace
Michels). Trade union officials' conservatism was therefore contingent
on the relative strength of the pressure placed on them by their members and the state.

CONFLICT MANAGEMENT

State response to this crisis during 1910–12 was to avoid stringent
action which could not be enforced because very large numbers of
men 'cannot be made to work if they will not work and they cannot
be imprisoned for striking'.[9] The more forcefully the state intervened,
the more likely it was to produce the situation it aimed at preventing
– and yet to do nothing could have the same result: 'a constant war
between parties growing bigger until it would reach something approaching a civil war'.[10] The pitfalls of forceful state intervention were
demonstrated in the early years of the war by the fate of the MOW
Act 'which did not prevent strikes from happening nor even reduce
them to negligible proportions'.[11] Again, in the May strikes of 1917,
'every one of the strikers was guilty of a breach of the law and
knew it but the knowledge had no restraining influence'.[12] After 1917
mass worker organization took on a more threatening dimension.
The threat of combined action was increasingly deployed in pursuit of
explicitly political ends. This was reflected in the formulation and implementation of state labour policy which took seriously the warnings
of Bagehot that 'a political combination of the lower classes, as such
and for their own objects, is an evil of the first magnitude.' In opting
for appeasement it also echoed his view that this evil could only be
averted by

'the greatest wisdom and the greatest foresight in the higher classes . . .
[who] . . . must avoid, not only every evil, but every appearance of
evil; while they still have the power they must remove, not only
every grievance but where it is possible every seeming grievance
too; they must willingly concede every claim which they can safely

concede, in order that they may not have to concede unwillingly some claim which would impair the safety of the country.'[13]

During the Railway strike in 1919 the MOL warned the Cabinet that although industrial conflict could be forcibly suppressed by the police or the armed forces, this could bring 'the conception of the class war dangerously into prominence' and at that time the loyalty of the police and the army was uncertain.[13]

The state adopted the approach favoured by the German government and took no action while appearing to seriously consider workers' demands. At the same time care was taken to reduce the opportunities available to the Triple Alliance for exercising its industrial muscle. This strategy was rewarded by late September 1919, when it became apparent that workers had lost interest in direct action and there would be no general strike. Public opinion 'much of which was labour opinion' had decided the issue and 'no single body can stand against an overwhelmingly hostile community.'[15]

THE ROLE OF TRADE UNIONS

The allocation of a share of state power to the trade unions was never envisaged at any point in this period. In the deliberations surrounding the Industrial Council in 1911, the idea of any devolution of state power was dismissed as a crude and unrealistic suggestion. Again, in the aftermath of the MOW Act, it was emphasized that the role of established trade unions was not to concern themselves with the detail of government policy but to impose it on their members 'to exert all their force to remove these suspicions and to encourage the men and – indeed, I will not say coerce, but bring every influence to bear on them.'[16] The MOL, commenting on the Whitley Scheme during 1916–18, noted that the problem with the latter as far as the trade unions were concerned was precisely that it offered them no executive powers. The whole issue was summed up by the Minister of Labour, who made clear to the Provisional Joint Committee of the NIC that the government had no intention of handing over 'to any body of people, however eminent' its responsibilities in the matter of legislation.[17]

The trade unions' role was industrial: to bargain with employers over wages, hours and working conditions, to discipline and control their members and to ensure the co-operation of their members to state policy formulated in the 'national interest'. The aim of consulting trade union officials and inviting them to participate at national level in conferences and committees was to bolster this role 'to develop such a sense of responsibility as will enable labour representatives, when considering demands to be put forward, to appreciate their possible results, not only from the individual workman's point of view but from the wider point of view of the general welfare, which is the individual's point of view in the long run'.[18]

NOTES

1. Report on Strikes and Lockouts of 1888 from the Labour Correspondent of the BOT, LXX 703.
2. Ibid.
3. PRO MUN 5/10/180/22, 1915.
4. Zeitlin, 1989.
5. Hobsbawm, 1984, p. 277.
6. PRO MUN 5/55 Intelligence and Statistics Department, July 1918.
7. PRO MUN 5/55 Report from the Ministry of Labour, 10th September 1919.
8. Ibid.
9. PRO CAB 37/110/63, April 1912.
10. Ibid.
11. OHMM vol. 1V, part 2, p. 9.
12. PRO LAB 2/254/13 September 1917.
13. Bagehot, 1949, p. 272.
14. PRO MUN 5/55, October 1919.
15. Ibid.
16. PRO MUN 5/73/324/15/8, December 1915.
17. PRO LAB 2/556/WA 7809, September 1919.
18. PRO CAB 24/90, May 1919.

Appendix: Methodology

This study is based on the following archival materials: Cabinet papers, the papers of the Board of Trade, the Ministry of Munitions, the Ministry of Labour, the Admiralty, the Ministry of Aviation and the Treasury at the Public Record Office, Kew. In addition, I have consulted the papers of the Royal Commission on Trade Unions 1867–69, the Royal Commission on Labour 1891–94, the Ministry of Labour and the Official History of The Ministry of Munitions at the Modern Records Centre, University of Warwick, together with newspapers and material on syndicalism and industrial unionism in Britain held at the Bodleian Library, Oxford and the Working Class Movement Library, Salford. It is a study of industrial conflict from above, not below. It is concerned with the way in which industrial conflict shaped industrial relations policy in a particular historical period. It could be argued that it relies too heavily on government records at the expense of trade union records, but this is indispensable for a study of the evolution of policy.

In the course of research for the book it became apparent that some sources, invariably cited as useful and reliable in those analyses which rely on government records, should be looked at more critically. The sources most heavily used in studies of industrial relations policy are Cabinet papers, private papers, biographies, diaries and memoirs of key political figures of the time and the Official History of the Ministry of Munitions. Although I, too, have used these sources directly and indirectly through the use of secondary texts, I have approached them with the following provisos in mind.

I have used Cabinet records in conjunction with others, following Davidson's observations (as noted in the introduction) that before 1911 industrial unrest was rarely discussed by the Cabinet and after this time the initiative in formulating industrial relations policy remained with the Board of Trade. As Mackenzie and Grove make clear, the part played by the Cabinet in policy making is restricted. Firstly, because of the limits of time and human reason, it can never intervene in practice at more than an infinitesimally small proportion of points at which decisions are required. A second difficulty arises out of the political functions of the Cabinet. Its business is to govern not the Civil Service but the nation. The Cabinet is made up of a group of party leaders who represent different interests within the party, the party itself is sensitive to the danger of failure at the next election and the Cabinet is constantly under pressure from public opinion. The Cabinet is less a central directing authority than an organ of co-ordination for the different departments of state which acts as a final court of appeal in specific controversies but which can do little to lay down in general terms forms of organization for the administration as a whole. Even during war or times of emergency, when the Cabinet may appear to offer comprehensive central direction, it remains the case that the small group of individuals who make up the Cabinet and their advisors can grasp only some of the complexities of the situation. Their leadership is largely political and directed to the nation as a whole. The Cabinet can affect administration directly only by limited and judicious intervention at key points.[1]

Cabinet Minutes are the organized record of decisions by the British government on all matters of importance, providing a continuous record of policy decisions and the main reasons for them, together with a network of cross references which ensure that nothing will be discussed in ignorance of action in related fields. However, they were designed as an instrument of administration and not as a historical record.[2] Mowat acknowledges that Cabinet papers 'will deepen our knowledge of what happened and of the information on which ministers or Cabinet decided to act' but warns that 'what the papers do not say, about motives or passions, the information they failed to supply to the government, will remain important, and light on these things will still have to be sought elsewhere.'[3]

Many writers have sought this information in the private papers, biographies, diaries and memoirs of politicians and civil servants. However, these sources vary widely in their reliability and usefulness. Turning to collections of private papers, it must firstly be noted that they are of historical value and many collections have been published. However, they rarely contain original government documents, since these have to be returned to the Cabinet Office. Lloyd George refused to return important documents after writing his memoirs[4], as did Addison,[5] but after his death in 1945 the more important documents were returned.

Biographies, while useful to the historian, are 'not a good way of writing history.' This is because the biographer's priority is to tell the story of someone's life, bringing out his personality and importance, and not to detail the individual's times, except in as much as they affect him or her. Biography 'tells us much personal and inner detail that would otherwise be lost, but it consistently turns the hero's face to the sun.'[6]

To a much greater extent the same is true of diaries and memoirs. The reliability of diaries as sources turns on several factors – whether they were written up each day or some time after the events, whether the entries were altered when hindsight changed an impression or an event. In addition, no diary has been published in its entirety and we have to trust the judgment of the individual who selected what was published. The status of diaries ultimately rests on whether the evidence of the diary is supported by evidence from other sources. A diary much used by historians of World War I is Thomas Jones's 'Whitehall Diary'. Its status as a source derives from its author, who was Deputy Secretary of the Cabinet Office from 1916, and it is therefore 'a first-hand record of a privileged observer.'[7] Nevertheless, while this work adds considerably to our knowledge and understanding of political figures and events at the time and the working of the Cabinet Office, it must be approached with the above reservations in mind.

As with diaries, the usefulness of memoirs depends on whether the author prefers 'frankness to discretion' and on freedom with his own manuscript. Ex-ministers and civil servants must have their manuscripts vetted by the Cabinet Office. Their reliability turns on the author's memory of events, on the wisdom of hindsight, on the desire to justify oneself and on whether they were written by the author, co-written or ghosted. As Mowat points out, the historian must use memoirs but with rigorously enforced safeguards, verification, confirmation from other sources, common sense and a general knowledge of the history of the time.[8]

The Official History of the Ministry of Munitions is the only official history of any part of the civilian side of World War I and is the standard reference for many writers on the latter half of the war. The Ministry of Munitions was set up in June 1915. In the first year of its existence it was proposed by a high-ranking official in the Department of Requirements and Statistics[9] that a record of its organization and executive activity be kept, because the Ministry's work was of 'peculiar significance to the political and social history of the country' and would contribute to 'the political intelligence of the nation'.[10]

The Cabinet, however, had already approved a plan to maintain a complete record of administrative action during the war to be used for the compilation of a War Book and saw the role of the proposed history of the Ministry of Munitions differently – as a reference work which would be useful in preparing for future wars and for the solution of problems in peacetime. It was to be 'the basis of any evidence to be laid before commissions of enquiry and as a guide for future action.'[11]

Heads of branches of the Ministry of Munitions were requested to provide statements of their work based 'partly on personal recollections . . . partly on reports and memoranda recorded in the current papers of the department.'[12] Initially the work was primarily in the hands of the heads of the branches concerned, who were left to decide for themselves what topics should be dealt with and where the emphasis should fall. There was no general plan and no attempt to cover large areas of ground which did not fall specifically within any single branch. Later the work became the responsibility of the Statistical Department of the Ministry which directed other branches to specific topics. It was found, however, that departmental accounts were badly written and that they reflected the preoccupations of their heads of department: examples included 'the Economic Structure of the Post-War World' or 'Trench Warfare Supplies'. Skilled researchers were recruited to plan the work, to widen its perspective and cover all the ground for which the Ministry was responsible, so that a history would be produced which could form the basis of useful research.

By the end of the war, however, the work was not complete, many of the skilled personnel had left, the Ministry faced dissolution and 'the scramble to get the work printed clearly led to serious faults in the History.'[13] In January 1920 the Treasury agreed to the employment of individual contributors, many of whom were students, on a piecework basis, which turned the history into 'a system of indoor relief' with 'all the disadvantages of complicated administration and unco-ordinated effort.'[14]

After the Armistice the Cabinet decided against the publication of the History. It was emphasized that 'there would be a good deal in the History which it would not be judicious to lay before everyone.' The work was to be made available to officials for official purposes only, and it was decided that expenditure on it would end with the expiration of the Ministry at the end of 1921. In March 1920 the Cabinet decided in favour of publishing those parts 'recording the activities in regard to industrial labour.'[15] The Ministry of Labour objected on the ground that this would lead to industrial conflict. It was agreed that these sections would be vetted by the Ministry of Labour before publication.

In the event the Ministry of Labour required the revision of the entire text and the removal of all direct references to official documents.

The History was not published. Two hundred and fifty copies were made available to Ministries and official bodies. Its usefulness as a source of information on government policy has been diminished, due to 'its dependence on one group of papers [which] somewhat unbalances the text.'[16] References are sparingly given and cannot be checked, since the schedule of destruction prepared by the Master of the Rolls put a time limit in no case longer than seven years on the papers used by the Ministry to compile the History. In consequence 'there is no comprehensive and reliable body of documents to verify the story which was compiled' and 'into the framework prepared for an economic and institutional discussion was fitted a description of administration.'[17]

My main aim in reviewing some of the most intensively used sources for the analysis of industrial conflict during 1910–21 has been to show that they should be used in conjunction with the papers of the departments of state from which industrial relations policy derived in this period, in order to avoid the confusion of political talk with administrative action. It has been a central contention of this book that a more accurate view of industrial relations policy in the period 1910–21 can be gained from a study of the papers of the departments from which it originated. These departments were the Board of Trade, the Labour Department of the Ministry of Munitions and the Ministry of Labour, which inherited the powers and responsibility for the management of industrial conflict conferred by the Conciliation Act 1896.

This insight was the result of a study of the evolution of the state's practical involvement in industrial relations from the mid-nineteenth century to the passing of the Conciliation Act 1896. My work in this area has relied to a great extent on the reports of the Royal Commissions of 1867–69 and 1891–94. Before such collections became the responsibility of the Labour Department of the Board of Trade, these Commissions gathered vast amounts of information, statistics and evidence from many sources, including trade unions, workers, employers and state departments such as the Board of Trade, the Treasury and the Local Government Board (Poor Law Commissioners). While it is true that the findings and recommendations of Royal Commissions do not always help to formulate policy and lead to action, and that they are sometimes appointed to avoid a crisis by delay and postponement (e.g. The Coal Industry Commission 1919), reports from both kinds of Commissions are sources in themselves and are also historical facts. Inaction on their recommendations is as much a decision of government as action.[18]

Locating the information on which ministers and Cabinet acted was, however, not simply a question of identifying the departments empowered to manage industrial conflict by the Conciliation Act. It is important to note here that some government papers do not reach the Public Record Office and many are accidentally or intentionally destroyed, whilst others, in spite of the thirty-year rule, are unavailable. In addition, not all of the available papers of state departments charged with responsibility for the formulation and implementation of industrial relations policy are equally useful. Documents which are ultimately published as official papers are usually the result of many drafts. These drafts are generally far more detailed and revealing than published papers in terms of how government policy developed. In the case of the Cabinet, drafts are difficult to locate and many no longer exist. Fortunately, the archives of the agencies listed above contain much internal correspondence on policy with regard to industrial conflict and many drafts of documents either for publication, submission to the Cabinet and for briefing Ministers. Access to these documents, however, is made difficult by other factors. Documents, especially in the LAB 2 class list (which include papers of the Board of Trade), are difficult to use because they cover the whole range of Ministry business, including general policy, industrial relations, establishment and trade boards and have been preserved in an uneven and disorganized way. There is an index to the LAB class at the PRO, named LAB 7, consisting of many docket books of subject indexes, which then have to be used with the indexes to LAB 2 (which take up many volumes). As a result, research in the LAB 2 class list can be time-consuming and unrewarding and may contribute to the failure of analysts of this period to appreciate the richness of material available concerning the state's relationship with organized labour and the nature of industrial disputes in Britain at this time. Fortunately, while browsing among dictionaries and reference works in the field of industrial relations in Warwick University Library, I discovered quite by chance that a listing and guide to LAB classes LAB 2, LAB 10, LAB 27, LAB 31 and LAB 34 had been compiled and a selection of the documents relating to industrial relations committed to microfilm, a copy of which had been deposited on the first floor of the library.[19] This saved much time at the Public Record Office.

NOTES

1. Mackenzie & Grove 1957, pp. 334–341.
2. Ibid.
3. Mowat, C.L., *Great Britain Since 1914*, Hodder & Stoughton, 1971.
4. Lloyd George, 1933–36.
5. Addison, London, 1934.
6. Mowat, 1971, p. 90.
7. Ibid., p. 102.
8. Ibid.
9. Godfrey Lloyd, Associate Professor of Political Science at the University of Toronto, seconded to the Ministry of Munitions in 1915.
10. AVIA 46/288, 6th April 1944.
11. Ibid., p. 3.
12. Ibid.
13. Ibid., p. 8.
14. Ibid.
15. Ibid., p. 12.
16. Ibid., p. 13.
17. Ibid., p. 14.
18. Ibid., p. 35.
19. Harvester Microfilm Collection, 1985.

Bibliography

Official Publications
Reports of the Royal Commission on Trade Unions, 1868–9. Cmd 4123.
Reports of the Royal Commission on Labour 1891–94. C-7421.
Memorandum on The Progress of the Labour Department of the Board of Trade, April 1893.
Report on the Strikes and Lockouts of 1896. Cmd 8643, 1897.
Report on Strikes and Lockouts in 1913. Cmd 7658, 1914–16.
Summary of the Reports of the Commissions on Industrial Unrest. HMSO.1917, Cd 8696.
Twelfth Report of Proceedings under the Conciliation Act 1896, 1914–18 (1919).
Minutes of Proceedings of the National Industrial Conference Provisional Joint Committee, 1st May 1919.
Official History of the Ministry of Munitions, 12 Vols (1920–24).

Primary Sources

Ministry of Aviation	AVIA 46	Files transferred to the Air Ministry after the disbanding of the Ministry of Munitions.
Cabinet	CAB 23	Cabinet minutes or conclusions of meetings of the War Cabinet including those withheld from circulated minutes on grounds of secrecy.
	CAB 24	Memoranda 1915–39: papers circulated to the War Cabinet (GT series) from other state departments which formed the basis of the Cabinet's discussions – for use alongside conclusions.
	CAB 27	Cabinet committees created 1917–22 – war policy, economy, demobilization, industrial unrest, finance, unemployment, Ireland.
	CAB 37	Cabinet papers from 1880 to 1916.
Ministry of Munitions	MUN 5	Papers of the Historical Records Branch of the Ministry of Munitions.
Ministry of Labour	LAB 2	includes most of the surviving general papers of the Ministry of Labour until 1933, covering the whole range of Ministry business including general policy, industrial relations, establishment and trade boards.
Home Office	HO 45	Correspondence and papers domestic and general, 1841–1939.

Trade Union Reports
National Union of Boot and Shoe Operatives Monthly Report, November–December 1900

Newspapers and Periodicals
The Forward
The Industrial Syndicalist
The Glasgow Herald
The Manchester Guardian
Railway Review
The Socialist
The Times

Unpublished works
Adams, K.J., 'Working Class Organization, Industrial Relations and the Labour Unrest 1914–21'. Ph.D. Thesis, Leicester University, 1989.
Aris, R. 'Industrial Unrest in Britain, 1910–12: implications for theories of the state.' M.A. dissertation, University of Warwick, September 1990.
Burdick, E., 'Syndicalism and Industrial Unionism in Britain Until 1918' Ph.D. Thesis, Oxford University, 1950.
Chewter, D.M., 'The History of The Socialist Labour Party of Great Britain from 1902 to 1921' M.Phil., Oxford University, 1964.
Elger, A.J., 'The Sociology of Trade Union Organization and Democracy'. Warwick University, 1989.
Elger, A.J., 'Trade Unions and Class Consciousness'. Warwick University, 1989.
Gordon, E. 'Women and the Labour Movement 1850–1914'. Ph.D. Thesis, Glasgow University, 1985.
Jacques, M., 'The Emergence of "Responsible" Trade Unionism; a study of the "new direction" in TUC policy, 1926–35' Ph.D. Thesis, Cambridge University, 1976.
Maguire, P., 'Unofficial Trade Union Movements and Industrial Politics 1915–22.' Ph.D. Thesis, University of Sussex, 1980.
The Official History of the Ministry of Munitions. Modern Records Centre, University of Warwick.

Secondary Sources
Adams, R.J.Q., *Arms and the Wizard*. Texas A & M University Press, 1978.
Addison, C., *Four and a Half Years*. Vols 1&2, Hutchinson, 1934.
Allen, V.L., *The Sociology of Industrial Relations*. Longman, 1971.
Amulree, Lord, *Industrial Arbitration in Great Britain*. Oxford University Press, 1929.
Andrews, I.O. and Hobbs, M., *The Economic Effects of the Great War on Women and Children*. Oxford University Press, New York, 1921.
Askwith, G., *Industrial Problems and Disputes*. Allen & Unwin, 1920; Sharp, 1950.
Bagehot, W., *The English Constitution*. World's Classics Edition, 1949.
Bagwell, P.S., *The Railwaymen*. Allen & Unwin, 1963.
Batstone, E., Boraston, I., and Frenkel, S., *Shop Stewards in Action*. Blackwell, 1977.

Beynon, H., *Working for Ford*. Penguin, 1973.

Blackburn, R.M., and Mann, M. *The Working Class in the Labour Market*. Macmillan, 1979.

Boston, S., *Women Workers and the Trade Unions*. Davis Poynter, 1980.

Bramble, T., 'Trade Union Organization and Workplace Industrial Relations in the Vehicle Industry, 1963 to 1991' in *Journal of Industrial Relations*, Vol. 35, No. 1, March 1993.

Brown, G. (ed.), *The Industrial Syndicalist*. Spokesman Books, 1974.

Burgess, K., *The Challenge of Labour*. St. Martin's Press, New York, 1980.

Burgess, K., *The Origins of British Industrial Relations*. Croom Helm, 1975.

Burns, E.M., *Wages and the State*. King & Son, 1926.

Butler, D. and Butler, G., *British Political Facts 1900–85*. 6th ed., Macmillan, 1986.

Carnoy, M., *The State and Political Theory*. Princeton University Press, 1984.

Challinor, R., *The Origins of British Bolshevism*. Croom Helm, 1977.

Chang, D., *British Methods of Industrial Peace*. Columbia University Press, New York, 1968.

Charles, R., *The Development of Industrial Relations in Britain 1911–39*. Hutchinson, 1973.

Clarke, S. (ed.), *The State Debate*. Macmillan, 1991.

Clarke, T., 'The Raison D'Etre of Trade Unionism' in T. Clarke & L. Clements (eds), *Trade Unions under Capitalism*. Humanities Press, New Jersey, 1978.

Clay, H., *The Problem of Industrial Relations*. Macmillan, 1929.

Clegg, H.A., Fox, A. and Thompson, A.F., *A History of British Trade Unions Since 1889*. Oxford, 1964

Cole, G.D.H., *A Short History of the British Working Class Movement*. Allen & Unwin, 1948.

Cole, G.D.H., *A History of Socialist Thought*. Vol. 3, part 1, Macmillan, 1954.

Cole, G.D.H., *Trade Unionism and Munitions*. Clarendon Press, Oxford, 1923.

Cole, G.D.H., *Labour in The Coal Mining Industry 1914–21*. Clarendon Press, Oxford, 1923.

Cole, G.D.H., *Workshop Organisation*. Hutchinson Educational, 1973.

Cole, G.D.H., *The World of Labour*. Harvester, 1973.

Conlin, J.R., *Bread and Roses Too: Studies of The Wobblies*. Greenwood, Westport, 1969.

Crompton, R., *Class and Stratification*. Polity Press, 1993.

Cronin, J., 'Coping with Labour' in J. Cronin and J. Schneer (eds), *Social Conflict and the Political. Order in Modern Britain*. Rutgers University Press, New Brunswick, NJ, 1982.

Crouch, C., *Trade Unions; the Logic of Collective Action*. Fontana, 1982.

Dangerfield, G., *The Strange Death of Liberal England*. Constable, 1936.

Davidson, R., 'Government Administration' in C.J. Wrigley (ed.) *A History of British Industrial Relations*. Harvester, 1982.

Davidson, R., 'The Board of Trade and Industrial Relations 1896–1914' in *The Historical Journal*, No. 21, 3 (1978).

Davidson, R., 'War-Time Labour Policy 1914–16: a re- appraisal' in *Scottish Labour History Society Journal*, No. 8, June 1974.

Davidson, R., *Whitehall and the Labour Problem in Late Victorian and Edwardian England*, Croom Helm, 1985.

De Ste Croix, G.E.M., *The Class Struggle in the Ancient Greek World*. Gerald Duckworth & Co., 1983.

DeLeon, D., *Flashlights of the Amsterdam Conference*. 2nd ed., New York Labor News Co., 1929.

DeLeon, D., *Industrial Unionism*. 10th August 1909.

DeLeon, D., *Reform or Revolution*, an address delivered at Well's Memorial Hall, Boston, 26th January 1896.

DeLeon, D., *The Burning Question of Trades Unionism*, a lecture originally delivered at Newark. N.J., 21st April 1904.

DeLeon, D., *The Socialist Reconstruction of Society*. Socialist Labour Party Press, Glasgow, 1905.

DeLeon, D., *Two Pages from Roman History*. Pamphlet produced by Socialist Labour Party Press, Glasgow, ND.

Desmond Greaves, C., *The Life and Times of James Connolly*. Lawrence & Wishart, 1976.

Dobb, M., *Wages*. Cambridge University Press, 1959.

Dunlop, J.T., *Industrial Relations Systems*. Holt, New York, 1958.

Evans, D., *Labour Strife in the South Wales Coalfield 1910–11*. Educational Publishing Company, Cardiff, 1911.

Flanders, A., *Trade Unions*. Hutchinson, 1968.

Foote, G., *The Labour Party's Political Thought*. Croom Helm, 1985

Fox, A., 'The Myths of Pluralism and a Radical Alternative' in T. Clarke and L. Clements (eds), *Trade Unions Under Capitalism*. Humanities Press, New Jersey, 1978.

Fox, A., *History and Heritage*. Allen & Unwin, 1985.

Gallacher, W., and Muir, J., 'Statement', *Glasgow Herald*, 30th March 1916.

Goldthorpe, J.H., 'The Current Inflation: Towards a Sociological Account' in F. Hirsch and J.H. Goldthorpe (eds), *The Political Economy of Inflation*. Martin Robertson & Co. Ltd, 1978.

Goldthorpe, J.H., Lockwood, D., Bechhoffer, F., and Platt, J., *The Affluent Worker*. Cambridge University Press, 1968

Goodrich, C.L., *The Frontier of Control*. Pluto, 1975.

Halevy, E., *The Rule of Democracy*. Peter Smith, New York, 1952.

Harvey, G., *Industrial Unionism and The Mining Industry*. Bealls, 1917.

Haydu, J., *Between Craft and Class*. University of California Press, 1988.

Hinton, J., *The First Shop Stewards' Movement*. Allen & Unwin, 1973.

Hinton, J., 'The Theory of Independent Rank and File Organization' in Clarke and Clements, 1978, *op cit.*

Hobsbawm, E., *Labouring Men*. Weidenfeld & Nicolson, 1964.

Hobsbawm, E., *Worlds of Labour*. Weidenfeld & Nicolson, 1984.

Hobsbawm, E., 'Class Consciousness in History' in Istvan Metzaros (ed.) *Aspects of History and Class Consciousness*, Routledge, Kegan Paul, 1971.

Holloway, J., and Picciotto, S. (eds), *State and Capital*. Edward Arnold, 1978.

Holton, R., *Syndicalism in Britain 1910–14*. Pluto, 1976.

Horvat, B., *Self-Governing Socialism*. International Arts and Sciences Press, New York, 1975.

Hunt, E.H., *British Labour History 1815–1914*. Weidenfeld & Nicolson, 1981.

Hunter, R., *Violence and the Labour Movement*. Arno Press, 1969.

Hyman, R., *Industrial Relations: A Marxist Introduction*. Macmillan, 1975.

Hyman, R., 'Comment' in *British Journal of Sociology*, Vol. 29, No. 4, December 1978.

Hyman, R., 'The Politics of Workplace Trade Unionism: Recent Tendencies and Some Problems For Theory' in *Capital and Class*, 8, 1979.

Hyman, R., *Marxism and the Sociology of Trade Unionism*. Pluto, 1971.

Hyman, R., 'Rank and File Movements and Workplace Organisation' in C.J. Wrigley (ed.) *A History of British Industrial Relations 1914–39*. Harvester, 1982.

Hyman, R., *The Worker's Union*. Clarendon Press, 1971.

International Labour Organization, *Conciliation and Arbitration Procedures in Industrial Disputes*. International Labour Office, Geneva, 1980.

Jaurès, J., *Studies in Socialism*, Independent Labour Party, 1906.

Jeffery, K., & Hennessy, P., *States of Emergency*. Routledge Kegan Paul, 1983.

Jessop, B., *State Theory*. Polity Press, 1990.

Johnson, P.B., *Land Fit For Heroes*. University of Chicago Press, 1968.

Jones, G.S., *Outcast London*. Penguin, 1976.

Jones, T., *Whitehall Diary*. Vol. 1, 1916–25, ed. K. Middlemas, Oxford University Press, 1969.

Kay, G., *The Economic Theory of the Working Class*. Macmillan, 1979.

Kelly, J., *Trade Unions and Socialist Politics*. Verso, 1988.

Kendall, W., *The Revolutionary Movement in Britain, 1900–21*. Weidenfeld and Nicolson, 1969.

Kidner, R., *Trade Union Law*. Stevens & Sons, 1979.

Kipnis, I., *The American Socialist Movement*. Monthly Review Press, 1952.

Landis, J.M., *The Administrative Process*. Yale University Press, New Haven, Mass., 1938.

Lane, T., *The Union Makes Us Strong*. Arrow, 1974.

Lapides, K., *Marx and Engels on the Trade Unions*. Praeger, New York, 1987.

Lenin, V.I., *What Is To Be Done*. Progress Publishers, Moscow, 1902.

Levine, L.L., *The Labor Movement in France*. Columbia University Press, 1912.

Lloyd George, D., *War Memoirs of David Lloyd George*. Vols 1 & 2, Odhams Press, 1933–36.

Lorwin, V., *The French Labour Movement*. Oxford University Press, 1954.

Lowe, R., 'The Erosion of State Intervention in Britain' in *Economic History Review* (31), 1978.

Lowe, R., 'The Failure of Consensus in Britain: the National Industrial Conference 1919–21', *History Journal*, 21 September 1978, pp. 649–675.

Lowe, R., *Adjusting to Democracy*. Clarendon, Oxford, 1986.

MacDonald, R., *Socialism in Society*. T.C. & E.C. Jack, 1907.

Mackenzie, W.J., and Grove, J.W., *Central Administration in Britain*. Longmans Green & Co., 1957.

Mann, M., *Consciousness and Action Among the Western Working Class*. Macmillan, 1973.

Marwick, A., *The Deluge*. Bodley Head, 1967.

Matthews, D., '1889 And All That' in *International Review of Social History*, Vol. 35, 1991.

McKillop, N., *The Lighted Flame*. Thomas Nelson & Sons, 1950.

McLean, I., 'The Ministry of Munitions, the Clyde Workers' Committee and the suppression of the "Forward": an alternative view' in *Scottish Labour History Society Journal*, No. 6, December 1972.

McLean, I., *The Legend of Red Clydeside*. John Donald, Edinburgh, 1983.

Michels, R., *Political Parties*. The Free Press 1968. Originally published in German, 1911; published in English 1915.

Middlemas, K., *Politics in Industrial Society*. André Deutsch, 1979.

Miles, R., *Racism*. Routledge, 1989.

Miliband, R., *The State in Capitalist Society*. Weidenfeld and Nicholson, 1969.

Miliband, R., *Parliamentary Socialism*. Merlin Press, 1973.

Mills, C.W., *The Power Elite*. Oxford University Press, New York, 1956.

Mitchell, B., *The Practical Revolutionaries*. Greenwood, 1987.

Mommsen, W., and Husung, H.G. (eds), *The Development of Trade Unionism in Britain and Germany*. Allen & Unwin, 1985.

Moss, B.H., *The Origins of the French Labor Movement* University California Press, London, 1976.

Mowat, C.L., *Great Britain Since 1914*. Hodder & Stoughton, 1971.

Nichols, T., & Beynon, H., *Living with Capitalism*. Routledge & Kegan Paul, 1977.

Orton, W.A., *Labour in Transition*. Philip Allan & Co., 1921.

Pelling, H., *A History of British Trade Unionism*. Penguin, 1963.

Pelling, H., *A History of British Trade Unionism*. Penguin, 1971.

Phelps-Brown, E.H., *The Growth of British Industrial Relations*. Macmillan, 1960.

Phillips, G.A., 'The Triple Alliance in 1914' in *Economic History Review*, 24, 1971.

Poole, M., *Theories of Trade Unionism*. Routledge Kegan Paul, 1981.

Porter, J.H., 'Wage Bargaining Under Conciliation Agreements 1860–1914' in *Economic History Review*, 23, 1970.

Price, R., *Masters, Unions and Men*. Cambridge University Press, 1980.

Redmayne, R.A.S., *The British Coal Mining Industry During the War*. Clarendon Press, Oxford, 1923.

Reid, A. in J.Zeitlin and S.Tolliday (eds), *Shop Floor Bargaining and the State*. Cambridge University Press, 1985.

Rubin, G.R., *War, Law and Labour*. Oxford University Press, 1987.

Sabel, C.F., *Work and Politics*. Cambridge University Press, 1981.

Schwartz, B., 'Conservatives and Corporatism' in *New Left Review*, No. 166, 1987.

Seretan, L.G., *Daniel DeLeon: The Odyssey of an American Marxist*. Harvard University Press, 1979.

Sharp, I.G., *Industrial Conciliation and Arbitration in Great Britain*. Allen & Unwin, 1950.

Schneer, J., *Ben Tillett*. Croom Helm, 1982.

Sturmthal, A., *Comparative Labour Movements*. Wadsworth Publishing Company, California, 1972.

Tarling, R., and Wilkinson, F., 'The Movement of Real wages and the Development of Collective Bargaining in the U.K.: 1855–1920.' in *Contributions to Political Economy*, Vol. 1, March 1982.

Turner, H.A., *Trade Union Growth, Structure and Policy*. Allen & Unwin, 1962.

Walby, S., *Patriarchy at Work*. Polity Press, Cambridge, 1986.

Ward, S., 'Intelligence Surveillance of British Ex-Servicemen 1918–1920' in *The Historical Journal*, XV1, 1 (1973), pp. 179–188.

Webb, S. and B., *History of Trade Unionism*. Kelley, New York, 1965.

Webb, S. and B., *Industrial Democracy*. Longmans, 1897.

Webb, S. and B., *Methods of Social Study*. Longmans, Green & Co., 1932.

Wolfe, H., *Labour Supply and Regulation*. Clarendon Press, Oxford, 1923.

Wrigley, C., 'The First World War and State Intervention in Industrial Relations, 1914–18' in C. Wrigley (ed.), *A History of British Industrial Relations, Volume 2: 1914–39*. Harvester Press, 1987.

Wrigley, C., *Lloyd George and the Challenge of Labour*. Harvester, 1990.

Wrigley, C., 'The Ministry of Munitions: an innovatory Department' in K. Burk (ed.) *War and the State*. Allen & Unwin, 1982.

Young, J.D., 'Daniel DeLeon and Anglo-American Socialism' in *Labour History*, Vol. 17, 1976.

Zeitlin, J., '"Rank and Filism" in British Labour History: A Critique' in *International Review of Social History*, Vol. 34, 1989.

Index